Immigration Structures and Immigrant Lives

Immigration Structures and Immigrant Lives

An Introduction to the US Experience

David W. Haines

ROWMAN & LITTLEFIELD
Lanham • Boulder • New York • London

Published by Rowman & Littlefield
A wholly owned subsidiary of The Rowman & Littlefield Publishing Group, Inc.
4501 Forbes Boulevard, Suite 200, Lanham, Maryland 20706
www.rowman.com

Unit A, Whitacre Mews, 26-34 Stannary Street, London SE11 4AB

British Library Cataloguing in Publication Information Available

Library of Congress Cataloging-in-Publication Data
Names: Haines, David W., author.
Title: Immigration structures and immigrant lives : an introduction to the
   US experience / David W. Haines.
Description: Lanham, MD : Rowman & Littlefield, [2017] | Includes index.
Identifiers: LCCN 2017021868 (print) | LCCN 2017038692 (ebook) |
   ISBN 9781442260115 (electronic) | ISBN 9781442260092 (cloth : alk. paper) |
   ISBN 9781442260108 (pbk. : alk. paper)
Subjects: LCSH: Immigrants—United States—Social conditions. | United
   States—Emigration and immigration.
Classification: LCC JV6475 (ebook) | LCC JV6475 .H33 2017 (print) |
   DDC 305.9/069120973—dc23
LC record available at https://lccn.loc.gov/2017021868

∞™ The paper used in this publication meets the minimum requirements of American
National Standard for Information Sciences—Permanence of Paper for Printed Library
Materials, ANSI/NISO Z39.48-1992.

Printed in the United States of America

Contents

Tables

Preface

No one can contest that the United States is a nation of immigrants. But what does that mean? Clearly the United States was founded by immigrants, and continuing waves of immigrants made it the populous, productive, and powerful country it had become by the beginning of the twentieth century. That makes the United States a nation of *former* immigrants and their descendants. With the reopening of the United States to immigration after the Second World War, the United States is today also a country of *current* immigrants. About one in seven Americans is foreign-born, and in some cities it is nearly one in two. Finally, despite concerns about current levels and types of immigration, it is hard to foresee any elimination of *future* immigration. Thus, for the United States, being a nation of immigrants is about the past, the present, and the future.

Furthermore, being "a nation of immigrants" does not convey the complexities of the way people move into and out of the United States. They do so for different purposes, for different periods of time—some temporary and some permanent—and with cascading effects over time for the migrants, for the nonmigrants whom they join, and for their children. The migration paths are sometimes consciously planned; yet sometimes they are unexpected, imposed by changing circumstances, and carry unpredicted consequences. Whether planned or not, migration inevitably reverberates through people's daily lives, their economic trajectories, their ways of understanding the world (and their place in it), and their interactions with an American society that vacillates between acceptance and rejection, inclusion and segregation. So the topic of US immigration is a complex one that involves the destinies of both the immigrants and American society overall.

How do you craft an introduction to a topic so broad, so variable, and so fundamental—both to the United States as a country and to the lives of migrants and nonmigrants within it? In this volume my decision has been, above all, to recognize the breadth and depth of the topic. In that aim, I have tried to:

Place immigration within the broader contexts of human mobility and global migration.

Recognize that migration is both a social process and an intensely individual one.

Reflect the multiple reasons for movement to America, from those fleeing loss and persecution to those seeking greater economic opportunity, and the many in between.

Recognize the way that migration is about the full spectrum of human life—of work, of belonging, of beliefs and convictions, and of life itself.

Recognize the complexity and unpredictability of immigrant life, the ebb and flow of hope and despair, and the frequent loss that accompanies progress in a new life.

Demonstrate the many different kinds of material that can illuminate American immigration, from ethnographic research to migrant accounts, demographic and economic data, political texts and tracts, and the humanities (especially literature).

Find common ground among the disciplines interested in migration, perhaps especially anthropology, cultural studies, economics, sociology, history, religious studies, and political and policy studies.

That is a very ambitious aim—and perhaps an impossible one. But in my effort to reach that goal, I hope this volume will spur people to recognize how profoundly important migration is on both social and personal grounds and how only a broad approach that integrates the social sciences and humanities can hope to be successful in understanding it.

In taking on this effort, I am indebted at Rowman & Littlefield to Leanne Silverman for early discussion of how a book like this might be constructed; to Kathryn Knigge and Patricia Stevenson for bringing the project to completion; to Debbie Justice for a most careful copyedit of the manuscript; and to a truly excellent set of reviewers—Caroline B. Brettell, Steven J. Gold, and Bernadette Ludwig, PhD—of the prospectus and manuscript. My own many years of teaching about migration (whether from a US, Asian, or European perspective) have been invaluable. The students in those classes, whether immigrant or not, have made that experience the most consistently enjoyable of my career. I have also been influenced by my own frequent focus on refugee issues. That has inured me to the frequent assumption in discussions of immigration that the core issue is one of rational decision making about economic futures. Finally, I have benefited from the careful reading of the entirety of this work by Rachel Kenderdine, Andrea Mendoza, and Kourtney Wilson and a more focused editorial review of the latter section of this work by Sheila Barrows. Finally, special thanks to Karen Rosenblum for sustaining my heart and my writing during this project. I am greatly indebted to them all both for their specific comments and for their assistance in making sure that this volume is consistent in opening up the many issues of US immigration, rather than closing them down with summary judgments or homogenized data.

I would also like to make a few personal comments about my own history. Like many Americans, my actual immigrant origins remain only partly known. There are indeed some markers: a semifamous ancestor from the early New England colonies on one side of the family and an unusually college-educated set of women from the late 1800s on the other side of the family. But those origins were never discussed in the family—to my knowledge—except in terms of lives after arriving in the United States. I heard nothing of my German ancestors on my mother's side except that they anglicized their name on arrival. The German Quakers on my father's side of the family only reemerged when a cousin recently took on the task of sorting out our ancestry. So immigration as a past experience has had little impact on my own development. What has affected me has been my own movement overseas as a child (Japan), as a soldier (Vietnam), as a foreign student (Japan again), and as a professor (Japan, Korea, and Italy). Those many journeys outward have been followed by returns to a home country that was always different from what it had been—in both fact and memory—and often difficult to navigate anew. Those movements back and forth have given me many of my keenest sensings of migration's joys and pains, losses and gains. We are who we are because of where we have been and how that has shaped our understanding of where we are now.

Introduction

Humanity on the Move

Mobility is a key aspect of all human societies. In even the most settled of societies, there is always some movement, whether as part of the food quest, to interact with other people (such as for marriage), or for spiritual purposes. Such movements may develop into the repetitive back-and-forth of seasonal migrations or into permanent migrations to new lands over the plains, beyond the mountains, and across the seas. As a result, human beings find themselves in places they have not been before, and the areas they once inhabited are peopled by others or even abandoned. Whether it is the initial human migration out of Africa, as documented by physical anthropologists; the initial peopling of the Americas, documented by archeologists; the colonial repeopling of the New World, documented by historians; or the contemporary surge in migration, studied by social scientists and illuminated by those in the humanities, the innate mobility of human beings is clear.

This introduction addresses these general issues of human mobility in three main parts: first, the basic mobility of human beings that can be seen in the anthropological record; second, the specific kinds of mobility that are usually categorized as migration, with particular attention to the borders and barriers that constrain movement and the varying definitions of such key words as *migration*, *emigration*, and *immigration*; and, third, some prefatory comments on the overall organization of the book.

HUMAN MOBILITY

Many discussions of migration rest on the idea that people originally live in one place but then move to another as a one-time event. That event is often described through the images of uprooting from the former place and putting down roots

1

in the latter. It is, however, a metaphor that applies far better to plants than to people. People, by contrast, are built to move. They come with legs, not roots. Upright posture provides a form of locomotion that puts the eyes at the highest point for assessing the horizon and leaves the hands free for carrying objects—or children. Human cognitive and vocal skills provide a way to think through and coordinate group movements, including explaining to people how to get places they have not seen and what they will find there.

This does not mean that the place where people currently live is unimportant to them and easily discarded for a move somewhere else. Indeed, the places that people live are often extremely important to them; they may well be unwilling to leave those places, and they may be willing to risk their lives to preserve them. But the record is also clear that people move and that they move for a variety of reasons, and for varying periods of time. Sometimes those moves are modest in distance and part of a daily round of activities. Sometimes those moves are more extensive and part of a seasonal round. At other times movement is linear to a new and unknown place and sometimes with no return. As people move across places, they are also moving forward in their own lives. Mobility and personal development go hand in hand: being a young adult often creates especially strong reasons for moving to seek a new life; parenthood may reduce mobility to provide a settled life for young children.

Consider some of the kinds of human mobility we know from the anthropo-logical record. The most basic human relationship to the land can be seen with hunters and gatherers. In such societies, people are almost always on the move. Whether hunting or gathering, people must follow what nature offers, and those resources will be in different places at different times of the year. So daily life is a movement across the land to gain those resources, with people sometimes working alone, sometimes in small groups, and sometimes in quite large groups. Sometimes the work of men and women is separate, with men doing more of the hunting and women more of the gathering, but sometimes it is also men, women, and children all working together, whether to hunt or to gather. The land that they inhabit is more a range of territory than a single place. The same applies to pastoralists, whose lives hinge on the animals they herd. They, too, are very mobile. The area they need to sustain their animals is often vast, and they must manage complex seasonal migrations, whether to seek fresh pastures higher on the hills or to search for fresh water lower in the valleys and plains. For them, the pressures of daily and seasonal life often work to separate men and women, sometimes with men and women herding different animals, and sometimes with men on the move with the herds and women settled in one place, perhaps grow-ing crops to supplement their pastoralist life. For both hunters and gatherers and pastoralists, one's destiny lies in constant movement.

With the cultivation of crops, the attachment to land changes. The invest-ment of effort in clearing and planting fields strengthens the linkages to a more narrowly defined place. Homes become not just quick shelters or transportable tents and yurts but also houses built for durability. Life becomes more settled

The first Americans probably crossed over a land bridge connecting the current Aleutian Islands, which are pictured here. (photomatz/Shutterstock.com)

and people generally less mobile on a daily or seasonal basis. The fields anchor people's lives, and the more effort they put into improving those fields, the more attached to them they are. The carefully terraced rice fields of Asia show the many generations of effort at improving the land. To lose that land—that very particular land that belongs to you—is to lose your life. In this case, then, one's destiny lies in *not* moving. For agriculturalists, the notion of migration as a drastic uprooting makes more sense. Through the roots of their crops, people are themselves rooted in the soil. But there is still mobility in agricultural societies. Fields are not always contiguous, and daily life may well involve some distances traveled. Furthermore, as agriculture becomes more intensive, other kinds of work emerge that do require mobility. Trade is essential to ensure a balanced diet—lack of salt and the iodine in it, for example, is extraordinarily damaging to human health. Trade is also essential as agricultural implements become more developed. Even an iron tip for a plow requires a trade network that connects to mining. War is another great mover of people in agricultural societies, sometimes temporarily and sometimes more permanently as war yields occupation by the victors of the territory won. Religion is still another mobility factor in agricultural societies: pilgrimages are crucial in most world religions (and in many localized folk religions as well).

This quick survey of the anthropological record suggests that humans are indeed mobile but their mobility depends a great deal on the way they relate to the environment and how they make their living. Some societies are inherently more mobile than others; yet even in relatively sedentary societies some people are moving at least some of the time. Those movements may be repetitive on a daily or weekly basis or on a more seasonal basis. They may also be one-time events that result in permanent changes. In many traditional societies, for example, marriage moves women (and sometimes men) from the places where they were born to new communities. In other cases, men (and sometimes women) are encouraged to seek their fortune elsewhere before returning as full adults to the places where they were raised. Mobility is woven into the very fabric of human life.

MOVEMENT AND MIGRATION, BARRIERS AND BORDERS

The question of which of these many forms of human mobility should be considered "migration" is complicated and perhaps arbitrary. Human mobility on a repeating daily or weekly basis is not generally considered migration. Seasonal changes, however, are often referred to as migration even if they are repetitive. Certainly those cases in which people make one-time moves across great distances are likely to be construed as migration even if they are not permanent. A semester abroad in Italy, for example, would probably not be considered migration, but a four-year job in Italy probably would be, and a permanent move to Italy certainly would be. So, for the purposes of this book at least, *migration* refers to movements that are more than episodic (you do not "migrate" when you take a vacation) and involve more than minimal distance (nor do you migrate to your job or to your classes). But that still leaves *migration* as a word that covers both one-time events (either temporary or permanent) and repeating events (whether seasonal or at some other longer interval). This is an issue of normal English usage, not some academic final determination.

Whether for movement in general or migration in particular, people's actions are based on a variety of factors that may involve any aspect of their lives, from economic necessity to religious commitment—or any combination of those aspects. Whatever the forces that fuel their movement, people will also face constraints as they move. The barriers are of many kinds. Some are quite physical and seemingly insurmountable: impassable mountains, burning deserts, large oceans. Some are more subtle: an unknown terrain that is hard to navigate, with unpredictable food and other resources. Some barriers involve other people, whether hostile, friendly, or simply hard to understand because of linguistic and cultural differences.

In the contemporary world, the barriers of the day are certainly the official political borders surrounding countries. However, these are not the only barriers that migrants must cross, and they are not always the most difficult. People who move from place to place—whether across national borders or not—all face a multitude of potential barriers: economic, social, physical, linguistic, cultural, religious. For some migrants, the barriers are formidable; for others—especially those with education and money—the barriers are easily surmounted. Even national borders are often rather porous. In the United States' case, the border with Mexico is partly walled and partly open except for "natural" barriers like deserts. The border with Canada, by contrast, is largely open, although travelers are supposed to cross it at designated places. Furthermore, the actual monitoring of border crossings may not happen at the border but internally within the country at workplaces or in random inspections and raids. After all, about half of the unauthorized migrants in the United States actually crossed the border legally with approved visas (or visa waivers). They just did not leave when those visas expired.

The frequent emphasis on national borders in discussing contemporary migration has some serious limitations. One is that it tends to downplay all the different kinds of barriers that migrants must overcome, barriers that are also borders in their own way. For example, an exclusive focus on national borders tends to divide considerations of international migration from those of internal migration, even though the two are similar in their dynamics and often connected in people's actual lives. Migrant histories, after all, are often a mix of internal and transnational moves. One other problem in the emphasis on national borders is that it has tended to divide the story of migration into two separate components, with the story of leaving one country as *emigration* and arriving in another country as *immigration*. A single migrant history thus becomes two very different stories based on the national perspectives of the "sending" and "receiving" countries. That single history also becomes a story of two sets of legal rights and constraints. The right to emigrate—to leave a country—is a fundamental principle of international law, but there is no equivalent right in international law to enter another country (except in the specific case of refugees fleeing persecution). To make matters worse, the use of the word *migrant* in normal conversation often refers to someone who is *not* an immigrant or emigrant: thus *migrant labor* implies a different set of people than *immigrant labor*, even though migrant labor often includes people who cross a national border to work and perhaps end up staying.

There is a further definitional problem, because the word *immigrant* is itself used in different ways. In the common, everyday sense in the United States, it means "people who come to this country to live," and that is generally how it is used in this book. But in a more legal sense it means "people who are approved by the government to stay in the United States permanently." Those two meanings may overlap much of the time, but they are not the same. People may come to the United States with temporary visas or with no papers at all and still intend to be "immigrants" in the sense of permanent residence and life in the United States. By contrast, people who have legal status as "immigrants" (technically "permanent resident aliens") may not intend to stay permanently in the United States, may return to their country of origin, may move on to yet another country, or may remain connected to multiple countries with lives that include continuing back-and-forth movements.

Overall, these comments on movement and migration, and the different words with overlapping meanings used to describe them, are a reminder that this process of human mobility is a complex one that looks different from different perspectives. In order to grapple with the full complexity of that movement, it is necessary to stay open to alternative perspectives that can help expand, rather than simplify, the understanding of people moving across space as their own lives move through time.

ORGANIZATION OF THE BOOK

The seemingly obvious topic of US immigration thus faces complexities both in its subject matter and in the very words used to describe it. Here the discussion has begun with a focus on human mobility. Human mobility has been a useful area of discussion in several disciplines and helps set the stage for understanding how migration is a very common human process but still a daunting one, with various kinds of barriers and borders that must be crossed. Beginning with general issues of human mobility helps show how today's mobility often reflects yesterday's mobility (thus extending the time frame for thinking about mobility) and how many different kinds of barriers there are to human movement (geographical, cultural, economic, political)—only some of which directly relate to the current public and scholarly emphasis on national borders.

The remainder of this book is divided into two parts that address the topic of US immigration from two fundamentally different perspectives: first, the overall history of immigration as a fundamental part of the development of the United States and, second, the lived experiences of the migrants themselves. Part I deals with the first issue—the history of immigration to the United States and the basic political and policy issues it raises. Specifically:

Chapter 1 provides an overview of world mobility and then focuses on the classic immigration history of the United States, particularly the great migrations of the 1800s and early 1900s before the immigration gates were virtually shut in the 1920s. Key themes are the durability of migration throughout American history and the very diverse people who have arrived—with different backgrounds, different dreams, and different destinies.

Chapter 2 focuses on immigration since the Second World War, when a variety of concerns, both domestic and international, began opening the doors that had been so resoundingly shut in the 1920s. This is the historical backdrop for the immigrants and their children who are in the United States now. Key themes are the variation in migrant origins, the many different channels by which people have come to the United States, and the varied trajectories of their lives after arrival.

Chapter 3 addresses the major political and policy issues raised by contemporary US immigration. The chapter outlines both the official and de facto US admissions policies and the political arrangements that sometimes exclude, but sometimes also include, immigrants. The many ways in which "illegal" immigration is a result of government policy receive particular attention. The chapter concludes by placing the United States in a broader context as one among many countries now experiencing high levels of immigration.

Part II focuses on the immigrants themselves and, albeit to a lesser extent, their children. Each of the chapters takes on a specific aspect of the immigrant experience and provides two paired comparisons of recent immigration groups. Specifically,

> Chapter 4 introduces the many reasons immigrants come, ranging along a continuum of escape from repression to the search for economic opportunity—with many variations in between. It continues with the vacillating responses that new immigrants face in the United States, from welcome to rejection (and sometimes simple indifference). Key themes are the varied reasons for migration (the United States as both a land of refuge and a land of opportunity), the wide range of local settings for their new lives, and something of how their new lives are both continuations and disruptions of their previous lives. The two paired comparisons at the end of the chapter are Cubans and Soviets, followed by Cambodians and Salvadorans.
>
> Chapter 5 focuses in more detail on the economic dimensions of a new life: on the world of work and how immigrants interact with it. The discussion attends to the different meanings of work and the strategies that immigrants use to maximize their situation—for example, by seeking jobs that permit accumulation of assets, jobs that produce steady income, jobs that can benefit from family labor (e.g., stores, restaurants), or simply jobs that permit them to pursue their more noneconomic goals. Key themes are the importance of individual factors but also of social and cultural resources. The paired comparisons at the end are Iranians and Indians, followed by Ecuadorans and Koreans.
>
> Chapter 6 turns from the practicalities of life in a new land to the challenge of creating a life that is meaningful in the long term. Immigrants often rely on formal religious institutions, whether building them from scratch, melding their own needs with those of existing American institutions, or actively joining in American religious congregations. But much of the meaning of life is found in domains that are not directly "religious" in the usual sense. Many immigrants, for example, find the meaning of their life in family, in the creative arts, and in political action—whether in the new country or the old one. Perhaps the key theme in the chapter is the range of options available in pursuing the meaning of life in a new context. The paired comparisons at the end are Mexican and Vietnamese Catholics, followed by African Christians from Sudan and European Muslims from Bosnia.
>
> Chapter 7 assesses how and where immigrants find a sense of belonging in their new lives in the United States. The discussion begins by sorting out the

multiple terms used for this process (for example, *acculturation, assimilation, accommodation, adaptation,* and *absorption*). One crucial implication of many of these terms lies in assumptions about how reciprocal or one-sided this process might be. The chapter continues by examining some of the actual data on immigrant integration over time and then considering what that process looks like when viewed in particular locations. The paired comparisons at the end are Mexicans in Los Angeles and Cubans in Miami, followed by Yucatecans in Dallas and Koreans in Washington, DC.

The epilogue briefly reviews the major themes of the book and refocuses the discussion toward the future and outward toward the global scene. The United States is only one of many countries where immigrants are now a sizable number and a noticeable presence. Furthermore, formal long-term immigration is only one form of contemporary transnational migration—and perhaps a decreasingly important one. This concluding discussion reinvokes the broader issues of human mobility and how to understand migration not simply as an uprooting experience but also as an experience that is quintessentially human and "normal."

A NOTE ON TABLES

A brief comment on the tables is also in order. The tabular material is drawn from various sources, but I have relied most heavily on standardized US government data. For part I, the major source is the Department of Homeland Security and its statistics of who is coming to the United States, especially its annual *Yearbook of Immigration Statistics*. This is a readily available source. The current website for all the yearbooks is https://www.dhs.gov/immigration-statistics/yearbook. Note that data are provided in three different formats: on the Web in a somewhat abbreviated version, in .pdf format that is complete, and as downloadable Excel files.

For part II of this book, the major source for tabular data is the US Census Bureau on the social and economic characteristics of those who have arrived in the United States. I rely especially on the Census Bureau's American Community Survey (ACS), which provides the kind of detailed information that used to be provided on the decennial census's long form. Without that level of detail, it is impossible to address issues about particular immigrant groups, whether in terms of country of origin, current location, or key economic and sociocultural situation. The sample size of the ACS, however, is not adequate for analysis of any but the largest immigrant groups, so merged data from multiple years are needed. For this book, most of the tabular data are taken from the merged data of the 2011–2013 surveys (for information on country-of-origin groups) and the 2011–2015 surveys (for information on foreign-born versus native-born more generally).

There are several advantages to relying on this standardized government data. It is the most comprehensive data, for example. Another advantage is its ready availability. Much of the information provided in this book can be re-created for more recent years and expanded to address other immigrants in other locations that could not all be covered in detail in a short introductory volume. These combined ACS data sets are available online, and it is possible to extract information through a structured query format for either sets of people or locations, or both. These can then be downloaded in various formats, including Excel spreadsheets (although with some size limitations). The easiest access is through American Fact Finder, at https://factfinder.census.gov/.

Two organizations that are especially skilled at compiling such government data (and other sources) on immigration are the Migration Policy Institute (http://www.migrationpolicy.org) and the Pew Research Center (http://www .pewresearch.org/). Although they remain good options for accessing data, there is far more flexibility in directly accessing the US census data, and it is a far wiser policy to tackle the numbers yourself on what is a highly politicized topic.

PART I

The United States and Immigration

1

~~

A World of Migrants, a Nation of Immigrants

The global flows of people and goods in recent centuries have transformed the existing land and people in places of origin and destination. Of these many flows of people, one of the most important has been to the United States. With a combination of people fleeing oppression and people seeking new economic opportunities, early European colonists produced a remarkably durable new republic by the end of the 1700s and the world's dominant economic and political power by the mid-1900s. That success was not without great human costs, especially to the Native Americans displaced by the European settlers and the people forcibly transported from Africa as slave labor. Yet the United States became a place where many newcomers could achieve dreams impossible in their home countries, even though they were often placed at the bottom of the social and political order in the United States. The reaction to these newcomers was sometimes positive but often harsh. Piecemeal exclusions of particular groups in the late 1800s culminated in a broader exclusion of immigrants in the early 1900s. The most powerful nation forged out of immigration forsook its heritage and, some would argue, as a result slid into isolationism and a massive economic depression. Only the Second World War would shake that pattern.

The aim in this chapter is to indicate the full range of migratory movements over the last few centuries and their implications for the United States. The discussion begins with an overview of the early peopling of North America and continues with the way immigration was viewed in the context of a new American republic and how it expanded greatly in both scope and origins during the 1800s. Those massive waves of immigration, however, set in play restrictionist forces that resulted in exclusionary legislation in the 1920s and the relative isolation of the United States during the 1930s, resulting in the exclusion of most immigrants and the more specific exclusion of refugees, especially Jews fleeing Nazi Germany. This chapter thus outlines both the epic flows of people into America and the abrupt shutdown of those flows.

A NEW LAND

With the fracturing of the supercontinent Pangaea roughly 150 million years ago, both North and South America drifted toward their current locations, ultimately docking with each other through a narrow land bridge that is now Panama. It was a drift into relative isolation with different destinies for both plant and animal life. One aspect of that isolation was the very late arrival of human beings to the Americas. The standard estimates—although subject to alternative theories and reconstructed timelines—are that human beings arrived across the Bering Strait, which was above water at the time, some twenty thousand years ago.[1] They then moved east across North America and south into Central and South America. Exactly how this migration took place may never be known, but one can imagine it as a gradual extension of hunting and gathering territories in new directions and then a range of adaptations to the different environments that the newcomers found. In most areas, hunting and gathering remained the core of economic life, but agriculture appeared in some areas and provided the basis for several very large, well-developed societies with cities, trade, government, and elaborate ritual lives. The Aztecs and the Incas remain the best known of these larger societies.

The Americas were thus a land of late human "immigration." They were also a land of low population density, less resistance to disease, and relatively low technological development compared to the rest of the world. That put the early Americans at an enormous disadvantage when Europeans began to arrive. Those Europeans came for many reasons: some to explore, some to pillage, some to convert. Some also came to settle. Particularly in the area that is now Canada and the United States, they saw a sparsely populated land, but one that responded well to the more intensive agricultural methods they used, and that would also provide the natural resources to fuel trade and eventually industrial development. There are many ways to tell this story—both its glories and its horrors—but one simple way is to consider population.

The figures in table 1.1 represent the efforts of Angus Maddison and his colleagues to provide a comprehensive grid of key population and economic data over the course of human history. These data are especially helpful in plotting the relative population sizes of different regions of the world. Up until AD 1500, the beginning of sustained European contact with the Americas, the population of western Europe, with a far smaller land area, dwarfed the combined populations of North and South America. By their estimates, the population of Europe in 1500 was more than twenty-five times as high as the combined population of North America, which they define as the current territory of Canada and the United States. The period immediately afterward made the population difference even sharper as European conquest brought death and disease. That cut the population of the Americas roughly in half according to their figures—and it may have been much worse. At the time of the first durable English settlements in North America, the population of North America was only a little more than 1 percent of the population of Europe. But that percentage would soon change. As the English settlements took hold, North America's population rapidly increased: it became roughly a tenth of the size of the western European population by the early 1800s, nearly a half by the early 1900s, and about three-quarters by 2000. This population growth in North America was one of the most explosive the world has seen.

Table 1.1. World population by region (in millions)

	Year						
	0	1000	1500	1700	1820	1913	2000
East/Southeast Asia	74	88	156	216	468	620	2,014
South Asia	75	75	110	165	217	320	1,355
West Asia	19	20	18	21	25	39	237
Africa	17	32	47	61	74	125	811
Western Europe	25	25	57	81	133	260	393
North America	1	1	2	1	11	105	318
Latin America	6	11	18	12	22	81	521

Source: University of Groningen, Angus Maddison Project, http://www.ggdc.net/maddison/maddison -project/home.htm. For particular data, see country-source references in the appendix of J. Bolt and J. L. van Zanden, "The Maddison Project: Collaborative Research on Historical National Accounts," *Economic History Review* 67, no. 3 (2014): 627–51.

Note: Figures for Eastern Europe and Central Asia are incomplete for early years and are not included here. Also definitions for subregions of Asia can vary.

The roots of that population explosion were very modest. The first lasting English settlement was in 1607 in Jamestown, Virginia. The three ships had a passable voyage, but the colonists' first year in the colony was devastating. Some two-thirds of the original settlers died before additional supplies and settlers arrived the following year. The new arrivals also suffered from mass starvation (and some reputed cannibalism). By the time a third round of supply ships reached them, only some 60 of the original 214 settlers survived. Circumstances improved thereafter, and Virginia would prosper. But several events in the very early history of Jamestown presaged the way in which the colony would develop. The first was the discovery that tobacco seeds would grow in Virginia, and grow very well. Thus the colony had a valuable export. The second was that growing tobacco was hard work. No one wanted to do it. That raised the question of how to get people to the colony who would grow and harvest tobacco rather than move on to far more appealing independent work in farming or trade. Thus in 1611 the colonists petitioned the British government to send convicts to the colony. The

British government acceded to this request and began to use "transportation" to the colonies to reduce the size of its prisons and poorhouses. One way to finance that transportation was to place those paupers and prisoners in servitude until they had paid off those costs. Thus new settlers would be indentured for some period of time after arrival until they were freed. Indentured servitude would be a major source of new settlers for many years. Also, in 1619 a ship with African slaves arrived, the slaves having been taken from a Dutch ship in the West Indies by a British ship, which then sailed to Jamestown. The settlers had a new form of bound labor, and one bound more firmly and more durably than indentured servants. While the situation of these initial African arrivals may have been somewhat flexible in terms of the strictures and duration of servitude, this nevertheless laid the basis for increasing use of African slaves for a plantation economy (first tobacco, then cotton) and the increasing rigidity and severity of the "peculiar institution" that was the American slave system.

The second durable English settlement in what would become the United States was in Massachusetts. Here the founding purpose was different. This was not a grand economic adventure but a purposive attempt to forge a new and better community for those with shared religious convictions. As with the original Jamestown settlers, a passable voyage (rough seas but only one death) was followed by very severe conditions. During the first winter, the death rate was high (45 out of 102). So these settlers, like those at Jamestown, paid a heavy early price. But other ships soon arrived, and the original group of Pilgrims was greatly amplified by a larger migration of Puritans, who would make Massachusetts the most populous of the colonies by the end of the century. As in Jamestown, early events presaged the particular undercurrents of this growing prosperity. In the matter of labor, for example, indentured servitude was used in the very first voyage—although most of the indentured passengers were on the *Mayflower*'s original companion ship (the *Speedwell*), which was ultimately unable to sail. As well, and unlike the completely male settlers of the original Jamestown ships, women were well represented on the *Mayflower* and its successor ships. From its very origins, this was a colony meant to be a full, functioning, and reproducing community in its new home. Somewhat more problematic in the initial years of the colony was a shifting balance of tolerance and intolerance. While the goal of the settlers was to flee intolerance in Europe, they were not interested in having any diversity of belief among themselves. It was not long, then, before the first purging occurred. In the mid-1630s both Roger Williams and Anne Hutchinson were banished for their views. Two decades later three Quakers would be hanged for their tenacity in preaching their radically egalitarian and nonhierarchical views in Massachusetts.

Although the Virginia and Massachusetts colonies had very different origins and goals, they both prospered and grew. That growth had its origins in migration, and continued to benefit from additional migration—whether of free settlers, indentured servants, or slaves. But much of the growth and prosperity was also the result of very high fertility among those who came to America. The

LANDING OF THE PILGRIMS

An 1877 vision of the original landing of the Pilgrims. (Engraving by Albert Bobbett, courtesy of the New York Public Library)

opportunities in the new colonies were expansive enough to support an increasing population. Those opportunities, however, came with loss to the original inhabitants. In the Virginia colony, relations with the Native Americans deteriorated very quickly. Despite some initial mutual accommodation—including the marriage of Pocahontas to John Rolfe—colonist actions in Virginia against the American Indians soon undermined hope for good relations. By 1622, the opposition to the colonists erupted in organized attacks: roughly a quarter of the colonists were killed in one coordinated attack. In Massachusetts, relations with the Native Americans were better, and those good relations lasted longer. But there, too, uneasy accommodation turned to war, and, with the so-called King Philip's War of 1675, hope of amicable relations was largely lost. The prosperity of the colonists was at the price of the dislocation and frequent death of the former inhabitants. Human mobility often has a darker side.

There would soon be other colonies with other destinies. They would share with Virginia and Massachusetts some measure of both economic adventurism and religious commitment. Their original populations were sometimes from different sources: Dutch (especially in New York and New Jersey), Germans (especially in Pennsylvania), and French (scattered in various colonies). Furthermore, those already in the colonies often moved to different places, just as they had often moved to different places before they came to the colonies. Many of those coming from the British Isles were also increasingly from the outlying Irish, Scotch, and Welsh lands rather than from England itself. Their movements were sometimes quite voluntary and sometimes relatively forced. Those coming from Africa as slavery took hold in the Southern Colonies were so fully forced that we have few records of their own experiences coming to the colonies and few artifacts of their passage—even their clothes were taken from them as they were packed into cramped and pestilent conditions on slave ships.

The Expulsion of the Acadians in the 1750s and 1760s provides an example of the complexity of these colonial migrations. The Acadians were French-speaking Catholics who had settled in what is now Atlantic Canada. They were industrious farmers, and their systems of water control to the fields made possible the development of the lands around the Bay of Fundy (with the world's highest tides) and, to a lesser extent, along the Gulf of Saint Lawrence. It was a lush landscape, then and still today. The problem for the Acadians was that Britain had gained control over their territory in the early 1700s. The Acadians were allowed to keep their lands and were even spared taking an oath of allegiance to the British that might have pitted them against their French-speaking brethren in still-French-controlled Quebec farther to the north. This agreement collapsed when war broke out again between the British and the French.[2] The expulsion had many stages in many places but has been particularly well described for the area of Grand-Pré, since the British officer who led the expulsion there later wrote about it in detail. He, John Winslow, arrived with troops in August 1755. The inhabitants were not told of the purpose of his visit and found out only two weeks later when he summoned all the men to the church, sealed the doors, and read them the proclamation that all their lands were to be seized and that they were to be expelled from their homes. The men were confined to the church as the British made preparations to expel them. By Winslow's account, the deportation was orderly and attempts made to keep families together. Whether that was even possible considering the circumstances and the large size of Acadian families is questionable. Whatever the case, the Acadians could do nothing as the ships transported them away. Their homes and fields were burned; it was a graphic reminder that their past was indeed gone. Here, in current migration terminology, former immigrants and their children had been transformed into forced emigrants.

But where did they go? Here there is another kind of migration story. They were sent to the British colonies to the south. Each colony was given a quota of expellees to settle based on population size. The largest quotas went to the prosperous colonies of Massachusetts and Virginia. Massachusetts, somewhat grudgingly, eventually accepted its quota but only after months of keeping the Acadians on the ships in Boston harbor had left them rife with disease. When allowed to disembark, they were dispersed out to localities where their lives were very difficult. They had, after all, lost not only their homes but also the fertile fields and animals that had been their livelihood. Many drifted into debt. That forced them to indenture themselves or their family members in order to survive. In Virginia, their fate was worse. The governor showed some initial sympathy, but there, too, the expellees were forced to wait aboard ship as their fate was decided. That fate was rejection. These expellees were routed on to England, where they were imprisoned. Those who survived imprisonment were returned to France at the conclusion of the war. Having no connections in France, many then returned to the Americas, particularly to the New Orleans area, which, at that time, was relatively hospitable to them.

Like many migrations, the Acadian expulsion had complicated origins and complicated outcomes. Imagining the full human experience of those expellees is difficult from the outside because of the fragmentary data. In this case, however, we also have the literary efforts of Henry Wadsworth Longfellow, whose *Evangeline* tells the story of the expulsion and its aftermath through a young couple, about to be married, who are pulled apart in the expulsion. They both land, alive, in the colonies to the south and spend the rest of their lives looking for each other. Instead, then, of being settlers in a new country, they become searchers through a new country for their past lives. There is little attachment to the new land because the overriding attachment is to the human connections that existed before arrival. Longfellow thus reminds us of how often arrival in a new land remains forever the loss of one's original land. Such loss is frequent—although not inevitable—for voluntary immigrants. It is inevitable for forced migrants, whether those we think of as refugees or those forced to a new land by servitude and slavery. What few accounts we have of arriving, foreign-born slaves, for example, are consistent on the continuing pain in the loss of family and home, as well as the pain in the loss of freedom.

A NEW COUNTRY

Through all these complicated skeins of movement, the new colonies grew and prospered. Ultimately they sought independence, in part because of their concern about how Britain was controlling migration to the colonies. In particular, Britain was forcing people into the colonies that the colonists did not want—especially felons and paupers—and also keeping from the colonies better-skilled settlers whom the English preferred to keep at home.[3] With independence it was possible to shape immigration more directly to national purposes.

By the time of the new country's first census in 1790, the total population was nearly four million, approximately 20 percent of whom were slaves. Virginia was by far the largest state (747,610, including 292,627 slaves), followed by Pennsylvania (434,373), North Carolina (393,751), Massachusetts (378,787), and New York (340,120). For the Southern states, the proportion of the population that was slave was high: Virginia at 39 percent and North Carolina at 26 percent (see table 1.2 for details). The 1790 census also provides a rough indication of the general ancestry of the nonslave population (see table 1.3). These figures should be used with some caution, since the categories are subject to some drift: "English" may well include some Scotch and Irish; "German" is clearly a language and

Table 1.2. US population by legal status, 1790

	Free	Slaves	Total
Maine	96,540	0	96,540
New Hampshire	141,727	158	141,885
Vermont	85,523	16	85,539
Massachusetts	378,787	0	378,787
Rhode Island	67,877	948	68,825
Connecticut	235,182	2,764	237,946
New York	318,796	21,324	340,120
New Jersey	172,716	11,423	184,139
Pennsylvania	430,636	3,737	434,373
Delaware	50,207	8,887	59,094
Maryland	216,692	103,036	319,728
Virginia	454,983	292,627	747,610
North Carolina	293,179	100,572	393,751
South Carolina	141,979	107,094	249,073
Georgia	53,284	29,264	82,548
Kentucky	61,247	12,430	73,677
Total	**3,199,355**	**694,280**	**3,893,635**

Source: US Census Bureau, *Census of Population and Housing, 1790*, 1793, https://www2.census.gov/prod2/decennial/documents/1790a.pdf.

Note: Maine still part of Massachusetts; territories not included.

regional marker and not a national one, since Germany as a unified country did not yet exist. But the results indicate that, for the free population, this was still very dominantly an English-populated country at just over 60 percent and, if the Scotch and Irish are included, at nearly 80 percent. Other than the English, the Germans were the major group, especially in Pennsylvania, and there were also other states where other ancestries were significant, perhaps especially the Dutch in New York and New Jersey. However, if slaves are included in the calculation, one would have to characterize the new United States as predominantly an Anglo-African country. Note as well that Native Americans are not included in these numbers, though, with the combination of war, disease, and constriction to reservations, their numbers were dropping sharply.[4]

This population of four million was the result of decisions by individual people to come to the colonies, of decisions about people (including slavery), and of a consistently high reproductive rate that had the colonies growing at a brisk 3 percent per year throughout the 1700s. By contrast, the current US rate is below

Table 1.3. Percent of population by ancestry, 1790

| | | | Irish | | | | | | |
	English	Scotch	Ulster	Free State	German	Dutch	French	Swedish	Not assigned
Maine	60.0	4.5	8.0	3.7	1.3	0.1	1.3		21.1
New Hampshire	61.0	6.2	4.6	2.9	0.4	0.1	0.7		24.1
Vermont	76.0	5.1	3.2	1.9	0.2	0.6	0.4		12.6
Massachusetts	82.0	4.4	2.6	1.3	0.3	0.2	0.8		8.4
Rhode Island	71.0	5.8	2.0	0.8	0.5	0.4	0.8	0.1	18.6
Connecticut	67.0	2.2	1.8	1.1	0.3	0.3	0.9		26.4
New York	52.0	7.0	5.1	3.0	8.2	17.5	3.8	0.5	2.9
New Jersey	47.0	7.7	6.3	3.2	9.2	16.6	2.4	3.9	3.7
Pennsylvania	35.3	8.6	11.0	3.5	33.3	1.8	1.8	0.8	3.9
Delaware	60.0	8.0	6.3	5.4	1.1	4.3	1.6	8.9	4.4
Maryland	64.5	7.6	5.8	6.5	11.7	0.5	1.2	0.5	1.7
Virginia	68.5	10.2	6.2	5.5	6.3	0.3	1.5	0.6	0.9
North Carolina	66.0	14.8	5.7	5.4	4.7	0.3	1.7	0.2	1.2
South Carolina	60.2	15.1	9.4	4.4	5.0	0.4	3.9	0.2	1.4
Georgia	57.4	15.5	11.5	3.8	7.6	0.2	2.3	0.6	1.1
Kentucky/ Tennessee	57.9	10.0	7.0	5.2	14.0	1.3	2.2	0.5	1.9
Total	**60.9**	**8.3**	**6.0**	**3.7**	**8.7**	**3.4**	**1.7**	**0.7**	**6.6**

Source: US Census Bureau, Historical Statistics of the United States, Colonial Times to 1970, September 1975, https://www.census.gov/library/publications/1975/compendia/hist_stats_colonial-1970.html, page 1168.

1 percent. The United States would thus have continued to grow without further immigration. So what was the US position on immigration going to be? The thinking at that time was not simply "for" or "against" immigration but rather hinged on several different considerations. Relying particularly on Benjamin Franklin, George Washington, and Thomas Jefferson—because they all focused on the issue in different ways at different times—the most general observation that can be made is that their views were mixed and fluid. In that mix and fluidity, however, were recurring core elements. From a moral point of view, one central issue was asylum. Their new republic stood for freedom in opposition to tyranny. Those who fled tyranny and sought refuge should, from their point of view, become part of this new land. Washington and Jefferson in particular stressed this concept. Washington wrote in a private letter in 1788, "I had always hoped that

this land might become a safe and agreeable asylum to the virtuous and persecuted part of mankind, to whatever nation they might belong."[5] Jefferson had
written in a similar vein in 1781: "It [has] been the wise policy of these states to
extend the protection of their laws to all those who should settle among them of
whatever nation or religion they might be and to admit them to a participation of
the benefits of civil and religious freedom."[6]

This commitment to the United States as a land of both civil and religious freedom, however, was not without limitation. Above all, there was concern that new
arrivals might not accept the basic tenets of a republic and that, especially by virtue
of settling in large numbers, they would remain separate from American society
and politics. Franklin was perhaps the most vociferous on the point, since in his
Pennsylvania there were large numbers of Germans who did indeed settle together
and retain their own language and customs. In a private letter, for example, he
noted, "Those who come hither are generally of the most ignorant Stupid Sort of
their own Nation. . . . But now they come in droves, and carry all before them. . . .
In short unless the stream of their importation could be turned from this to other
colonies . . . they will soon so out number us, that all the advantages we have will
not in My Opinion be able to preserve our language, and even our Government
will become precarious."[7] In a public document, he wondered, "Why should Pennsylvania, founded by the English, become a Colony of *Aliens*, who will shortly be so
numerous as to Germanize us instead of our Anglifying them, and will never adopt
our Language or Customs, any more than they can acquire our Complexion."[8]
Jefferson and Washington were more careful in their wording, but they echoed
similar concerns. Washington cautioned that settling new arrivals in large groups
would impede them from becoming "assimilated to our customs, manners and
laws" and thus keep them from becoming "one people" with those already in the
country.[9] Jefferson warned that new arrivals "will bring with them the principles
of the governments they leave" or, worse yet, have abandoned those principles for
"an unbounded licentiousness" that leaves no room for any "temperate liberty."[10]

To these concerns about asylum and assimilation, Franklin, Jefferson, and
Washington added a concern about the future growth of the United States. Despite his railing against the Germans, Franklin could also extol the benefits of
further immigration. "Strangers are welcome here," he wrote, "because there is
room enough for them all, and therefore the old Inhabitants are not jealous of
them."[11] Jefferson proclaimed that previous migration to the United States had
demonstrated that openness to new settlement was "worthy of being continued
in future times."[12] And Washington, perhaps most eloquently of all, proclaimed,
"The bosom of America is open to receive not only the opulent and respectable
stranger, but the oppressed and persecuted of all nations and religions, whom we
shall welcome to a participation of all our rights and privileges, if by decency and
propriety of conduct they appear to merit the enjoyment."[13] The final phrase in
Washington's statement is a reminder that this acceptance of newcomers is not
unconditional. Those coming to the United States need to either share the values
of the new republic or assimilate to those values over time. The intolerance of

difference seen in the early years of the Massachusetts colony is echoed here in concerns that newcomers may debase the common good. In the Massachusetts colony, those reasons for rejection were largely religious in nature. With the founding of the United States, there was a heightened concern with political and cultural factors, particularly when differences were tied to foreign policy. Thus, in the very early years of the republic, concern about French infiltration led to draconian policies against foreigners. The Alien and Sedition Acts signed by President John Adams in 1798, for example, greatly extended the period before newcomers could gain citizenship.[14] These laws were ultimately rescinded, but they presaged other virulent—and sometimes hysterical—reactions against immigrants. Those reactions have continued into contemporary times.

A LAND OF IMMIGRATION

In the founding of the republic, the issue of slavery had not been resolved, and the international slave trade was not to be subject to federal government control for twenty years, nor was there to be any other control of immigration except by the states themselves. The new republic did, however, create a system of relatively rapid naturalization, partly out of concern to entice new settlement and partly out of concern to facilitate assimilation of newcomers into American society.[15] The net result—except for the period when the Alien and Sedition Acts were in effect—was that migration to the United States was initially largely unregulated at the US receiving end, although other countries might well limit the ability of their citizens to emigrate to the United States. During the early 1800s, then, there were few barriers to those seeking the opportunities that the United States had to offer. There were some changes, however, as the international slave trade was eventually abolished, which triggered a massive expansion of the internal slave trade between the "Old" and the "Deep" South. There was also some increasing regulation of shipping as an indirect control of migration. By and large, however, if people wanted to come to the United States, they could.

Records on migration into the United States began to be collected regularly in 1820. From these data (see table 1.4), one can see surging, although erratic, numbers. From 130,000 arrivals in the 1820s, the numbers increased to roughly a half million in the 1830s, a million and a half in the 1840s, and approaching three million in the 1850s. Even in the 1860s, with the Civil War, over two million immigrants arrived. The numbers climbed again in the 1870s and reached their peak with over eight million arriving in the first decade of the 1900s. (The precipitous drop thereafter will be discussed later in the chapter.) Another way to look at this surge in immigration, which coexisted with a continuing strong increase in children born to those already in the country, is to consider the percentage of the foreign-born in the United States (see table 1.5). Those data are available from US census data beginning in 1850. The initial figure for 1850 shows about one in ten persons (9.7 percent) as foreign-born. The number jumps to about one in seven in 1860 (13.2 percent) and remains quite consistent thereafter into the early 1900s—and again today.

Table 1.4. Immigration by decade, 1820–2009

	Arrivals per decade
1820s	129,000
1830s	538,000
1840s	1,427,000
1850s	2,815,000
1860s	2,081,000
1870s	2,742,000
1880s	5,249,000
1890s	3,694,000
1900s	8,202,000
1910s	6,347,000
1920s	4,296,000
1930s	699,000
1940s	857,000
1950s	2,499,000
1960s	3,214,000
1970s	4,248,000
1980s	6,244,000
1990s	9,775,000
2000s	10,299,000

Source: US Department of Homeland Security, *Yearbook of Immigration Statistics: 2015* (Washington, DC: US Department of Homeland Security, Office of Immigration Statistics, 2016).

The immigrants arriving during the early years of the republic were similar to those who had arrived in colonial times, with the exception of the abolition of the African slave trade. But there were changes over time in the origins of these immigrants (see table 1.6). In the 1820s, origins were still largely English and Irish, with much smaller numbers of French and Germans.[16] In the 1830s, Ireland was the major source, followed by Germany, with England in third place. The same pattern held in the 1840s and 1850s—although with a lengthening lead of Germany over England. For the 1860s, 1870s, and 1880s, Germany was the main source, trailed by England and then Ireland. By the 1880s, however, people from many other countries were also arriving in large numbers: at least one hundred thousand each from Austria, Hungary, Italy, Sweden, and Russia. During the next two decades, it was Austria, Hungary, Italy, and Russia that became the dominant source countries. This was a tidal shift in immigrant origins from western and northern Europe to eastern and southern Europe. That shift is seen in

Table 1.5. US population and percent foreign-born, 1850–2010

	Total	Foreign-born (%)
1850	23,192,000	9.7
1860	31,443,000	13.2
1870	38,558,000	14.4
1880	50,156,000	13.3
1890	62,622,000	14.8
1900	75,994,000	13.6
1910	91,972,000	14.7
1920	105,711,000	13.2
1930	122,775,000	11.6
1940	131,669,000	8.8
1950	150,216,000	6.9
1960	179,326,000	5.4
1970	203,210,000	4.7
1980	226,546,000	6.2
1990	248,710,000	7.9
2000	281,422,000	11.1
2010	308,746,000	12.9

Source: Updated version of Campbell J. Gibson and Emily Lennon, "Historical Census Statistics on the Foreign-Born Population of the United States: 1850–1990," Population Division Working Paper no. 29, US Bureau of the Census, Washington, DC, 1999, https://www.census.gov/population/www/documentation/twps0029/twps0029.html.

increasingly vivid form in the 1890s, 1900s, and 1910s. Yet there were also immigrant origins beyond those European sources. From midcentury on, for example, there were sizable numbers from China and then from Japan later in the century, with smaller traces from many other places—although there were very few from Central and South America and few from Africa. There were also many arrivals from Canada and the Caribbean, although many of them were not originally from those places but coming through them to the United States.

Such discussions by national and regional origin cannot fully convey the complexities of the reasons and dynamics underlying migration to the United States during this period of mass migration and the fates of these migrants after arrival. Consider five cases from around 1850 as examples of the range of migrant origins and destinies: Irish, Germans, Chinese, Mexicans, and West Africans.

In the Irish case, migration to the colonies and the United States was hardly new. The migration flow included a wide range of people, some Protestant and

Table 1.6. Cumulative arrivals by origin, 1820–1919

	1820–1869	1870–1919	Total
Europe	6,394,900	23,025,125	29,420,025
Austria-Hungary	3,375	4,065,076	4,068,451
Austria	2,700	1,649,142	1,651,842
Hungary	483	1,570,050	1,570,533
Belgium	15,594	115,374	130,968
Denmark	18,551	278,348	296,899
France	240,040	283,780	523,820
Germany	2,215,719	3,278,971	5,494,690
Greece	166	358,258	358,424
Ireland	2,335,339	2,013,420	4,348,759
Italy	22,627	4,078,108	4,100,735
Netherlands	29,615	184,859	214,474
Norway–Sweden	118,768	1,718,748	1,837,516
Norway	0	632,595	632,595
Sweden	0	1,086,153	1,086,153
Poland	3,463	161,719	165,182
Portugal	10,466	202,696	213,162
Russia	2,976	3,229,739	3,232,715
Spain	22,572	96,839	119,411
Switzerland	57,944	198,763	256,707
United Kingdom	1,297,536	2,559,502	3,857,038
Asia	90,698	836,704	927,402
China	90,004	255,004	345,008
Japan	138	232,611	232,749
Turkey	295	319,086	319,381
Americas	306,722	2,262,911	2,569,633
Canada	230,603	1,650,932	1,881,535
Mexico	19,494	224,794	244,288
Caribbean	47,912	295,897	343,809
Central America	1,030	24,268	25,298
South America	7,529	59,643	67,172
Africa	714	16,834	17,548
Total	**6,990,035**	**26,234,767**	**33,224,802**

Source: US Department of Homeland Security, *Yearbook of Immigration Statistics: 2015* (Washington, DC: US Department of Homeland Security, Office of Immigration Statistics, 2016).

Note: Numbers will not sum to the total, since only major origins are included.

some Catholic, some political exiles and some with more economic consider-ations. By the middle of the 1800s, however, the situation in Ireland had a new intensity. Irish Catholics had largely been relegated to small plots of land as Eng-lish Protestant landlords gained control of the land. On those small plots, survival hinged on one crop: the potato. When that crop failed them in the 1840s, they were at the edge of famine and soon passed over it. The economic crisis had po-litical undertones: even when the Irish were starving, the English were still send-ing food from Ireland to England. That is a useful reminder of the intersection of political and economic factors in many migration decisions. In contemporary terms, these Irish fit much of the refugee definition, forced to flee by the results of ethnic and religious persecution. And the Irish fled in massive numbers. Their families who remained often held wakes for them before they left, for to leave Ireland was much like death in its finality of separation. But death was not only metaphoric; with famine had come disease, and the ships that took the Irish to the United States were crowded, and below board those diseases often spread with virulence. For these Irish, the voyage to the United States may have been for the preservation of life, but the voyage itself was also through death. Nor did arrival end their misery. Reaction to them in the United States was often harsh. They were derided by many as virtually subhuman, and "No Irish need apply" was a frequent notice on help-wanted announcements.

The situation of the Germans arriving at that same time was quite different. People from the German states had long been a major migrant group to the United States, but for those coming at midcentury the reasons were more sharply political. Political movements across the German states had held the promise of a new republican form of government that would unite those many states and would do so in opposition to the monarchists who then dominated most of them. But the plans failed, and those who had dreamed this liberal dream of a new Germany were forced to flee. Some remained in neighboring countries, hop-ing that conditions would change and they could return. Many, sooner or later, found their way to the United States. They were, in many ways, ideal immigrants: well educated and closely aligned to American republican ideals. They prospered. They also brought ideals from home that slavery was inherently wrong, and those ideals put them squarely in the middle of the debates about slavery in the 1850s. They were thus both lauded and excoriated. On the positive side, Abraham Lincoln found them a congenial group, and the transcripts of talks to German American societies show their appreciation of him—and his ability to reach through to their sentiments as Germans and as new Americans. On the negative side, however, they were labeled as intemperate and intrusive, as "the worst kind of crazy visionaries ever thrown by circumstances upon our shores."[17]

The Chinese at midcentury, unlike the Irish and Germans, were a new migra-tion stream. They came from coastal areas of China that had long been outward looking and the source of emigrants. Prior to the California Gold Rush, there had been very few Chinese in the United States, but the demands for labor on the West Coast expanded greatly, and, from probably less than a thousand before

1850, their numbers climbed to some twenty thousand in 1852 alone. Over three hundred thousand Chinese would come to the United States by the end of the century. Although conditions in China were not good, there was less desperation among Chinese emigrants than in the case of the Irish, and the appeal was more the increased economic opportunity of the United States. Coming from southern China, which already had economic connections of various kinds with the United States, these Chinese knew of economic opportunities in the United States and had the connections to make the journey possible—including the ability to borrow money for the costs of passage. There were also enterprising employers and steamship companies that, in pursuit of profit, made their passage easier. Most of the migrants were men looking for temporary work before returning to China. Many stayed, however, and their desire for wives created a continuing stream of female Chinese migration to the United States even after further arrival of male workers was prohibited. Despite the immense contributions of the Chinese to the California economy—and the completion of the transcontinental railroad—public reaction against them soon reached critical levels, and they, like the Irish, would be derided as nearly subhuman. In the Chinese case, the labor that was once wanted had turned into people who were not.

The situation of Mexicans in the United States at midcentury reflected a very different set of dynamics. The United States had grown in surges. The initial thirteen colonies became the original states, but they were soon joined by new states formed out of the splitting of the original colonies (e.g., Maine from Massachusetts) and out of territory that came to the United States at the conclusion of the Revolutionary War (e.g., the northwest that became all or parts of Ohio, Indiana, Illinois, Michigan, Wisconsin, and Minnesota). The country also acquired new land with the Louisiana Purchase of the Mississippi drainage in 1803, Florida from Spain in 1819, and Texas by voluntary accession in 1845 (about a decade after it had declared independence from Mexico). But the continental United States as we know it today was not completed until 1848, when negotiations with Britain fixed the northern boundary of what is now the State of Washington and war with Mexico yielded the immense areas of the Southwest and the southern part of the West Coast.[18] Suddenly much that had been Mexico was now the United States. That included the people. The lands at the time were sparsely populated, with a population split between those of Mexican and US origins. For the Mexicans, they had not crossed a border, but a border had crossed them, and they became foreigners in their own land. The treaty ending the war labeled them explicitly as subject to Mexico unless they chose to become US citizens. The mechanism for naturalizing was not overly difficult, and most opted for it. Their fates in their new country varied, generally better in what is now New Mexico (and reflected in that state being the only officially bilingual state) and less so in California. But the incorporation of Mexicans into US society at midcentury meant that the United States–Mexico border would always be a border between many people of the same origins.

A final example involves the last slave ship bringing West Africans to the United States before slavery was abolished. The international slave trade (but not the domestic slave trade) had been abolished decades earlier, and the net of international antislavery patrols had tightened. The slave population in the United States was thus, unlike the general US population, almost entirely native-born by midcentury. But there were still a few attempts at importing slaves. The very last such attempt occurred shortly before the beginning of the Civil War. Some 125 slaves were procured from West Africa, brought to Alabama, hidden in the swamps, and then moved to their final destination, usually on the plantations of those who had organized this last clandestine slave ship. Slavery represented the rawest form of labor migration to the United States: forced, violent, degrading. Yet the story of this last slave cohort has some interesting and positive aspects. These Africans, for example, stuck together, often in opposition to US-born slaves. They were, after all, Africans, not Americans. The US-born slaves, in turn, seemed to largely look down on the Africans, having absorbed US notions of savagery in Africa. Yet they also could respect the pride and determination of the Africans. There are cases in which the Africans stood up to slave owners and got away with it. In particular, they would not allow the beating of African women. On one occasion, they actually whipped a white supervisor who tried to whip one of the women. What is perhaps most intriguing is the way this group of Africans, from many different linguistic, cultural, and religious origins, determined to remain a group through slavery and then through Emancipation at the end of the Civil War. The community they founded together became known as Africatown. They could not return to Africa, as they had continued to hope, and so made a piece of Africa in Alabama.

The variety of motives and dynamics seen in these five cases continued through the rest of the 1800s and into the early 1900s. Sometimes economic motives tended to prevail, whether with an intent to remain in the United States or to return to the country of origin. Sometimes it was ethnic, political, and religious factors that propelled migrants to the United States, usually permanently, since there was little to return to. Through the years, there were changes in origins, particularly from northern and western Europe to eastern and southern Europe. There were also changes in destinations as the United States went from being extremely rural—a reported 95 percent in 1790—to being less than two-thirds rural by the end of the century and about evenly split between rural and urban by 1920. Increasingly, migrant destinies in the United States lay in urban areas. By 1900, for example, the foreign-born population was about one in seven of the total US population, but it was a third or more in cities like New York, Chicago, Boston, San Francisco, and Detroit and a quarter or more in many other cities on both coasts and in the Midwest. There was still also some settlement in rural areas and small towns. Special trains would take new arrivals directly from their landing point to western destinations that sometimes still had land for homesteading. The urban case, however, was becoming the far more common pattern toward

Ellis Island at its peak activity in the early 1900s. (Edwin Levick, courtesy of the New York Public Library)

the end of the 1800s. That tended to make immigrants more visible. The dense settlements of migrants at the center of cities were hard to ignore with people who looked different, dressed different, acted different, and lived in often squalid conditions. The standard claim is that the Lower East Side of New York City was, at the end of the 1800s, the most densely populated place in the world. New kinds of housing were developed to make that density possible. They came to be known as tenements. The conditions in them were poor and often awful, with no internal water or toilets or electricity.

CLOSING THE DOOR

The miseries of tenement life were often in the public spotlight in the late 1800s. The work of Jacob Riis was especially important. Himself an immigrant, Riis roamed the streets of New York relentlessly trying to grasp its full immigrant dimensions. The portrait that emerges in his words and photographs is one part sympathy, one part support, and one part stereotype. Here are both the depths and the caricatures of immigration at its peak: the clean Germans, the orderly blacks, the penurious Jews, the amalgam of international and internal migration that was making New York America's dominant city. Riis was hardly the only one to observe the often-abject needs of migrants in cities. The settlement-house movement, for example, would locate middle-class Americans to the inner cities to bring American culture and values to these new arrivals. By 1900, there were more than a hundred settlement houses in US cities. Such a strong public and personal commitment underlined how serious the problems were.

While the severity of the problems moved some people to aid immigrants, it raised doubts among others about the usefulness of continuing immigration at its current levels and with its increasingly eastern and southern European origins. There had always been negative views of immigrants in the United States among some portion of the public, but for roughly the first hundred years of the republic's existence those views had resulted only in indirect and partial attempts to actually curb immigration. Restrictions were from time to time introduced to prohibit entry to persons of dubious moral quality (criminals, prostitutes) and those likely to become public charges. In 1882, however, Congress had gone further and banned one entire group of immigrants: the Chinese.[19] With the massive flows of immigrants around the turn of the century, support for broader restriction of immigration grew, and Congress was more willing to act.

One central question in the overall debate about immigration was how important immigrants actually were to the overall US economy and to particular industries. Another central question was the enduring one of whether these new immigrants could indeed assimilate to American life. Even if they *could*, there was the additional question of whether they *would*. There were thus two possible lines of objection to the migrants in terms of assimilation. First, some argued that the immigrants were not capable of adapting, and this had racial bases. Second, others argued that the immigrants might be able to adapt but might not want to. They might be content in their old ways or simply have divided loyalties that would undermine US institutions. Theodore Roosevelt, for example, was adamant that all people should be treated by the same standard but equally adamant that there was no place in the United States for divided loyalties. Immigrants were obliged to assimilate. He is worth quoting at length because of that double adamancy:

> We should insist that if the immigrant who comes here does in good faith become an American and assimilates himself to us, he shall be treated on an exact equality with every one else, for it is an outrage to discriminate against any such man because of creed, or birthplace, or origin. But this is predicated upon the man's becoming in very fact an American and nothing but an American. If he tries to keep segregated with men of his own origin and separated from the rest of America, then he isn't doing his part as an American. There can be no divided allegiance here. . . . We have room for but one language here and that is the English language, for we intend to see that the crucible turns our people out as Americans, of American nationality, and not as dwellers in a polyglot boarding house; and we have room for but one, soul loyalty, and that loyalty is to the American people.[20]

The "polyglot boarding house" to which he referred was exactly the tenement as seen in New York's Lower East Side and all the other housing that had been divided and subdivided to maximize rents from poor immigrants.

It was this polyglot mix of foreign immigrants, with their foreign ways and foreign languages, that appalled many Americans. Clearly the living conditions of the new immigrants were poor, but did the people themselves cause those conditions, or did those conditions cause their blight? Furthermore, could these people change? Was there hope? Congress, through a special committee formed in 1907 (called the Dillingham Commission after its chairman), commissioned forty-one volumes of studies and reports that focused on the immigrants in their daily lives, as involved in different industries, and in their interactions with the native-born. There were both positive and negative views. Anthropologist Franz Boas, for example, provided research on the physical changes among immigrants between the arriving "first-generation" immigrants and their children. He noted that even supposedly racial features such as head shape, which people often used to distinguish northern/western Europeans from eastern/southern ones, changed over time. If physical features could change over one generation, he argued, how could one believe that immigrant attitudes would not also change in the direction of assimilation?

Overall, however, the negative views won the day. In 1921, the Emergency Quota Act capped the number of immigrants who could arrive at 3 percent of their total population in the United States in 1910. That restricted the overall number and rolled back the calculation date to when there had been fewer immigrants from eastern/southern Europe and more from northern/western Europe. In 1924, the Immigration Act capped overall immigration at 150,000, with immigration from any individual country capped at 2 percent of its total population, and reset the calculation date for that 2 percent back to 1890, when there had been yet fewer immigrants from eastern/southern Europe and yet more from northern/western Europe. The legislation also banned all Arab and Asian migration and precluded almost any migration from Africa. Latin American immigration was not included, but it had been at very low levels in any case.

The number of immigrants promptly dropped. As seen in tables earlier in this chapter, arrivals plummeted from six million in the 1910s to four million in the 1920s to under a million each for the 1930s and 1940s. The percentage of the population that was foreign-born also began to drop—from roughly 13 percent in the 1920s to a low of 4.7 percent in 1970—just as new legislation was opening up the doors again. At the same time, the population growth of the United States also slowed, dropping to well below half of the figure for the early 1900s and below a fifth of the figure from the early period of explosive growth in the colonies. The United States was still growing, but slowly. It was no longer a nation of immigrants in terms of its past, present, and future but a nation of immigrants only in terms of its past, a nation not really of immigrants but of the descendants of immigrants. That would change.

2

~~

The Reopening of the United States:
Refugees and Immigrants

In the early 1900s the United States, the paragon of an immigrant society, closed its doors to the very migration that had created and sustained it. The proportion of the US population who were newcomers fell to levels unknown in US history. But the reincorporation of the United States into global politics with World War II had implications not only for foreign affairs but also for immigration at home. The war period had fostered a sharp debate about whether the United States should be a refuge for the world, and the postwar period brought an increasing affirmation that—to at least some degree—it should be. The resettlement of hundreds of thousands of displaced persons after the war renewed the image of the United States as a beacon of hope. In addition, the return of US soldiers with foreign wives was a reminder that migration is also a matter of the heart that creates families as well as relocating them. Changes to immigration law in 1965 and increased refugee flows in the 1960s and 1970s made newcomers again a vital and noticeable part of American society. The United States was back to normal; once again, roughly one in seven Americans was foreign-born. Some fled oppression; others sought economic opportunity. Some were temporary residents; others came for the duration. Most came through legal channels; many—and the numbers began increasing—were undocumented. They came from all corners of the world drawn to a country that promised a place of both refuge and opportunity.

This chapter focuses on the story of renewed US immigration and sets the stage for the more specific discussions in part II of the lived experience of immigrants in the United States. Key topics for discussion include the response to refugees during World War II and its aftermath; refugees from Cuba, the Soviet Union, and Southeast Asia from the 1960s to the 1980s; the burgeoning migration from Asia and Latin America that stemmed from immigration-law revisions in 1965;

and the increase in undocumented migration at the end of the twentieth century as one important example of how migration as a human process is often at odds with the formal legal systems governing migration.

A LAND OF REFUSAL

The plunging number of immigrants to the United States in the 1930s was not solely the result of the restrictive legislation of the 1920s. The Great Depression also had an effect, as unemployment swelled from 4.2 percent in 1928, just before the stock market crash, to a high of 19 percent in the late 1930s. The United States was a less attractive destination, which helps explain how even the lower immigration quotas were not fully met during this period. However, there were other factors at work. Perhaps the most painful was the US response to Jews trying to flee Germany, especially after the "night of broken glass" (*Kristallnacht*) in 1938 when Nazi-organized violence claimed synagogues, stores, and human life. About twenty-six thousand Jews were arrested and put in detention.

The pressure on the Jews had been severe even before then. In earlier days, those Jews with enough money to leave might have found a haven in the United States. Jews from throughout Europe had been a major element in the mass migrations to the United States of the late 1800s and early 1900s. New York, their major destination, was at the time effectively the largest Jewish city in the world. While many of those Jewish immigrants remained in poor economic circumstances, many prospered and were more than willing to provide support for Jews trying to flee Nazi Germany. They were, for example, willing to provide the affidavits of support that guaranteed new immigrants would not become public charges. But the forces of restriction were strong in the United States, and Jews were often denied visas even when there were available slots under the reduced-quota system.[1] The most graphic example of refusal was the voyage of the *St. Louis*. In May 1939 passengers boarded the ship in Hamburg, Germany, and, after a stop in Cherbourg, the total number on board reached 937, of whom some 900 were German Jews. Many were well off, but not all. The individual stories were varied, including one man who had been released from detention in Germany on the condition that he leave the country immediately. The ship sailed for Cuba, where it was expected that the passengers would disembark and from there mostly make their way to the United States. The Cuban authorities, however, kept the ship isolated in the bay, and, while relatives could talk to passengers as they bobbed in boats alongside the *St. Louis*, they could not board, and only a few of the *St. Louis* passengers were allowed to disembark. The Cubans eventually evicted the ship from Cuban waters, and it then steamed up the East Coast of the United States.

The situation of the *St. Louis* was well covered in the US media. Many of the *St. Louis* passengers had connections in the United States; many already had the affidavits of support they needed for visas. Furthermore, there was a well-organized religious community that actively sought to help them and that had strong connections with the administration of Franklin Roosevelt. Those connections included his treasury secretary (Henry Morgenthau Jr.) and Roosevelt's wife, Eleanor, who was a diligent supporter of refugee causes. It was often she who sent notes to FDR asking for action on particular refugee cases and she who was in active personal correspondence with individual refugees and with those, like Albert Einstein, who were agonizingly aware of the dangers in which their coreligionists lived in Nazi Germany. But all was to no avail. The pleas from the *St. Louis*, and from the supporters of its passengers, were without reply. The *St. Louis* continued steaming northward, was rebuffed as well by Canadian authorities at Halifax, and then returned to Europe.[2]

Other plans to aid Jewish refugees also failed. One of the most striking was the unwillingness to help Jewish refugee children, even though the government arranged to open its doors to English children and thus keep them away from the dangers of war. Simultaneously, the US government placed Japanese Americans in detention, suggesting that the country was a refuge neither for those trying to flee danger nor for those already legally residing in the United States. For many people, these issues of refusal and detention were necessary to the war effort and the human-rights issues were secondary. Thus the refusal of refugees and detention camps for Americans were tolerated. At the same time, however, those affected by those policies, both Jews and Japanese, volunteered to fight in the war, and they fought courageously and with great loss of life for an America that they still believed to be their country.

A NEW WORLD

The new world that emerged in the course of the Second World War was one that put the United States at the center. That greatly affected its immigration policies. Three crucial decisions are worth noting. First, the US exclusion of certain nationalities, like the Chinese, seemed increasingly inappropriate given the importance of countries like China as allies in the war effort. On a country-by-country basis, the United States began rescinding exclusionary policies. In 1943, the Chinese Exclusion Act of 1882 was formally rescinded. Similar actions took place over the next few years: Indian and Filipino exclusions ended in 1946, Japanese and Koreans were deemed admissible as wives in 1947, and finally all origins were made acceptable for immigrant admissions in 1952. The United States became officially open to all countries of origin, even though the actual numbers were often limited by small quotas. While restrictions continued, at least the total-exclusion measures were gone.

The second key development was the War Brides Act of 1945. Servicemen were marrying foreign brides, and this would continue with the long occupations of Germany and Japan. Some one hundred thousand spouses and minor children would enter the United States under the provisions of the law by 1948, when it expired. The act was limited to military personnel (active duty or honorably discharged) who were US citizens, and the spouses were subject to medical examination—although not to exclusion for medical conditions. One crucial element of the legislation was that spouses and minor children would *not* be subject to any immigration-quota limitations. The War Brides Act was a core foundation for current US immigration policies that allow marriage partners to legally enter the United States without any numerical limit—although still subject to government review to be sure that the marriages are bona fide.

The third key development involved people in Europe displaced after the war from their former homes and unwilling or unable to return. There were numerous displaced-person camps in Europe, and the numbers displaced were in the millions. Even two years after the war, there were still at least a million displaced. President Harry Truman was insistent that the United States should help the DPs (displaced persons). Using his own presidential authority, in December 1945 he made the first steps toward accepting some of the DPs. His statement deserves attention for its eloquence on behalf of refugees and on behalf of a new US commitment to world affairs. He began the statement with the "appalling dislocation of populations in Europe" and the many who "have no homes to which they may return."[3] He then noted how little of the immigration quotas had actually been used during the war and thus that slots were available. By his authority, consular

President Harry Truman's support for displaced persons was strong and crucial. Here he speaks to an international migration organization at the White House (1951). (Copyright unknown; courtesy of the Harry S. Truman Library)

resources were directed toward reviewing these displaced-person cases. Truman also began an effort for broader legislation that would move beyond the existing quotas to settle more of the DPs. Congressional action in 1948 and 1950 did just that, allowing far larger numbers of displaced persons into the United States. Interestingly, Truman considering vetoing the 1948 bill because he thought it too restrictive. He claimed that it formed a "pattern of discrimination and intolerance wholly inconsistent with the American sense of justice."[4] Nevertheless, he signed it, and under its provisions and extensions 415,000 displaced persons entered the United States. The United States was again a place of refuge.

As the confrontation with communism deepened in the postwar period, the situation of those escaping communist tyranny to find freedom resonated well with the full spectrum of US political opinion, from liberals who had sought to let in Jewish refugees before and during the war to the deeply conservative who saw the new clash with communism as a moral and even religious imperative. Two later refugee flows helped crystallize this new understanding of refugee admissions. The first was the Hungarian uprising of 1956. It was a mass uprising that seemed to threaten the Soviet hold on Eastern Europe. It was, however, soon crushed by Soviet Red Army tanks. Many of those involved in the uprising fled to neighboring Austria. President Dwight Eisenhower moved quickly to allow some of them to resettle in the United States. This was a more formal governmental program than had existed in the past, including a government-run processing center at Camp Kilmer in New Jersey. This US action to aid Hungarian refugees was, as Eisenhower noted in a short statement, "clearly in the national interest" and reflected US commitment to "continue, along with the other free nations of the world, to do its full share in providing a haven for these victims of oppression."[5] His invocation was of a dual obligation to help refugees and to provide a fair share of the burdens of addressing world problems.

The second flow, and a far larger one, came from Cuba. The crucial event was the victory of Fidel Castro's forces and his triumphant entry into Havana in January 1959. Some Cubans had left even before then, but the numbers soon escalated. Cuba had long been closely tied to the United States, and the creation of a communist state less than a hundred miles away, where there would soon be an attempt to station Soviet nuclear weapons, caused consternation as an issue of foreign policy but also considerable governmental and public sympathy for those fleeing the new regime. As refugees began arriving in greater numbers in Miami, Eisenhower again made refugees a federal government commitment as he opened a refugee-assistance office in Miami, beginning what would be a long federal involvement with Cuban refugees. He commented in January 1961, as he was preparing to leave office, that he took such action in accord with "long-standing traditions of the United States" and noted how "[o]ur people opened their homes and hearts to the Hungarian refugees four years ago. I am sure we will do no less for these distressed Cubans."[6] Incoming president John Kennedy stressed a few days later the importance of the "tradition of the United States as a humanitarian sanctuary" and how it had often "extended its hand" to refugees.[7]

Over the next fifteen years, some 650,000 Cubans would enter the United States. Special legislation provided automatic legal status for them once they landed on US soil,[8] and the US government provided support for them, including efforts to help them move on to other cities from Miami. The Cubans were, in many ways, ideal refugees. Early research showed a population that was relatively well educated and held distinctively strong family ties. Cuban women, who often were not in the labor force when in Cuba, began working in the United States. Even when the individual jobs of Cuban refugees in the United States were not as good as those they had held in Cuba, the combination of two working spouses permitted a settled life and good educational opportunities for the children. Furthermore, in Miami and other major settlement areas, like the New York metropolitan area, the Cuban community provided a high degree of mutual support, including an increasing number of jobs within a strong ethnic economy. All those factors created a positive image of Cubans to the rest of the country. The inevitable accolade of "the Cuban success story" may at times have been overstated; yet there was much truth to it, and it helped sustain the refugee-program efforts on their behalf. That the Cubans remained firmly conservative and anticommunist helped them bridge the frequent political divisions between Democrats and Republicans.

Another set of refugees, smaller in size but also politically significant, were Soviet Jews. Their acceptance can be seen in part as a reaction against the earlier exclusion of Jews from Germany. Most of these Soviet Jews were so-called breakoffs who had left the Soviet Union for Israel but then switched destinations to the United States. (At that time, they could only legally leave the Soviet Union if their official destination was Israel.) In the 1960s the numbers were very small, but by the end of the 1970s about sixty thousand had arrived in the United States. The US government again was directly involved, although there was also very strong support from Jewish organizations at both the national and the local levels. The Soviet Jews tended to cluster in New York, with about a third of the total, and had a high educational profile—roughly half with at least some college education. This was thus another refugee group that had the potential for economic success in the United States. Their experience also raised some intriguing questions about whether they were religious or political refugees. Many American Jews found them surprisingly nonreligious but also had to acknowledge that they had been severely discriminated against in the Soviet Union. Nevertheless, the Soviet case, with its religious basis, provides a useful complement to the Cuban case with its political basis. America was once again a haven—an asylum in the early phrasing of Washington and Jefferson—for refugees fleeing religious persecution, political persecution, or some combination of the two.

The commitment to providing refuge from communism came into play again following the collapse of US-supported governments in Southeast Asia in 1975. An initial wave of 125,000 refugees fled as Saigon in Vietnam and Phnom Penh in Cambodia fell to communist forces in April of that year. Only a few Cambodians were able to escape, but far more were able to do so from Vietnam, sometimes by air but usually on boats that left Vietnam, with the passengers then rescued on the seas and taken to temporary reception centers that were set up quickly, and by most accounts very effectively, by the US military. The refugees were then transferred to camps in the United States for processing. By the end of 1975, they had all been processed out to local communities, with the assistance of voluntary agencies and individual sponsors. This early set of refugees included people of differing educational, occupational, and religious backgrounds, but many had relatively high educational and occupational backgrounds and considerable experience dealing with Americans. Survey data from their early years in the United States suggest their initial adjustment was quite positive in economic terms, with levels of work surpassing native-born Americans. Once again, refugees appeared to be rather successful new arrivals. Humanitarian commitments combined with personal connections between Americans and Vietnamese as former allies together created another "success story" of refugees in America.

The resettlement of refugees from Southeast Asia was initially seen as a one-time event. The relatively few number of escapes from Vietnam during 1976 and 1977 seemed to confirm that. The numbers escaping, however, surged in the late 1970s as a massive boat exodus strained the ability of neighboring countries in Southeast Asia to manage the numbers fleeing. The refugees faced an increasingly uncertain reception: sometimes relatively open reception, sometimes placement in fortified, closed detention camps, and sometimes outright rejection—ships turned back to sea and to almost certain death. In addition, the disruption of the Vietnamese invasion of Cambodia in 1978 opened up borders to many who had been sealed within the communist Khmer Rouge regime and its killing fields. They could now flee and did so in massive numbers, ending up mostly in camps just over the border with Thailand to the west. Furthermore, there were already numerous refugees from Laos (especially ethnic Hmong from the highlands) who had escaped from communist control and were also in camps along the Thai border. The result was a massive international humanitarian and political crisis. Under the auspices of the United Nations, international agreements were developed to allocate these refugees for resettlement in various countries. The United States, because of its size and its responsibilities for this particular crisis, took on the largest number of the refugees. The numbers arriving in the United States soon dwarfed the experience of 1975, and the wide range of cultural and economic backgrounds of this new wave of refugees presented difficult program challenges. Some of the problems reflected cultural diversity and general lack of preparation for life in an advanced industrial economy. However, the new arrivals had been through the aftermath of the communist victories, and those experiences were often horrifying. The Cambodian experience included mass killings that, among other effects, left many women and children without husbands and fathers, thus both emotionally bereft and lacking those who would normally provide economic support for the family. The horrors were less for those from the other countries but still significant. Many of the Vietnamese had suffered imprisonment, harassment, fear, and economic deprivation. For all, the hazards of flight had been followed by extended, enervating, and sometimes dangerous stays in temporary refugee camps before acceptance for resettlement.

The peak year of arrivals from Southeast Asia was 1980. The number admitted that year was 167,000, making it the biggest year of formal refugee arrivals the United States had seen.[9] That same year, however, there was also a major influx of Cuban refugees as Fidel Castro opened the port of Mariel to all who wished to leave and added to that at least some people he released from prisons and mental institutions. President Jimmy Carter quickly indicated US willingness to accept these people, while also trying to institute some sort of orderly process. The flow, however, continued at a disorderly pace, and by the end of the year the total number of Cubans reaching the United States was approximately 125,000. Furthermore, a smaller but still significant exodus by boat from Haiti was taking place, and these people were also accepted. That was another 25,000 people, yielding a combined total of 317,000 for that year.

Ironically, Carter had just signed the Refugee Act of 1980. That bill had attempted to regularize the very irregular way in which refugees were admitted and resettled. Its provisions included adhering to the United Nations definition of refugees and setting up a single coherent program for their resettlement rather than the separate programs of the past for such particular refugee groups as the Cubans, Soviets, and Southeast Asians. These new Cuban and Haitian arrivals did not quite fit into that new system, and they were assigned a different legal status by the government. They became "Cuban-Haitian Entrants" rather than refugees, even though they would receive the same services and assistance as those legally defined as refugees. Whatever the precise legal definitions, the raw number of arrivals in 1980, whether legally "refugees" or "entrants," represented a crucial turning point for American-refugee commitments. If all these different kinds of refugees are added together for 1980, that number is equal to about half of immigrant admissions to the United States.[10] That number was, for many Americans, too high and the resettlement program too uncertain in its success. Public opinion, always ambivalent about newcomers, turned negative. The aim thereafter would be to reduce the number of refugee admissions and to provide a more orderly, effective resettlement program for that reduced number.

A RISING TIDE OF IMMIGRATION

The decline in refugee admissions after 1980 would not, however, result in a decline in overall immigration. There was a different and ultimately stronger dynamic that would soon make refugee admissions a very minor part of the overall number of people admitted to the United States as permanent residents. To understand that dynamic it is necessary to backtrack from 1980 to the early 1960s, from a Refugee Act sponsored by Senator Ted Kennedy to an overall revision of immigration law prompted by his older brother, President John Kennedy. John Kennedy's views on immigration were laid out in detail in his book *A Nation of Immigrants*, which was first published in 1958, two years before his election as president. In that book, he reviewed the great contributions of immigrants to America for the work they did and the way they invoked the founding dream of the United States. As he put it, with their two great hopes ("the hope for personal freedom and the hope for economic opportunity"), each "new wave of immigration rekindled the dream" of a better life in America.[11] Interestingly, he classified US immigrants in three categories: first, religious refugees, second, political refugees, and third, those with other economic interests. For him, America as refuge took precedence over America as land of opportunity.

For a Kennedy of Irish Catholic descent, immigration was a good thing. However, John Kennedy found in the US immigration policy of his day some unacceptable elements. Above all, he opposed the quota system that largely limited arrivals to Europeans. There were no longer any complete bars to particular nationalities; those had been abolished in 1952. Yet the resulting quotas were extremely small. This, thought Kennedy, reflected "strong overtones of indefensible racial preferences."[12] Furthermore, he found the piecemeal approach of targeted exemptions from immigration law to be counterproductive. He sought a new legal basis for immigration that would be generous, fair, and flexible. "With such a policy we can turn to the world, and to our own past, with clean hands and a clear conscience."[13] When it came time as president to introduce proposals to rewrite immigration law, he commented again that it was time for an "immigration law that serves the national interest and reflects in every detail the principles of equality and human dignity to which our nation subscribes."[14] Legislation roughly conforming to Kennedy's concerns was finally passed in 1965 under President Lyndon Johnson, two years after Kennedy's assassination. As Johnson signed that bill (usually referred to as the Hart-Celler Act after its congressional sponsors) in front of the Statue of Liberty, he similarly noted that it repaired a "very deep and

President Lyndon Johnson signed the 1965 Hart-Celler Act on Liberty Island in New York Harbor (1965). (Yoichi Okamoto, courtesy of the LBJ Presidential Library)

painful flaw in the fabric of American justice. It corrects a cruel and enduring wrong in the conduct of the American Nation."[15]

Abolishing discrimination in immigrant admissions was not the only crucial part of the legislation. The 1965 Hart-Celler Act attempted to rationalize the kinds of skills that immigrants should have and increased the kinds of family members who were granted either automatic legal status or preferential treatment. Nevertheless, the general regional inclusiveness of the law was probably its greatest legacy and can be seen in changes over time in immigrants' countries of origin. Above all, the data show a plummeting proportion of immigrants coming from Europe (see table 2.1). Comparing decades since the 1940s, for example, the proportion of immigrants from Europe dropped to only about an eighth (12.3 percent). The proportion coming from Asia increased especially sharply to a full third (33.5 percent) of the total. The proportion from the western hemisphere also grew overall, whether in the particular case of Mexico or more generally from the Caribbean, Central America, and South America. There was also a sizable increase in the proportion coming from Africa.[16]

The 1965 legislative changes altered not only the proportions among origin countries but also the overall numbers. The Hart-Celler Act itself did not abolish quotas completely—originally setting an overall quota at 170,000, which was increased periodically thereafter—but it did expand the kinds of family members who would not be subject to that overall quota. Spouses, for example, had been placed outside the quota in the War Brides Act of 1945. Now, however, parents

Table 2.1. Regional origin of immigrants compared (%), 1940–2015

	1940–1969	1990–2015
Europe	45.8	12.3
Asia	8.1	33.5
Americas	44.5	46.0
Americas subtotals		
Canada	14.4	2.1
Mexico	11.8	20.2
Caribbean	9.0	10.9
Central America	2.4	5.6
South America	5.3	7.2
Other America	1.6	0.0
Africa	0.7	6.5
Oceania	0.8	0.6
Not specified	0.2	1.1

Source: US Department of Homeland Security, *Yearbook of Immigration Statistics: 2015* (Washington, DC: US Department of Homeland Security, Office of Immigration Statistics, 2016).

of citizens were also exempt. Furthermore, other kinds of family had some preference under the quota-based part of immigration. This tended to fuel chain migration, as family members in the United States helped family members overseas come to the United States. The combination of a rising overall quota and an increasing number of family members not subject to the quota created a dynamic of increasing immigration to the United States. That increase was not seen immediately, but by the time of the peak in refugee admissions in 1980 it was becoming established. Annual immigrant-admissions numbers, for example, were about three hundred thousand when the legislation was passed in 1965; reached five hundred thousand in the late 1970s, six hundred thousand in the late 1980s, and eight hundred thousand in the late 1990s; and have been around one million each year since then (see table 2.2).[17]

The crucial effects of the 1965 Hart-Celler legislation were thus increased numbers and a radically changed pattern of regional origins, especially the decline in the proportion of arrivals from Europe, the very large increase from Asia, and the more moderate increase from the western hemisphere. A consideration of the major origin countries for the decade spanning 2000–2009 illustrates the new contours of US immigration that had their genesis in the Hart-Celler Act, although modified by other legislation over time (see table 2.3). By far, the largest single-origin country is Mexico, with 1.7 million authorized immigrants arriving during that decade. (The additional numbers of unauthorized migrants will be discussed later in the chapter.) Mexican immigration is, of course, nothing new. The border between Mexico and the United States has been crossed in many ways for many years in both directions. As noted, many Mexicans were incorporated

Table 2.2. Increase in annual admissions, 1966–2015

	Annual average
1966–1970	374,273
1971–1975	386,595
1976–1980	493,239
1981–1985	557,730
1986–1990	893,461
1991–1995	1,045,625
1996–2000	770,480
2000–2005	980,388
2005–2010	1,119,823
2010–2015	1,030,355

Source: US Department of Homeland Security, *Yearbook of Immigration Statistics: 2015* (Washington, DC: US Department of Homeland Security, Office of Immigration Statistics, 2016).

Note: There was a surge in admissions from 1989 to 1991 that represents the effects of the amnesty created by the 1986 Immigration Reform and Control Act.

into the United States after the Mexican-American War ended in 1848 and the borders shifted. They continued to cross that new border for temporary as well as permanent residence. Mexicans were often the preferred seasonal workers in agriculture well back into the 1800s, and, when restriction was implemented in the early 1900s, the western hemisphere—and thus Mexicans—was exempt from any quota. Mexican migration has a very long history in the United States, and the contemporary numbers show it.

Table 2.3. Admissions from selected countries, 1940s vs. 2000s

Selected origins	1940s	2000s
Germany	119,403	122,373
Poland	7,774	117,921
Russia	605	167,152
United Kingdom	131,794	171,979
Yugoslavia	2,039	131,831
China	16,072	591,711
India	1,692	590,464
Korea	83	209,758
Philippines	4,099	545,463
Vietnam		289,616
Canada	160,911	236,349
Mexico	56,158	1,704,166
Cuba	25,976	271,742
Dominican Republic	4,802	291,492
Haiti	823	203,827
Jamaica		172,523
El Salvador	4,885	251,237
Guatemala	1,303	156,992
Brazil	3,653	115,404
Colombia	3,454	236,570
Ecuador	2,207	107,977
Peru	1,273	137,614
Total from all countries	**856,608**	**10,299,430**

Source: US Department of Homeland Security, *Yearbook of Immigration Statistics: 2015* (Washington, DC: US Department of Homeland Security, Office of Immigration Statistics, 2016).

Note: The list only includes countries with over one hundred thousand admissions from 2000 to 2009. Separate numbers for Jamaica and Vietnam not available for the 1940s.

The next three origin countries by numbers, and at nearly a tie, are China with 592,000 during the decade, India with 590,000, and the Philippines with 545,000. The three account for nearly half of the overall Asian total. The dynamics of the migrations are rather different. Chinese have long been in the United States, and their numbers have often been supplemented by Chinese-origin immigrants coming from places other than China. Many of the Vietnamese refugees, for example, were ethnic Chinese fleeing anti-Chinese policies of the Vietnam government. Their origins often lay in southern China, exactly the places from which early Chinese migrants to the United States came. In recent years, however, the influx from China has been more wide ranging, including, for example, large numbers of Chinese foreign students in the United States who were able to convert their US education into permanent-residence status. The number also includes migrants from Taiwan, which has a long relationship with the United States. So this large group of Chinese is quite heterogeneous in terms of background.

In the Indian case, similarities in language, education, and technological interests made the United States an attractive destination and have made Indians attractive employees, especially in the high-tech sector. There were some early Indian migrants to the United States, largely because they were viewed as possible labor replacements for the Chinese on the West Coast, but the numbers were very small. Again, like the Chinese, education or temporary employment in the United States often has provided the basis for later legal permanent-resident status. Families then followed. The resulting India-origin population in the United States is extremely heterogeneous in cultural background, with broad representation of the country's many language groups: Hindi, Urdu, Malayalam, Bengali, Marathi, Gujarati, and many others. Yet, while facility in English provides a bridge between India and the United States, the religions of the Indian migrants (primarily Hinduism but also some Islam) tend to keep them separate in the United States. The Indians in the United States thus present a particularly good example of being both similar and dissimilar to the native-born population.

The case of the Philippines is similar to the Indian case in having English as an additional language that is fully entrenched in the country-of-origin educational system. But, unlike the Indian case, the historical connections between the United States and the Philippines are extensive and deep. The Philippines became a colony of the United States as a result of the Spanish-American War of 1898 (when Cuba also came under US control). Already at that time some Filipinos had come to the United States, like the early Indians, as potential replacements for the Chinese in California.[18] With colonization and continued links after Philippine independence in 1946, the migration connections between the countries were strengthened in many different ways. Filipino men, for example, often worked on US ships and for the US Navy. Educated Filipinos often looked to the United States for further education. More recently, doctors and nurses trained in the Philippines according to US-oriented health-care curricula have found ready employment in a United States where there are frequent shortages in medical personnel. Those strong ties to the United States are not, however, the full story of global migration from the Philippines. Filipina women, in particular, have long journeyed abroad to work in many countries in domestic work and health care, and their remittances are a major contribution to the economy of the Philippines. They are officially recognized as "new heroes" of the country.

The next set of major origin countries for the first decade of this century—all in the two hundred thousand range—include Korea and Vietnam from Asia and Colombia, Cuba, the Dominican Republic, Haiti, and El Salvador from the Americas. All these countries have special historical relationships with the United States. For Vietnam and Korea, US support in civil wars ended with two very different outcomes: Korea remains divided and technically at war, but there is a stable, democratic, and very productive South Korea that is strongly tied to the United States. Vietnam is now unified, but only through the disappearance of a US-supported South Vietnamese government. Yet both the Korean and the Vietnamese cases have yielded large numbers of migrants of various kinds—students, family members, spouses, and refugees. Similarly, for the western hemisphere countries, there was also US involvement and, again, very different outcomes. US actions, for example, were instrumental in the overthrow of the Rafael Trujillo regime in the Dominican Republic, while they were utterly ineffective in keeping Fidel Castro from claiming and maintaining power in Cuba. Yet for these two countries—as for Colombia and Haiti—frequent US involvement has created special connections that have, in turn, served as pathways for refugees and more routine economic migrants.

The final case involves El Salvador. During the 1980s the US government opposed a leftist government in Nicaragua and thus was supportive of rightist rebels against that Nicaraguan government. It was also, not surprisingly, supportive of a rightist government in neighboring El Salvador that faced leftist insurgency. With deteriorating political and economic conditions in El Salvador, many Salvadorans fled to the United States. For the most part, they crossed into the United States without authorization. Their attempts to claim legal asylum were not very successful, since they were fleeing a US-supported regime. Over time, however, many obtained legal status in the United States, sometimes through renewed asylum claims and sometimes through other legal provisions. Some, for example, were able to utilize the amnesty provisions of the 1986 Immigration Reform and Control Act (IRCA).[19] Others were able to obtain at least temporary legal status—and work permits—through the temporary protected status (TPS) program. Even though many of them remain undocumented, they are still a major immigrant population even in terms of the official, authorized admissions figures used in this discussion of origin countries (and seen previously in table 2.3).

TEMPORARY OR PERMANENT? LEGAL OR UNAUTHORIZED?

The above description suggests the broadening array of origin countries and the different factors that underlie their importance. However, the data also obscure a more complete understanding of who is moving across US borders and for what reasons. The word *immigrant*, after all, has a variety of meanings. In normal speech it implies that someone has moved from somewhere else to here and that the move is more or less permanent. In US legal terms, however, an immigrant is someone who has come to the United States with official approval to reside on a permanent basis. With that approval, new arrivals are, again in legal terms, "permanent resident aliens." The two usages of the term *immigrant* are similar in that they emphasize the perspective of the receiving country (immigration rather than emigration) and the permanency of migration. Both usages, however, also elide the more complex issues of human mobility, including the many different kinds of movement, the ways those different kinds of movement are linked together, and the different kinds of barriers people face when they move—only one set of which are actual national borders.

Consider first the issue of whether migration is permanent. There is far more temporary migration in the world than permanent migration. People travel, they go to school, they find jobs. Those are not automatically permanent moves. People often travel and return, but not always. They may go to school (especially university) somewhere else and expect to return but then stay or move on to another place entirely. They may take a job somewhere else that they view as temporary but stay, or they may initially view that job as permanent but then move on. So moving to another place is often uncertain in duration: people may not plan to stay, but then they do; they may plan to move on or return home but then do not. Whether they are "immigrants" in the general sense of permanence is not always clear. Of the many migrants who have come to the United States over the years and generally been called immigrants, and generally been counted as legal immigrants, many have gone home. Extensive data from the early 1900s show that, with the reduced cost and time of a voyage by steam rather than by sail, many migrants did indeed go home. They sometimes did so as part of a plan, and sometimes they did so when economic conditions in the United States worsened. Data from that period, for example, show a very high percentage of Italians returning home—well over half. However, many other migrants to the United States have not been able or willing to return. During the same period when so many Italians were returning home, virtually none of the Jews from Russia and eastern Europe went back. There was, effectively, nothing to return to except renewed persecution.[20] Those from the Caribbean at that time were in between, with roughly a third returning. Those who returned, of course, sometimes came again to the United States for another limited time—or perhaps that next time they stayed permanently.

The question of whether migration to the United States is permanent can also be approached by looking at the level of commitment migrants have to life in the United States. Are they involved in their communities? Are they in a general sense "good citizens"? One marker of their commitment that is often stressed by the receiving society is naturalization: whether they do or do not choose to become legal citizens of the United States. For well over two centuries the US rule has been that anyone who is a legal permanent resident—an "immigrant" in legal terms—can apply for naturalization after five years. There are hurdles (proof of regular residence in the United States and basic understanding of the US political system), but they are not onerous for the majority of immigrants. Applying for citizenship is often taken as a litmus test for whether people wish to firmly attach themselves to the United States for symbolic or practical reasons. Part of the citizenship oath, after all, is to disavow attachment to any other nation-state, so it is a good test of how people view their respective attachments to their country of origin versus the United States.[21] There are differences in naturalization rates between migrants by their country of origin, by the length of time they have lived in the United States, and by their current circumstances, including the depth of their personal connections in the United States as well as in their country of origin. The decision to naturalize may take some time, and rates tend to rise the longer people live in the United States. Some people, however, never take citizenship. This can pose problems in terms of their interaction with American society. Both the US government and the American people—since the birth of the republic—have tended to be wary of (and sometimes very hostile toward) immigrants who are not fully committed to the United States, whether they actually return to their country of origin or simply fail to seek citizenship. The prevailing view on the US side has generally been that, if people are let in as legal immigrants, they should indeed be permanent immigrants in word and deed, fully committing to American life, and thus inevitably becoming citizens.

Many of the people counted in the official "immigration" statistics are thus not immigrants in the everyday sense of permanently changing the location and country in which they live. The reverse is also often the case: people who come temporarily may end up staying. As immigration to the United States has become more formalized and regulated, this distinction has become more important and more troublesome in terms of government policy and public attitudes. Even with greatly expanded numbers of people arriving as permanent legal residents, limitations in the number and kind of people approved leaves many other people without immediate access to permanent-resident status. Their only option may be some kind of temporary "nonimmigrant" status. There are many such temporary statuses in current US law, and they will be discussed in the next chapter. As one historical example, however, consider the Mexican Farm Labor Agreement of 1942, usually called the Bracero Program. The program originated during the Second World War when the need for labor in the fields suggested the utility of formalizing the long-existing, largely unregulated flow of Mexican agricultural labor into the Southwest. During most years, it brought some two hundred thousand Mexican workers across the border, returning them at the end of the harvests. Some of those returns were routine; others were forced deportations when workers resisted return—suggesting that from their perspective they were indeed "immigrants" to the United States. But the workers were decidedly not "immigrants" according to US law or according to US authorities. Although they were legally in the United States as temporary workers, if they overstayed their contract or moved to a different job, they were then quite explicitly "illegal immigrants."

In addition, there were other Mexicans who followed the same path as this special category of temporary workers—the braceros. They lacked any legal status in the United States, whether permanent or temporary. They were thus fully unauthorized and undocumented and generally termed *illegal immigrants*. This separate stream of unauthorized migrants had many roots. One was doubtless that workers had long crossed the border for agricultural work in the United States and neither they nor their employers saw the need to formalize their informal arrangements. Another reason was that the Bracero Program itself was disliked by virtually everybody. The braceros found it intolerable in its abuse of workers. Even with the direct involvement of the Mexican government in the program, in part to protect them, the conditions remained poor both in the work itself and in the housing and support provided to them. Conditions were even worse in those places (like the Northwest) where there was no presence at all of the Mexican government. From the employers' point of view, the program was also a problem. It was bureaucratic, limited their managerial discretion, and created higher wages than they would have had to pay otherwise. Having more compliant unauthorized workers was to the employers' benefit. With them, they did not have to be concerned about government regulations or labor activism. While those in the Bracero Program might (and did) complain about working conditions, the unauthorized workers were far less likely to do so.

The Bracero Program was terminated in 1964, a year before the Hart-Celler Act opened up more opportunities for permanent legal migration to the United States. The issue of temporary labor migration, however, was not resolved. There were attempts to create a better version of a temporary-labor-migration program, but they never succeeded in creating one that worked in the Mexican case. The result was that what was once a three-pronged migration (legal permanent migration, legal temporary migration, and nonlegal migration whether temporary or permanent) was largely reduced to two prongs: Mexicans could apply for permanent-residence status, or they could move illegally across the border. They might also find some way to legally cross the border and then work illegally on the other side. As before, employers often supported the use of undocumented workers, since it suited their business needs for low wages, low costs, and low levels of labor agitation. As in earlier years, Mexican workers might not have liked the situation, but it remained an acceptable way to earn a far higher wage than they could in Mexico.

The Mexican case is far from the only one in which people come to the United States by illegally crossing the border or by coming to the United States legally for one purpose (tourism, education) but then violating their visa by overstaying or by working without authorization. Over the years about half of this combined category of illegal immigration has involved Mexicans. The other half includes a wide range of origin countries for a wide range of purposes: sometimes as a way to work and sometimes as a way to avoid repression in countries of origin—as with the Salvadorans who have also often been undocumented. The reasons people are undocumented are often valid and are often accepted by at least some

Americans. Many people we would normally consider as bona fide refugees, for example, must cross the border illegally in order to effectively claim asylum from within the United States. Only then can they obtain the legal counsel and representation they will need to move through a complex, legalistic asylum application and adjudication process.

The reopening of the doors for migration to the United States since the Second World War thus shows an expansion of a wide range of channels by which people come to the United States for a range of purposes and often with uncertain long-range destinies. One channel involves those who seek refuge in the United States. Refugees have been crucial as the moral and foreign-policy issue that helped open the doors to immigration after World War II and that remains a crucial part of US immigration policy. Another channel rests on the importance of family ties as a basis for admission that has both unlimited quotas for some (spouses, for example) and quota-based limits for others (siblings, for example). Yet another channel is the more economic one, but it, too, is complicated. That channel is generally split between those with strong educational and occupational skills—who are prime candidates for legal immigration status—and those who work at more manual jobs and find it harder to enter the country legally. For all these kinds of formal legal immigration, there are also shadow channels that sometimes involve legal temporary status, sometimes involve unauthorized presence in the United States, and sometimes involve different legal statuses at different times. The lived experience of immigrants in all these channels will be the focus of part II of this book. But the web of current law and regulations pertaining to immigration, and to the broader range of temporary statuses that complement permanent migration, deserves additional discussion, as does the often-vitriolic discussion by the US public about the relative merits of immigration. Those issues of contemporary immigration politics and policy are the focus of the next chapter.

3

Migration Politics and Policies

Although immigration is once again a central feature of American life, it continues to generate a mixed response from the native-born. Sometimes the response is rejection and victimization of the immigrants. Sometimes, however, the response is positive. Furthermore, immigrants themselves have often mobilized very effectively on their own behalf. The story of US immigration thus has a volatile political dimension involving both the native-born and the newcomers. The political battles are fought out at the local, state, and national levels. Competing claims about the value of immigration result in policies that sometimes encourage immigration but also sometimes discourage and penalize it. At the national level, the competing claims have often resulted in paralysis. Such paralysis reflects inherent contradictions in American views of immigrants. One crucial political contradiction, for example, is that those who are often most fierce in their opposition to the cultural and social challenges of immigration are often those most invested in the free flow of labor, on which their businesses depend.[1] Like other countries, then, the United States is torn between the desire for cultural continuity (and thus relatively low levels of migration from relatively known sources) and the desire for economic and societal growth (and thus relatively high levels of migration from a broader range of countries).

This chapter begins with a sketch of the political dynamics surrounding immigration and then focuses on the current legal-immigration system and the categories of migrants entering in recent decades. The aim is to provide a better grounding in the details of who comes to the United States. That discussion necessarily includes those who come as legal, permanent residents and those who come in more temporary legal statuses that may—or may not—turn into more permanent arrangements. The concluding section of the chapter places the US experience within the broader global intersection of economic, political, cultural, and demographic forces, especially how a once-exceptional United States is now surpassed by other countries in the level of immigration (especially Australia, Canada, and New Zealand) and matched by a number of other countries whose experience with extensive immigration tends to be more recent (for example, the United Kingdom, Spain, and France).

THE POLITICS OF IMMIGRATION

US politics can be fractious in its contests among varying interests at the individual, group, locality, sector, and national levels. In the case of immigration, *individuals* may support policies that serve their own interests or those of their families; *groups* may use immigration issues to advance their own goals as effective social and political entities; *localities* may struggle to control the relative balance of the positive and negative effects of migration; *sectors* such as agricultural business may have their own specific interests in the availability of particular kinds of labor; and at the *national level* political campaigns may attempt to sway voters to their views about how immigration affects the country overall. At all these levels, immigration issues are contentious for several reasons. One reason is that immigration is an issue that goes back to the very origins of the United States, so the views about it, both pro and con, can be fierce. Another problem is that there are actually several different "immigration" issues and the views on one of them may not automatically predict views on another. There is also a great deal of misinformation about immigration, which, in turn, means the political discussion and public attitudes about migration are often warped at the core. Politics and public attitudes about immigration are thus deep in resonance, characterized by multiplicity, and often occluded.

The historical discussion in the previous two chapters has highlighted several very durable elements of US immigration and of the thinking about US immigration. History suggests that these issues are never fully resolved and that, at any point in time, the overall view of the value of immigration may shift toward acceptance or rejection. One key theme is the notion of the United States as a refuge for the religiously oppressed, for the politically oppressed, and for those whose lives in other ways pressure them to flee. Another key theme is growth. If immigrants clearly benefit the country, it becomes far less likely that they will be rejected. If they are seen as working hard, that also makes them more acceptable.[2] Conversely, if immigrants are seen as unproductive, then opinion shifts toward rejection. If they are seen as posing some additional threat to public safety or public morals—remember those beer-drinking Germans mentioned in chapter 2—then the shift toward rejection will be more pronounced. Accusation of immigrant involvement in crime or acts of terror is especially effective in portraying them as a threat to American values and American security. Finally, there has long been a tendency to expect that immigrants will assimilate to the United States by accepting its core political and social values or by already being connected to the

United States—through family ties, for example. These issues of refuge, growth, security, assimilation, and connection play out in different ways at different times. If those arriving are fleeing known persecution, contributing to American growth, law-abiding foes of foreign aggression, at least trying to fit in, and already related to America or Americans in some way, then the forces of acceptance are stronger. If, by contrast, those arriving seem to be falsely claiming refuge, undermining American growth, threatening American security, not fitting in, and unconnected to America or Americans, then the forces of rejection are stronger.

If all these criteria are applied to legal immigration—that is, to those who are admitted as legal permanent residents—then the consensus position is likely to be fairly positive with a broad, if informal, coalition of Americans seeing immigrants as productive newcomers. Some of those supporters may be politically to the left and value a more diverse United States; others may be politically to the right and value the energy and skills that immigrants bring to work settings and the conservative family values that they bring to the society as a whole. Within that coalition, there is likely to be continuing debate on exactly how many immigrants should come in and what their background characteristics should be. There may be calls for research to assess precisely how much these newcomers do contribute and how policy might more carefully choose them before the fact. There may also be debate about the nature of the family ties that count as a basis for immigration. There has been periodic objection, for example, to having special preferences for siblings and adult married children. Are these truly core family connections in American terms, even if they are argued to be core family connections in other cultures? Another item of debate is likely to be the relative emphasis on high-skilled jobs versus more manual occupations. Which kind of immigrant skills are actually needed and in what numbers? Even within this informal coalition in support of legal immigrants, there are thus still issues in dispute. People may support legal immigration in general, for example, but think the numbers allowed in should be a bit smaller or a bit larger, or perhaps a bit more oriented toward economic rather than familial criteria.

There are, however, some aspects of immigration that are disputed far more stridently. One involves refugees of uncertain or unknown origins. Refugees represent one of the core commitments of American history, from the very founding of the first colonies to those fleeing religious and political persecution today. The general commitment to refugees may be accompanied by actual personal or political connections to particular refugees. In the Cuban and Vietnamese cases, for example, the long personal connections and political resonances between Americans and the refugees greatly facilitated refugee acceptance and resettlement. On the other hand, refugees often come from relatively unknown places with which the United States and Americans have had limited contact. They also come from places that are in turmoil. There is always some risk that within refugee flows are some of the very people who created the conditions that forced people to flee. In US Republican campaign diatribes against Syrian refugees in 2016, all these negative issues came together: people who were unknown, from a different regional and religious background, and with the risk of importing terrorism with them to the United States. Donald Trump, for example, at one point proposed excluding all Muslims because of their religious differences and at another point proposed excluding refugees from the Middle East.[3] That put the United States in the somewhat odd position of not accepting people from the very regions from which they were likely to be fleeing. Meanwhile, in 2016, the Democratic president, Barack Obama, was increasing the number of refugees coming into the United States and increasing the number of Syrian refugees in particular. Here was a very sharp political divide, a broken consensus about America and refugees that continued to roil the United States through 2017.

Another aspect of immigration that tends to provoke debate—even anger—involves unauthorized migrants. Those migrants are about an equal number of people crossing the border illegally and people coming to the United States legally, as tourists or students, for example, and then staying after their visas expire. About half of the total are from Mexico. There are also sizable numbers from Central America who arrive across the Mexico–United States border, as well as many from outside the western hemisphere whose routes to the United States are often complex and costly. The overall number of unauthorized migrants rose sharply in the 1980s and 1990s, although leveling off—and slightly declining—over the last decade. The current estimate is that there are about eleven million unauthorized migrants in the United States. Note that some of these unauthorized migrants are refugees who will make claims for asylum after they arrive in the United States, some of which will be successful. They are thus only temporarily unauthorized. Many other migrants are also only temporarily unauthorized while they are caught between the expiration of one kind of visa and its renewal or substitution by another kind of visa. In the public mind, and certainly in the 2016 presidential campaign, this complex set of unauthorized migrants seems reduced to an image of Mexicans streaming across the border. The 2016 slogan "build a wall, and make Mexico pay for it" is somewhat ironic, since the number of unauthorized border crossings has been dropping, much of the border is already fortified, and the effect of that fortification is known to be counterproductive in at least some ways. Living lives on both sides of the border becomes more difficult as the border is sealed, effectively locking people into the United States as well as locking them out. Temporary migrants thus become permanent ones simply because they cannot risk going back and forth across the border as they once did.

If there is a single crucial trend in these political debates about immigration, it is how polemical and polarized the debates have become. The pragmatic issues of exactly how many and what kinds of migrants represent the most beneficial public policy have been overshadowed by more strident emotional appeals. Some people strenuously argue that the United States has lost control of its borders and must regain them. Other people strenuously argue that the United States has lost its moral core as it turns away refugees and demonizes newcomers. Yet others emphasize how the country has lost the ability to recognize the contributions of economic migrants to its economy, including those unauthorized workers who

In Silicon Valley immigrants work from the top of the system as heads of companies through mid-level technicians to the service people who provide support. (jejim/iStock.com)

have long been welcomed by US businesses as good, low-wage labor. Not even the situation of those brought to the United States at a young age has been enough to produce any kind of political resolution. In 2001, for example, the DREAM Act (Development, Relief, and Education for Alien Minors) was jointly introduced by a Republican (Orrin Hatch of Utah) and a Democrat (Dick Durban of Illinois). They sought to address the situation of those who had been brought to the United States as children, without legal authorization, but who had demonstrated their commitment to the United States, with an emphasis on educational achievement. The bill was never passed. Despite periodic efforts to introduce similar legislation, even this seemingly middle-of-the-road approach to address the situation of young people involuntarily brought to the United States as children made no progress in Congress, leaving it to President Barack Obama to set up such a program on an administrative basis. That effort, Deferred Action for Childhood Arrivals (DACA), was implemented in 2012, providing two-year renewable work permits and exemption from deportation. That administrative action provoked yet more reaction from Republicans, who claimed the proper role of Congress was being bypassed. These issues were also fought out in the courts with varying results. DACA was challenged but upheld; an extension of DACA, Deferred Action for Parents of Americans (DAPA), was blocked by a district court in Texas in 2016.

The general election in 2016 saw the explosion of these concerns about refugees and unauthorized migrants into major campaign issues. There was also concern about the overall role of immigration in American society, whether the numbers being admitted were too high, and whether those coming in were fitting in well enough.[4] Through these debates has run a current of fear about the practical and cultural effects of immigration. Also running through these debates has been both misinformation and lack of information. Americans, for example, routinely over-estimate the percentage of the foreign-born and the percentage of the foreign-born who are unauthorized. Data from the Pew Research Center, for example, suggest 35 percent of Americans think the total percentage foreign-born is 40 percent or higher (versus the correct figure of 13 percent), and 36 percent think the percent-age of that number that is unauthorized is 45 percent or higher (versus the correct figure of 26 percent). There are also misunderstandings of the processes by which immigrants come to the United States, the degree to which those processes can be controlled, and the relative proportions of formal permanent residents versus those who are in the United States legally but for temporary purposes. The political and public debates are often based on fragmentary or erroneous views of current US immigration and exactly who is and who is not a legal immigrant.[5]

THE US LEGAL IMMIGRATION SYSTEM

The misunderstandings about US immigration have many roots. One is the frequent confusion between "immigration" as a general form of more or less permanent migration to a new place and "immigration" as a legally defined process by which a government decides who will be a fully legal permanent resident. Another is the confusion about, and frequent overlap among, those with legal status and those without such status. For that reason, it is necessary to bring into the discussion the way the current US legal-immigration system actually works. The approach taken here is not to review the development of immigration law in the United States but to consider the results: who actually gets into the United States as a legal permanent resident—as an "immigrant" in the technical legal sense.

The growth in legal immigration since the 1965 legislative changes has led to current annual arrivals of about one million people each year as permanent resident aliens. Those numbers have been steady for about the past two decades. The numbers by region for legal immigrants (not including the unauthorized) now indicate roughly one-third each from Asia and Latin America, a bit above a tenth from Europe, and a bit below a tenth from Africa. In terms of specific source countries, a few stand out—particularly Mexico (16 percent of the total) and China, India, and the Philippines (about 6 percent each). All these cases make sense: Mexico as our most populous neighbor, China and India as the world's most populous countries, and the Philippines as a former colony and close political ally. The more impressive figure, however, may be the sheer num-ber of countries from which immigrants now come. Twenty-six countries have been averaging at least ten thousand admissions per year, and many, many more have contributed at least some immigrants. Those numbers underscore the great national, linguistic, and cultural breadth of those coming to the United States.

These people are admitted to the United States as permanent resident aliens through a variety of specific categories. Table 3.1 presents the major categories of admission to the United States over the last decade. There are three major categories. The largest one—and accounting for fully two-thirds of all legal immigration—involves family. There are two major components to that family category of immigration. The larger family-related component of immigration—at nearly 45 percent of total admissions each year—includes immediate relatives of US citizens. They are mostly spouses, but also some unmarried children under the age of twenty-one and some parents. This category is not subject to any numerical limitation, and it is hard to imagine how it ever could be. There are, however, concerns about the potential abuse of this unlimited category of immigrant. Anybody interested in coming to the United States would immediately recognize that this is a major category of admission to the United States and one that is subject to no numerical limitation. There is concern about marriage fraud, and there can be processing delays. Immediate family members nevertheless remain the largest single category of legal immigration and also the least controlled.[6]

The other part of family-based immigration—and the smaller one at about 20 percent of the total—involves a series of preference categories that *are* subject to numerical restrictions. The priorities stem in part from the legal status of the United States–based relative. For example, the spouse of a citizen is (as noted above) *not* subject to any numerical restriction, while the spouse of a noncitizen permanent legal resident *is* subject to numerical restriction. Such a spouse must wait in a queue after being approved until a "slot" is available. Relatives are also prioritized by the closeness of their relationship to the United States–based relative. Unmarried children, for example, have a higher priority than married children; both have higher priority than siblings. Overall, about two hundred thousand people a year, roughly one-fifth of all immigrants, are such sponsored relatives. There is a large backlog of applicants for these slots, and the result can be a long wait. Filipinos who had applied in the 1990s to join family in the United States, for example, were only being processed about twenty years later. The waiting time has been similar, although not quite as long, for Mexicans. These delays reflect the nearly three million people who queue up each year for the roughly two hundred thousand slots available for these family preferences.

The second major segment of US legal immigration involves economic-based criteria and accounts for about 15 percent of total admissions. This segment represents more formal government decisions and control about the kind of new people—not just relatives—who ought to be admitted to the United States. Many other countries more sharply emphasize economic factors in a broader range of immigrant admissions, often using some kind of point system that is based directly on potential immigrant economic contributions—or that attempts to balance economic factors with family ties and cultural compatibility (for example, English-language skills). The United States, however, has largely been content with this smaller economic stream for immigrant admissions. Among other reasons, to raise the number of explicitly economic migrants would either increase the overall number of immigrants or reduce the number of family-based immigrants. Both would face political obstacles.

Table 3.1. Recent immigrants by class of admission (annual average)

	Number	%
Immediate relatives of US citizens	479,969	44.35
Spouses	274,699	25.38
Children	90,069	8.32
Parents	115,201	10.64
Family-sponsored preferences	216,067	19.97
Unmarried sons/daughters of US citizens and their children	24,816	2.29
Spouses, children, and unmarried sons/daughters of alien residents	100,554	9.29
Married sons/daughters of US citizens and their spouses and children	24,966	2.31
Brothers/sisters of US citizens (21+ years of age) and their spouses/children	65,732	6.07
Employment-based preferences	161,770	14.95
Priority workers	39,114	3.61
Professionals with advanced degrees or aliens of exceptional ability	50,783	4.69
Skilled workers, professionals, and unskilled workers	59,632	5.51
Certain special immigrants	8,375	0.77
Employment creation (investors)	3,866	0.36
Refugees	96,087	8.88
Asylees	58,767	5.43
Diversity	46,177	4.27
Parolees	2,199	0.20
Children born abroad to alien residents	624	0.06
Nicaraguan Adjustment and Central American Relief Act (NACARA)	355	0.03
Cancellation of removal	11,795	1.09
Haitian Refugee Immigration Fairness Act (HRIFA)	1,149	0.11
Other	7,253	0.67
Total	**1,082,211**	**100.00**

Source: US Department of Homeland Security, *Yearbook of Immigration Statistics: 2015* (Washington, DC: US Department of Homeland Security, Office of Immigration Statistics, 2016).

Note: Data are ten-year averages calculated for 2005–2014 from data in the 2015 edition of the *Yearbook of Immigration Statistics*.

The third major segment involves a set of categories that, for the sake of convenience, can be called "humanitarian admissions." The United States has long prided itself on being a haven for the oppressed and the persecuted. The percentage of all immigrants who are refugees or other kinds of humanitarian cases has varied greatly, from the years after World War II, when they were a very major part of US immigration, to the virtual shutdown of the refugee program in the months after the terrorist attacks of September 11, 2001. The figures for the last decade suggest something more moderate and not very different from the equivalent figure for economic-based migrants: about 15 percent of the total number of admissions. The two farthest wings of US immigration—those based on economic benefit versus those based on humanitarian need—together provide almost a third of total US legal immigration and complement the overwhelming core of contemporary US immigration, the roughly two-thirds who are family.

The basic numbers thus show that US immigration is based on three main principles: family reunion, economic development, and humanitarian relief. Those are all important goals, all reflect fundamental features of US history, and all remain highly appropriate in the contemporary world. But what is the proper mix? If a million immigrants a year is a reasonable number—not too few, but not too many—then increasing the number of people admitted under any of these three categories would be at the expense of the other categories. Furthermore, except for immediate relatives of citizens, there are long waiting lists for all these categories of immigration: long pending applications for family sponsorship, long lists of people who want to work in the United States, and long lists of people who need refuge in the United States. So to change the mix would require a decision to have one category of immigrant bear the cost of increased numbers in other categories. It would pit those who want to bring in their family members against those looking for fresh labor—and both of them against those more concerned about refugees and asylum seekers.

Another important characteristic of the US legal-immigration system is that about 60 percent of new admissions each year are people who are already in the United States (see table 3.2). Thus over half of new *admissions* are not new *arrivals*. They are already in the United States, living under a variety of legal statuses, including being undocumented. Not surprisingly, the characteristics of the immigrants coming from abroad and those already in the country differ in terms of country of origin and legal-admission category. The result is that there are two somewhat different US immigration systems, depending on whether legal permanent-resident status involves a new arrival or a change in legal status for someone already in the United States.

Humanitarian admissions provide a particularly good example of the differing effects of these two systems: legal admission before physical arrival versus legal admission after physical arrival. In the humanitarian case, there are many admissions categories: some are temporary (as in temporary protected status—TPS), while others yield permanent legal status, or at least a path toward it. Some are potentially available to all groups, while some are limited to a specific group.[7]

Table 3.2. Overview of recent immigrant trends

	Admissions			Naturalizations
	Total admitted	Already in country	Immediate relatives	
2005	1,122,257	738,302	436,115	604,280
2006	1,266,129	819,248	580,348	702,589
2007	1,052,415	621,047	494,920	660,477
2008	1,107,126	640,568	488,483	1,046,539
2009	1,130,818	667,776	535,554	743,715
2010	1,042,625	566,576	476,414	619,913
2011	1,062,040	580,092	453,158	694,193
2012	1,031,631	547,559	478,780	757,434
2013	990,553	530,802	439,460	779,929
2014	1,016,518	535,126	416,456	653,416
2015	1,051,518	542,315	465,068	730,259

Source: US Department of Homeland Security, *Yearbook of Immigration Statistics: 2015* (Washington, DC: US Department of Homeland Security, Office of Immigration Statistics, 2016).

Some are for groups as a whole, but some are for particular individuals (such as cancellation of removal). The two main legal statuses in terms of numbers stem from the US Refugee Act of 1980. That law created two separate tracks, one for people whose status is determined before arrival in the United States (thus legal admission *before* physical arrival) and the other for people whose status is determined after arrival in the United States (thus legal admission *after* physical arrival). The standard is the same, but the processes are quite different.

There is a legal definition of *refugee* in US law,[8] and that definition largely matches international standards. But by whom and where does the application of this definition to particular people take place? How do people who have fled—who are refugees in the general sense—become refugees in the more specific legal-immigration sense? This is where the two tracks arise. The first track is the one for refugees who are identified overseas, often in refugee camps just across the border from the countries from which they have fled—for example, the Southeast Asian refugee camps of the late 1970s and early 1980s in Thailand, Malaysia, the Philippines, Indonesia, and Hong Kong or the massive refugee camps today in East Africa. This track has some procedural advantages. The refugees are together as groups, so there can be efficiency in processing and a better chance to be sure that the people really are bona fide refugees. A claim to have fled across the border, for example, is more easily verified near that border, and the conditions causing flight are likely to be better known. Furthermore, defining legal status before arrival in the United States provides for a far more orderly resettlement process after arrival. The inevitable problems of adjustment to a new country are not further exacerbated by questions about legal status. The many organizations who reach out to these newcomers to offer assistance in their new lives have more assurance that these people really are refugees.

The second track occurs when refugee status is sought by people who themselves make the journey to the United States either claiming to be refugees at the border or—and the wiser practical strategy—entering the country illegally and then finding the community and legal resources to file a claim for refugee status. This way of claiming refugee status is a more individualized and legalistic process. It takes place farther away from the country from which the refugees have fled, making it more difficult for those adjudicating the case to know of the severity of conditions in that country and whether those conditions may have changed. These people are thus not yet legally "refugees," whatever their personal experiences may have been. Rather, they are technically only "asylum seekers." The public reaction to asylum seekers is often confused, precisely because their legal status remains uncertain. The legal terminology becomes even more confusing, since asylum seekers who are approved as meeting the refugee standard become, again in legal terms, not refugees even then; instead, they are *asylees*. There are still many organizations that aim to aid these newcomers, including making sure they gain access to legal representation, without which their claim is in far greater jeopardy. Yet, still, the process is shrouded in uncertainty—for the asylum seekers, for those who seek to aid them, for the government as it attempts to impose consistent migration controls, and for the general public who are likely to be, at the least, a little confused.

These dual tracks for refugees are a reminder of the extent to which US immigration policy is both about accepting people from somewhere else and about accepting people who are already in the country. Clearly people who arrive in the United States claiming refuge cannot be sent back to some camp in another country to await proper processing there; clearly people who are waiting in camps cannot be told that they must make a clandestine trip to the United States in order to gain direct access to the US legal system. While people may well be confused about these twin tracks to become "refugee" or "asylee"—including refugees themselves—the need for each track is still manifest. Here, then, policy and operational complexity may seem to burden the system and confuse the citizenry; yet the complexities are necessary to meet the goals of humanitarian relief both overseas and in the United States.

The details and complexities of these humanitarian-admissions are mirrored in other aspects of US immigration policy, including family reunion and the economic categories of admission. The overall system is complex in its categories, subcategories, policies, and procedures. Just as there are many different kinds of humanitarian migration statuses, so as well are there many different kinds of family-sponsored immigrants (married children, unmarried children, siblings, parents) and economic-based immigrants. Many of these categories operate as virtually independent immigration programs, each with its own particular logic. A few examples may help indicate how specialized immigration law and policy can be.

Consider, for example, nurses and preachers. One set of people ministers to the body and another to the spirit. Both occupations are important, and both tend to be rather underpaid, considering the skills and education required. So there is likely to be a shortage of each group in at least some areas in the United States. Foreign nurses and preachers thus become candidates for special consideration as immigrants. In the case of nurses, processing is under one of the categories of employment-based immigration and has fairly extensive requirements in terms of education and diploma in country of origin. The overall numbers for that category are not large, and the nurses must compete among each other and among other people in that category. Yet the result is something of a special immigration channel for nurses. In the case of preachers, there is a special category of employment-based immigration specifically for religious ministers, and it requires proof of already belonging to an established religious denomination in the United States. Again, the numbers have been small (about one thousand in recent years), but that in itself helps indicate how detailed is the interest in even very small categories and subcategories of admission to the United States.

Both the nurse and the minister cases represent an attempt in US immigration policy to address quite specific employment needs. This is not a grand policy of skills-based migration but rather a more focused set of mini-programs to address quite specific employment gaps. While such programs have the disadvantage of complexity—separate programs for separate groups—they have the decided advantage of addressing particular needs that have become apparent enough to attract governmental attention. It may seem a somewhat disorganized approach to immigration policy, with a little piece here and a little piece there, linked together in an uncoordinated fashion, but it addresses the component issues and may actually work fairly well through an inveterate American tinkering with the details.

As another example, consider the Diversity Visa Program. The logic is fairly simple: Because existing streams of immigrants to the United States create future immigration for their relatives, yesterday's immigrants bring today's immigrants, and today's immigrants bring tomorrow's immigrants. The result is large numbers of immigrants from particular countries—and often from particular places within those countries. But shouldn't the United States be open to everybody on an equal-opportunity basis? Here again is a kind of special need, and the answer again has not been to change the entire immigration system but simply to add a separate program for people from countries underrepresented as sources of immigration to the United States.[9] People in such countries now have the opportunity to apply for a special kind of immigration slot, with the results chosen by random lot. This is the Diversity Visa Program—the diversity lottery—with roughly fifty thousand people selected each year by random number from a Web-based application system operated by the US Department of State. This is another example of American tinkering: it is not necessary to revise the whole immigration system—just add another component or subcomponent to achieve a particular goal. Aiming at those specific goals individually may be more practical and efficient than any reconstruction of overall US immigration policy.

The fence on the United States–Mexico border divides countries and lives. (Arturo M. Enriquez/iStock.com)

THE TEMPORARY OPTIONS

One further complication to US immigration—and a frequent cause of public confusion—involves the vast number of people who come to the United States legally but not as approved permanent residents. These are *nonimmigrants* in government terminology. And the numbers are huge. There are nearly two hundred million land-border crossings each year from Canada and Mexico. Many of these involve preapproved "trusted-traveler" programs, and many of these do not appear in formal visa statistics. Under the North American Free Trade Agreement (NAFTA), even more routine border crossings were originally planned, but the free movement of labor has been a far slower process than the free movement of goods. In any case, there are high numbers of routine border crossers who continually refresh the daily links and interactions among Canadians, Mexicans, and Americans.

There are also more carefully monitored border crossings that are tracked in government statistics. The statistics have become increasingly precise over the last few decades. Data include the kind of entry into the United States, the period of time allowed in the country, and the general conditions that govern that temporary time in the United States. Data from the most recent year available appear in table 3.3. Note first of all that these data cover only about 40 percent of known arrivals in the United States. That is, nearly 60 percent of border crossings are Canadians and Mexicans moving back and forth across the border for work, shopping, or just visiting. Nevertheless, review of the narrower group of I-94 arrivals provides some general insight into the proportions and range of "nonimmigrants" coming legally to the United States.

The overwhelming number, more than sixty million, are tourists. Depending on the country from which they come, they may have to obtain a visa before traveling or simply enter "visa-free" because their country is considered a safe and reliable origin, in part because data indicate that most of these temporary migrants do indeed return to their country of origin. Sometimes the designation of "visa-free" has been problematic. For many years, for example, South Koreans

Table 3.3. Nonimmigrants by class of admission, 2015

	Number	%
Estimated total of all admissions	181,300,000	100.00
Total I-94 admissions	76,638,236	42.27
Temporary workers and families	3,722,543	2.05
Temporary workers and trainees	2,306,962	
Temporary workers in specialty occupations (H-1B)	537,450	
Agricultural workers (H-2A)	283,580	
Nonagricultural workers (H-2B)	120,207	
Spouses and children of H-1, H-2, or H-3 (H-4)	205,521	
NAFTA professional workers (TN)	787,180	
Intracompany transferees	917,613	
Treaty traders and investors	449,732	
Students	1,990,661	1.10
Exchange visitors	576,347	0.32
Diplomats and other representatives	438,477	0.24
Temporary visitors for pleasure	61,017,237	33.66
Temporary visitors for business	8,008,659	4.42
Transit aliens	689,990	0.37
Commuter students	100,495	0.06
Alien fiancé(e)s of US citizens and children	35,266	0.02
Legal Immigration Family Equity (LIFE) Act	1,627	0.00
Other	74	0.00
Unknown	56,860	0.03

Source: US Department of Homeland Security, *Yearbook of Immigration Statistics: 2015* (Washington, DC: US Department of Homeland Security, Office of Immigration Statistics, 2016).

Notes: For simplicity, subcategories of temporary workers are only included if they number more than one hundred thousand. Note that I-94 forms are *not* required for routine border crossings by Canadians and Mexicans.

coming to the United States were required to obtain a visa. The South Koreans were annoyed at this because their country is such a close ally of the United States, and the movement of people back and forth between the two has been extensive and durable over time. Nevertheless, the data kept showing that a few too many Korean visitors to the United States were overstaying their visas. Eventually, South Koreans did receive visa-free status. More recently, issues of security have raised the possibility that many current visa-free origin countries might be effectively downgraded and their citizens required to have an advance visa to enter the United States. One complication is that visa-free designations are often reciprocal between countries. To rescind visa-free status for a country might well provoke that country to rescind visa-free status for Americans. There are also economic implications. Tourism, for example, is such a big industry that there is always opposition to rules that make it harder for people to come as tourists to the United States. Restrictive rules are bad for business.

The second biggest number, at about 3.7 million entries per year, involves temporary workers. The largest subcategory includes intracompany transfers: managers and professionals who are not changing their employer but only changing the place where they work for that employer. There are various periods of time possible, including renewals, but there is an absolute cap of seven years in the United States. These transfers account for about a fourth of the total number of temporary workers. Comprising nearly as large a subcategory are professional workers covered by NAFTA, who usually have at least a college degree. They must belong to a designated set of professional categories and have a prearranged job with a US employer. They then receive a three-year visa, which can be extended indefinitely. Note that there is no cap at all on the number of these visas or the number of times they can be extended for additional three-year periods. The next set of temporary workers in terms of numbers includes H-1B professionals, particularly in the high-tech sector, and with very strong representation of people from India. Like the NAFTA workers, they must work at the professional level, usually have at least an undergraduate degree, and have an employer in the United States who seeks to hire them. The visa is for three years, renewable for an additional three years. With a year's return to country of origin, it is possible to again become an H-1B worker. Parts of the H-1B program are capped in terms of number, especially for those coming directly from the origin country. Other parts are not capped, especially for those with US graduate degrees or those who work in university or nonprofit settings. There are also other temporary workers for agricultural and nonagricultural work. These are smaller sets, though there is often debate about making them larger. The hope is that more temporary but legal workers would reduce reliance on unauthorized workers, especially in agriculture. But there is also great opposition to such an increase, based in part on the many problems in the former Bracero Program. Note also that there are visas for the families of these temporary workers, although those visas generally preclude working.

The third biggest category involves students. Their origins are diverse, but as of 2015 the source countries with over one hundred thousand students included Canada (253,000), China (521,000), India (180,000), and Mexico (273,000).[10] The vast majority are in higher education, about evenly split between under-graduate and graduate programs. More than half are in business, management, engineering, math, and computer science, and nearly all (94 percent) are on visas that allow them to work half-time during the school year and full-time during nonschool portions of the year—although the students must maintain full-time academic status. The visas run as long as full-time study continues, even if that is longer than originally planned. Foreign students are often a source of contention in other countries where student and trainee visas are used as a back door for bringing in workers. In the United States, this problem is generally avoided by the emphasis on university-level education and the requirement that any work be based at the university or with companies affiliated with it.

These three large groups of tourists, temporary workers, and students provide an opportunity to consider again the links between permanent and temporary migration. A tourist visa, for example, may serve as a way to see the United States for the first time, to create a more extensive attachment through repeated visits, or to continue and solidify ties with family already in the United States. Out of that huge number of tourist visits there are at least some future students, workers, and permanent immigrants. For temporary workers and students, the increased length of time and fuller immersion into US institutions and cultural lifeways are likely to bring an increased interest in more permanent migration to the United States. Permanent migration may actually be the reason for coming to the United States as a student or worker in the first place. Furthermore, that interest in permanent migration may well have strong support from the companies and universities in which the students and workers have been embedded. There are frequent applications for permanent residency that are supported by the employers who now know the migrants and their abilities well, and there is similar support for students who have been educated to US standards and often in exactly the technical fields in which the native-born show less interest.

Thus it is that when it comes time to "admit" someone as a legal immigrant (i.e., as a permanent resident alien), the number of them who are already in the country is very large: well over half for all classes of admission. That percentage is especially high for those being admitted on economic grounds. For them, about 85 percent are already in the United States. The economic segments of US immigration turn out to be like the emphasis on family admissions in that they prioritize existing connections as a good basis for immigrant admissions. The economic migrants are already connected to the United States, having worked in US companies and studied at US universities. The resulting gain to the United States may well be a loss to the countries of origin, as these students and workers constitute what is usually called a "brain drain." Yet there are offsetting factors, too. Those new permanent residents, and often later new citizens, provide useful economic ties to their original country, often send invaluable remittances, and may, as circumstances evolve, end up returning later in life. Human mobility, after all, is rarely kept in check. People move short distances and long, temporarily and more permanently, as their lives and those of their families evolve over time.

To this discussion of permanent- and temporary-migration statuses must be added the issue of unauthorized migration. Many people would argue that the unauthorized represent a kind of tacit, shadow immigration policy that is managed directly by employers and workers, or sometimes simply as an unauthorized family-reunion policy. Others react to the unauthorized as if they were criminals rather than simply people bending the law for understandable purposes and with the frequent consent—and sometimes instigation—of US employers and relatives. That divide in opinion remains one of the most volatile aspects of immigration politics and one of the most contorted aspects of immigration policy. It is such a major tension point at present because the number of unauthorized migrants escalated so rapidly during the 1980s and 1990s, before leveling off in recent years (see table 3.4). This issue of unauthorized migration is likely to remain, as suggested earlier in this chapter, a very contentious one.

Table 3.4. Selected data on unauthorized migration

	Apprehensions	Removals	Returns	Estimated number in US
2005	1,291,065	246,431	1,096,920	10,500,000
2006	1,206,408	280,974	1,043,381	11,500,000
2007	960,673	319,382	891,390	11,780,000
2008	1,043,759	359,795	811,263	11,600,000
2009	889,212	391,341	582,596	10,750,000
2010	796,587	381,738	474,195	11,600,000
2011	678,606	386,020	322,098	11,500,000
2012	671,327	416,324	230,360	11,400,000
2013	662,483	434,015	178,691	11,100,000
2014	679,996	407,075	163,245	11,000,000
2015	462,388	333,341	129,122	11,300,000

Sources: US Department of Homeland Security, *Yearbook of Immigration Statistics: 2015* (Washington, DC: US Department of Homeland Security, Office of Immigration Statistics, 2016); Jeffrey S. Passel and D'Vera Cohn, "As Mexican Share Declined, U.S. Unauthorized Immigrant Population Fell in 2015 below Recession Level," Pew Research Center, April 25, 2017, http://www.pewresearch.org/fact-tank/2017/04/25/as-mexican-share-declined-u-s-unauthorized-immigrant-population-fell-in-2015-below-recession-level/; and Bryan Baker and Nancy Rytina, *Estimates of the Unauthorized Immigration Population Residing in the United States: January 2012*, Office of Immigration Statistics, US Department of Homeland Security, March 2013, https://www.dhs.gov/sites/default/files/publications/ois_ill_pe_2012_2.pdf.

Notes: "Removals" are what used to be termed *deportations*, while "returns" are people simply stopped at the border. For new unauthorized population numbers, Pew estimates are used for 2013, 2014, and 2015 to supplement the earlier estimates from Baker and Rytina.

THE UNITED STATES IN COMPARATIVE PERSPECTIVE

The United States is often portrayed as unusual in the extent of its immigration experience. But much of its experience is paralleled by other countries. The other English colonies—Australia, Canada, New Zealand, and to some extent South Africa—have seen similar migration influxes from similar European countries, combined with complex mixes of indigenous groups. Their societies were constructed largely through European settlers, but they have been increasingly open to diversity of origins in recent years, although marred by outbursts of what is usually called "nativism" (even though the Europeans were hardly the original natives). Yet many other countries also have long histories of people moving in and moving out for various reasons, including shifting demands for labor and surges in refugees crossing borders. These other countries also have many foreigners among them, some to stay temporarily and some to settle permanently.

The overall number of migrants more or less permanently in another country (i.e., not simply short-time visitors like tourists) has risen and fallen with economic and political changes. Since the late 1900s, the overall number of such migrants throughout the world has risen from around 160 million in 1995 to nearly 250 million by 2015. Given the overall increase in world population, the more important question may be whether the *percentage* of international migrants has changed. The basic answer is yes: the percentage of the foreign-born overall has risen from 2.8 to 3.3 percent. However, the differences between world regions, and between what the United Nations terms developed versus developing countries, are more striking (see table 3.5). In developing countries, while the overall

Table 3.5. Percent foreign-born by world region

	1995	2005	2015
World	2.8	2.9	3.3
Developed	7.9	9.7	11.2
Developing	1.5	1.4	1.7
Africa	2.3	1.7	1.7
Asia	1.3	1.4	1.7
Europe	7.3	8.8	10.3
Latin America and Caribbean	1.4	1.3	1.5
North America	11.3	13.8	15.2
Oceania	17.3	18.1	20.6

Source: Economic and Social Affairs, Population Division, "Trends in International Migrant Stock: The 2015 Revision," United Nations, December 2015; data are drawn from Excel tables available at http://www.un.org/en/development/desa/population/migration/data/estimates2/estimates15.shtml.

Note: Figures generally refer to those permanently in another country, but the exact definitions vary by country.

numbers have grown, the percentage of foreign-born remains about the same. In developed countries, by contrast, the overall numbers have grown, and the percentage of the foreign-born has also risen, from 7.9 to 11.2 percent. The largest increases have been in Europe (from 7.3 to 10.3 percent), in North America (from 11.3 to 15.2 percent), and in Oceania (from 17.3 to 20.6 percent). The North America and Oceania numbers are driven directly by the experience of the former English colonies, but note especially that the United States has by far the lowest percentage among those countries: the US figure is about 13 percent, and the others are much higher—Canada at 20 percent, Australia at 26.7 percent, and New Zealand at 22.4 percent (see table 3.6). Many European countries now also match or exceed the United States in the proportion of foreign-born. The most populous European countries (France, Germany, and the United Kingdom) are at about the same percentage as the United States, some are a bit higher (Austria, Belgium, Sweden), and some are much higher (Switzerland, Luxembourg).

There are thus many countries that share a relatively high percentage of the foreign-born. These countries also share some of the same streams of incoming migrants. Some of those are likely to settle permanently, whether that was their original intent or not. Others are likely to be more temporary. Some are highly valued (professionals, investors, students); some are likely to receive an ambivalent and sometimes hostile reception (temporary workers, asylum seekers). Exactly as there have been flare-ups in negative reactions to immigration in the United States, so also have there been similar negative reactions in most of these other countries. Two of the migration channels fueling those negative reactions deserve particular attention: low-wage labor and refugees.

In economic terms, developed countries are magnets for people in developing countries. Whether the conditions in those developing countries are relatively good or relatively poor, the wages and opportunities in developed countries are far higher. Wages are often five to ten times higher.[11] So people move toward those higher wages. As in the United States, sometimes they cross borders illegally. In Europe, much of that traffic is across the Mediterranean. It is actually a two-stage process: across the desert from Sub-Saharan Africa to the coast—especially Libya in recent years—and then across the sea to Italian islands that are very close to North Africa, less than a hundred miles in some cases. Each stage of that journey poses grave risks, including frequent death. Arrival in a southern European country is usually not the end of the journey—rather, it is only an entry point into the rest of Europe because of the open-border provisions of the European Union.[12] Migrants tend to move through that southern entry point to countries further north, especially Germany. Some aim for the United Kingdom, but that requires another clandestine crossing, since Britain retains its own border controls, and migrants have died trying to cross the channel tunnel illegally. Many other workers, however, come in legally, again because of open EU borders.[13] The net result in recent years has been a surge of workers into northern and western Europe. The response has often been negative. When the United Kingdom voted to leave

Table 3.6. Percent foreign-born in selected countries

	2003	2013
Australia	23.5	26.7
Canada	18.1	20.0
New Zealand	19.1	22.4
United States	11.6	13.1
Austria	14.1	16.7
Belgium	11.4	15.5
Chile	1.4	2.5
Czech Republic	4.7	7.1
Denmark	6.3	8.5
Estonia	17.5	10.1
Finland	3.0	5.6
France	10.9	12.0
Germany	12.9	12.8
Hungary	3.0	4.5
Iceland	6.8	11.5
Ireland	10.7	16.4
Israel	29.5	22.6
Italy		9.5
Luxembourg	34.3	43.7
Netherlands	10.7	11.6
Norway	7.6	13.9
Portugal	7.1	8.1
Slovak Republic	3.2	3.2
Slovenia	0.0	16.1
Spain	8.8	13.4
Sweden	12.0	16.0
Switzerland	23.1	28.3
United Kingdom	8.6	12.3

Source: Organisation for Economic Co-operation and Development (OECD), International Migration Data-base, "Foreign-Born Population," 2016, https://data.oecd.org/migration/foreign-born-population.htm.

Note: Exact methods of calculating the number vary by country and are subject to updating (i.e., it is a live-data system). Note that the former English colonies are listed first as what are usually viewed as tradi-tional immigration countries.

the European Union in 2016, migration was a major factor. In particular, workers from fellow EU member Poland had come in very large numbers to Britain, even though the government had asserted that such a large flow would not occur. There was annoyance at the numbers coming in and annoyance at a government that many felt had misinformed them—even though much research suggests that these workers are beneficial to the economy, that they generally take jobs others do not want, and that they often create new jobs.

In terms of refugees, a major flash point has been the Syrian refugee crisis. In the summer and fall of 2015, major flows of Syrian refugees, mixed with other migrants, moved toward Europe. They initially moved across land borders and, when those were closed, across the sea from Turkey to Greece and then north, until border controls were reinstated there. In 2015 alone, more than one million refugees and migrants reached Europe, with the highest number by far in Germany. It was the largest refugee crisis in Europe since the Second World War. The European response was varied, with some countries very accepting—especially considering the large numbers—and some very resistant. The Syrians had the misfortune of coming after several decades in which foreign workers and asylum applicants had created an increasingly bleak response to immigration from the native-born. Terrorist attacks, especially the Paris attacks of November 2015, helped channel those concerns into ones of fear and insecurity. Right-wing parties made progress in most European countries as a result. This turn against migrants turned the United Kingdom against the European Union, threatened to bring Angela Merkel's long tenure as chancellor of Germany to an end, and affected nearly every European country in some way.

This combination of ambivalence (at best) about low-wage workers, uncertainty (at best) about asylum applicants, and prevailing anxiety about security was accompanied by renewed attacks on those who seemed to challenge traditional European values. As in the United States, this brought a surge of concern about Islam in terms of its perceived threats to physical safety, cultural institutions, and the economic situation of the native-born. It also brought about a fundamental rethinking of immigration and border-control policies and how countries should deal with new arrivals who are sometimes invited, sometimes come uninvited, and often bring the challenges of difference and uncertainty. In that sense, the US experience is not unusual. Indeed, the challenges posed by immigration in the United States may be less than in many other developed countries. Current US immigration numbers are not particularly high compared to other developed countries and no higher than in most periods of US history. The challenges of immigration in the United States today may thus be as much about the complexities of an ever-tightening web of global connections and the shared experiences of advanced industrial societies as about the unique historical nature of the United States as a nation of immigrants. Whatever the case, the lives of the immigrants move forward within the particular options and constraints of the United States. That lived experience of immigrants in the United States is the focus of part II.

PART II

Immigrants and the United States

4

⌒

To Live: Moving Forward but Looking Back

Whatever their reasons for migrating and whatever their backgrounds, immigrants to the United States must forge new lives that balance the skills, dreams, and legacies they have brought with them and the opportunities and constraints they face in the United States. Out of that mix of what they bring and what they find come the trajectories of their new lives and those of their children. In some cases, the transition to living in the United States is relatively smooth. Well-educated immigrants with solid English-language skills often find a relatively easy path. If they have been able to bring family with them, and perhaps some financial capital, they may do even better. By contrast, many refugees come from situations of chaos and horror, with disrupted family ties, and limited abilities to synchronize with American society. For them, the transition is much harder. To live in America is thus a varied experience, harder for some and easier for others, but for all with both boon and burden, a new life that may look at times like a dream realized and at other times like a hope delayed or a dream denied.

The discussion in this chapter begins with the hazards of the passage to America, then continues with the range of conditions immigrants face after arrival: opportunities, constraints, and sometimes just problems. How immigrants fare after arrival depends greatly on their background characteristics, reasons for migration, effects of migration itself (especially the heavy losses sustained by refugees), and the general fit (or lack of fit) between immigrants and the localities in which they settle. They must, in effect, find a new way to live. That attempt to create a new life and to navigate through diversity is clear in a variety of materials on immigration, but the emphasis in the early part of this chapter is on some examples from American literature. The latter part of the chapter—like all chapters in part II—has two paired comparisons of more recent immigrant groups that demonstrate the range of experience in how immigrants forge new lives in the United States. The first of the paired comparisons focuses on Cuban and Soviet refugees arriving in the 1960s and 1970s, especially the fortunate timing of their arrival, their good occupational and educational fit with American society, and the strong political support for them. The second of the paired comparisons focuses on Cambodians and Salvadorans. For both, economic and educational backgrounds were more mixed with greater challenges in adjusting to the United States. Both also bore the scars of conflict. For the Cambodians, those scars were of an almost unbelievable holocaust. For Salvadorans as well, the degree of violence in the home country was often significant, and the lack of legal status in the United States posed additional burdens.

DIFFICULT PASSAGES

People have come to the United States in many ways, at many times, and for many reasons. In earlier periods, the passage to America was often difficult. The voyages of the first colonists to Jamestown and Plymouth Rock resulted in few deaths, although much discomfort. The trips were long, arduous, and unpredictable. Later crossings were often less fortunate. The death toll for those Acadians traveling along the East Coast from what is now Atlantic Canada was high, and the conditions on slave ships were horrifying. Perhaps the highest death tolls came on the Irish famine ships. Conditions below deck were crowded, and the passengers were generally already weakened by famine and often ill. On some ships, the death toll reached one in four. With the famine in Ireland had come disease, and that disease traveled with them to America, often erupting during the voyage.

With steam replacing sail, the trip across the Atlantic became safer and faster. In colonial days, the trip might well take a month or two. But during the nineteenth century the duration of the voyage dropped rapidly. By 1900, crossings of less than a week were possible. For most immigrants, then, the passage itself became routine and the rupture of ties to the home country far less. It became much more feasible to move back and forth between the old and new worlds. Of the many immigrants in the decades before the restrictions of the 1920s, the number returning home was very high, especially for such groups as the Italians and Greeks. For many immigrants since then, the passage to the United States has become, in practical terms, even more routine. But that has not been the case for everybody. For refugees in particular, the images of ships at sea, of danger, and of delay remain all too frequent. Small, leaky boats crossing the Caribbean, and even occasional large ships crossing the Atlantic and Pacific, remain a necessary way for those seeking refuge who do not have the proper documentation. For the many migrants crossing the border between Mexico and the United States, the dangers have become worse, as border fortifications have turned what was once an easy stroll into a harrowing march across formidable, hot, and sometimes deadly terrain.

This continued difficulty of passage—for some, but not for all—is a reminder of how strong the motivations to move can be. Even in the face of brutal treatment from nature and from people, and with a known possibility of death, people chance the journey. Sometimes their motivation is life itself. If they were to stay in their country of origin, they might not survive. Sometimes their motivation is for a more meaningful life. They may survive in their home country but face a degree of oppression and restriction that undermines any hope of a life worth living. Sometimes their motivation is for others. Perhaps they can survive, but they may fear a life without hope for their children. Such people may or may not be refugees in formal legal terminology, but they reflect the reality that migration is not simply the hope for a better life but the determination to find a place where one can truly live, rather than merely survive.

Even for those with the resources to plan their move, who have legalities in place and have a quick, safe passage, the journey may still present difficulties to overcome. The uprooting from home may be bearable for some, even liberating, yet devastating for others. Those separating from family, friends, and lovers might seem to face the most emotional stress, but even those traveling together as family groups may sense the passage in very different ways, placing stress on their relationships as their responses to migration diverge. Children may react differently from adults, older children from younger children, men from women. The passage to hope is thus often through the shoals of difficulty and danger, loss, pain, and uncertainty. It is also a passage to new local contexts that provide an unpredictable mix of acceptance and rejection, opportunities and limitations, security from old dangers but susceptibility to new ones.

TROUBLED ARRIVALS

Having survived the passage, arrival presents immigrants with additional challenges. Even when conditions at the destination are themselves fine, there can be other problems. Sometimes passengers are not allowed to land even when in sight of shore. The spurned Acadians in colonial days and the spurned passengers of the *St. Louis* in the runup to the Second World War are examples, as are the boats interdicted by the US Navy at sea off the coast of Florida in recent decades. During the periods of open immigration before restriction in the 1920s, the screening of passengers led to some being rejected, largely for reasons of health. The numbers rejected were not high—perhaps 3 percent—but those were painful reminders that reaching one's destination was not full arrival. More recently, the images of refugees being blocked at US airports provide another reminder that physical arrival is not the same as legal admission.

New arrivals face an additional set of problems as they move to specific localities in the United States. Over the course of American history, some have settled at their port of entry, and others have spread out across the country. During the early days of the republic, many moved to rural areas in what was still a largely rural country. During the later 1800s, as the railroad made the West more accessible and there were still opportunities to buy land at low prices, many—like the Norwegians and Swedes—continued to move to rural areas. Yet cities were growing during that same period, and increasingly that is where immigrants settled. Both rural and urban destinations posed their own problems. Some illustration from classic American immigration fiction helps illuminate those difficulties. In her novel *My Ántonia*, Willa Cather describes both the beauty and the harshness of the West experienced by members of an immigrant family from Bohemia (in the current Czech Republic) who move to the American West toward the end of the 1800s. They arrive to find a house and plot of land that are overpriced and barely adequate for survival. The first winter finds them freezing in a home dug into the earth. The youngest child sleeps in a small area hollowed out of the dirt in that basement-like house. A visitor reacts negatively to the child sleeping in an animal-like burrow, but the family explains it is the warmest place in the house. Cather's story turns out well, but the potentially fatal consequences of a harsh environment, misinformation from a compatriot, and poor preparation for a different kind of life are staples of the early immigrant experience in the West.

In the cities challenges were different but also often severe. By the late 1800s, the same time setting as for Cather's novel, immigrant arrivals in US cities were straining the infrastructure. Existing houses were split into apartments and new kinds of buildings created for the immigrants. The buildings were small, smoky, and dark. They were unventilated, with no indoor plumbing, running water, or bathrooms. Stephen Crane describes them in his 1893 novella *Maggie: A Girl of the Streets*, as Maggie endures the violent arguments of her family and the constant intrusion of neighbors in cramped quarters. When they returned home, they "plunged into one of the gruesome doorways. They crawled up dark stairways and along cold, gloomy halls." This was the life of the tenement.

The issue of housing is a crucial one for new arrivals, especially those with limited funds. These dark and gloomy tenements had some advantages. They were often in areas where earlier immigrants from similar origins had settled. During early industrialization, these tenements were often close to places where immigrants could work and were also close to markets, close to schools, and close to religious and community institutions. But tenement life also put them in areas of crime, with poor public services. Perhaps above all, it put them in areas where they could be financially exploited. Those low-rent, small tenement apartments, for example, often yielded profits to landlords that were greater than the better, larger housing in other areas of the cities. Smaller apartments yielded smaller rents but higher overall rents per square foot. Furthermore, the tenement apartments rapidly ran down, were often ill maintained by landlords, and were only grudgingly renovated when public shock at housing conditions forced change, gradually creating a regulatory bottom line for ventilation, heating, electricity, and indoor running water and toilets.

Another crucial aspect of immigrant life is evident from the housing example. While immigrants may arrive looking for the opportunities that America provides, they in turn are seen as an opportunity for profit by those already in the

United States—and often by their own compatriots. In his 1906 novel, *The Jungle*, Upton Sinclair describes the housing scam used against his protagonist, Jurgis, and Jurgis's family. A fellow immigrant lawyer tells them the contract to purchase a small house is fine, but they soon discover the house is a wretched framework under a new coat of paint and with a ruinous payment plan that ultimately causes the family to lose the house. A century later, immigrant housing is now generally far better. But cramped subregulation housing still exists—especially for low-wage, and sometimes trafficked, labor—and the potential for housing scams remains high. In addition, events like the US housing crisis of the mid-2000s can place many people, including immigrants, under water with mortgages that have high payments but no possibility of exit.

In some ways, the housing situation is worse now for many immigrants since the cheapest housing is often in depressed inner-city areas that have fewer jobs than they did a century ago. Extensive commuting then becomes necessary. Those areas also tend to have poorer schools and fewer community resources. As before, they are often areas of high crime. Some is petty, and some is more serious. Again, immigrants may be the targets. Sometimes they are the targets of the criminals, and sometimes they are viewed as the criminals and thus the target of law enforcement and public concern. Often their "crimes" involve only different cultural traditions. The temperance movement of a century ago, for example, had many of its roots in a negative reaction to Irish- and German-immigrant drinking that, most horrifically to society at large, involved drinking with both families and friends, and doing so even on Sundays. The joke in New York City when a law was passed to close saloons on Sunday was that when eight thousand front doors closed, eight thousand back doors opened.

For immigrants, the overall navigation of a new environment can thus be difficult. Part of the difficulty is that the logic of the new environment, and the language skills needed to navigate it, may not be immediately available to new immigrants. For English-speaking arrivals, adjustment to a new life in the United States is inevitably easier. English can be a channel for understanding how to navigate through the new society and a mechanism to ease potential strains with other groups. But language alone may not be enough. While there are many examples of hostility to immigrants who appear different physically and sound different linguistically, there have also been many immigrants, like the Irish, who were (usually) English speakers and from a culture quite similar to the dominant English culture of the early colonies.

Whatever the language, there was still hostility toward them. That hostility sometimes erupted into full-scale violence. Among the worst cases from the latter 1800s were an 1855 mob attack that destroyed a hundred buildings and killed over twenty Germans in Louisville, Kentucky; a lynching of seventeen Chinese in Los Angeles in 1871 in retaliation for an assault on a police officer; an 1891 break-in to a police station to seize and lynch eleven Italians in New Orleans; and the shooting of nineteen Slavic miners in Lattimer, Pennsylvania, in 1897 during a mine strike. The strike itself was based on various labor abuses in terms of wages, working conditions, and forced use of an overpriced company store—another reminder of how often immigrants are ill used for the profit of others.

A century later, immigrants were still often the focus of attacks. In the 1992 Los Angeles riots, for example, Korean businesses were often targeted by rioters. Koreans have been very active in small businesses in the United States, identifying particular sectors where their efforts might be rewarded. In New York City, for example, they became a major part of the fresh fruit– and vegetable-marketing networks. In Los Angeles (as in other cities) they ran convenience stores in more run-down neighborhoods, exactly where the riots took place. The reasons for such attacks on immigrants are varied and sometimes accidental. Recent immigrants are often seen not in terms of their origins but in terms of racialized stereotypes. Vincent Chin, as one example, was a Chinese American man in Detroit, in his mid-twenties and about to be married, who was beaten to death in 1982 with a baseball bat by a Chrysler plant superintendent and his nephew.[1] In an odd twist, they thought he was Japanese and thus responsible for problems in the US auto industry. As another example, Amadou Diallo, a Liberian-born Guinean, was shot to death by NYPD officers in 1999. There are diverging accounts of the incident, but the basic facts seem to be that Diallo was unarmed but was shot nineteen times when he pulled out his wallet, admittedly in dim light. In this case, an immigrant was drawn into a broader racialized framework in which he was seen as a risk. He had only been in the United States for three years and was in fact undocumented. Life in a new land can be dangerous.

Marriage continues to be crucial for immigrants; in this case a Korean couple marries in New York City (2011). (Lee Snider Photo Images/Shutterstock.com)

A WAY TO LIVE

The life of a new arrival in the United States has its hazards and outright dangers, but it also has its opportunities. Whatever the original motivation for migrating, the flow of immigrant life is reshaped within a new context in a new country. People continue to move through their lives as they move through a new geographical terrain and new cultural and linguistic matrices. Much of the shape of that new life will be about individuals, much will be about groups, especially the family. Much will have to do with what migrants have brought with them, whether practically, emotionally, or spiritually. Much will have to do with the way they are seen and treated by other people in their neighborhoods, workplaces, schools, businesses, community groups, and religious settings.

In individual terms, much of the shape of immigrant life hinges on very elemental factors like age, sex and gender, educational experience, and English-language ability. There are some relatively predictable patterns in how these factors affect new immigrants. In terms of age, the general rule for migration is the younger the better in terms of absorbing the new context. For those who arrive as very young children, language and culture are quickly absorbed. As those children grow up, they will go through what other American children go through and will, in that sense, be fully American, whatever their legal status. Thus it is that most (but not all) Americans are sympathetic to the "dreamers" who may have been brought to the United States illegally but who have demonstrated through school that they are indeed "good" Americans. Youth is also generally good for employment. The young are generally stronger, healthier, more resilient, and less emotionally torn between the new and old countries. Older people may have important skills, but much of what they know is tied more to their old life context than to their new one.

Differences by sex and gender once had relatively predictable effects for immigrants but less so in recent years as defined gender roles have eased in the United States. On the other hand, many immigrants come from societies that are considered very traditional in terms of basic gender roles. But even so, there are still unpredictabilities. Women in many societies that are putatively patriarchal nevertheless have significant economic independence. So the situation of immigrant women in the United States can be an unpredictable mix of strong orientation to the home and also strong initiative and skill in the workplace. Two classic immigrant novels highlight this unpredictability. In the first, again Willa Cather's *My Ántonia*, the protagonist is an outgoing young Bohemian immigrant woman who moves from a farm to a town, where she works, forms friendships with other unattached young immigrant women who have somewhat dubious reputations, and is maneuvered into a disastrous marriage. But she rebounds, marries an immigrant man from similar origins, moves back to the farm, and has a large, raucous, and happy family. She herself drifts back into speaking Bohemian, while her children learn English naturally at school. She, then, might be seen as a case of a "traditional" home-oriented woman stepping back into country-of-origin patterns. Those dubious friends of her youth, by contrast, turn out to be very astute businesswomen who move on to the cities, carefully apply hard-won skills to new situations, and prosper financially. Cather suggests a special kind of liberating experience for these young immigrant women, an ability to capitalize on their first-generation energy without automatically absorbing the conventions of either old or new countries.

Another example of the complexity and unpredictabilities of immigrant life comes from the 1925 novel *Bread Givers*, by Anzia Yezierska. In a crowded urban setting, a young Jewish woman fights her way free of an extremely oppressive father who seems intent on using his daughters as economic assets, either through their work or by marrying them off. Her sisters are all maneuvered by him into disastrous marriages, although more so in emotional than economic terms. She wonders about her father: "Shall I let him crush me as he crushed them? No. This is America, where children are people." She finally escapes, learns to live alone and free from the intrusions of her family. She finds an apartment: "My hands clutched at the knob. This door was life. It was air. The bottom starting point of becoming a person." She studies, she works, she achieves a solitude that eases her spirit. Eventually she becomes a teacher—a crucial option for many immigrant women—and meets a man, also a teacher, who shares her passions. Finally, for her, marriage becomes possible, as she recognizes that "to marry myself to a man that's a person, I must first make myself a person."[2]

These two interior views of immigrant women suggest, above all, unpredictability in the trajectories of immigrant lives as people move through the stages of life in a new context. The trajectories cannot be conveyed in snapshots of life at a particular moment. Lives that may appear fortunate at one time may become disastrous; lives mired in despair may well be resurrected. The trajectories may swerve back and forth between the new and the old, between discovery and rediscovery. In *My Ántonia* and *Bread Givers* the main subjects are women, but something of the same unpredictability is seen in the books' male characters as well. Ántonia's father, for example, is a distinguished man who cannot adapt to life on the plains. His violin rests unused in a corner, and his sadness inexorably claims his life in suicide. Yet his grave, visited constantly by Ántonia, stands the test of time, fending off numerous attempts to build roads across the small plot where that grave lies. In *Bread Givers*, the great patriarch is ultimately alone and feeble. He remains "unchanged—as tragically isolated as the rocks." Here is a hint, too, of the varied trajectories of immigrant men's lives—sometimes triumphant, as in the classic autobiographies of immigrant success in America, but sometimes also these painful roads into loss of status, isolation, and despair.

The trajectories of male and female immigrants overlap in some ways and not in others, sometimes because of home-country legacies, and sometimes because of US conditions. But there are also more generic skills, aptitudes, and beliefs that immigrants bring with them that can have decisive effects on the trajectories of their lives. Sometimes these are described as "human capital." Of course, one thing that immigrants sometimes bring with them that is extremely useful is actual capital. Money helps, and a lot of money helps a lot. But skills, aptitudes, and beliefs are also important. Language proficiency may be the most crucial single element. It is best to have English proficiency on arrival, but the young, with exposure and education, can achieve it even after arrival. For adults it is far more difficult. Literacy, especially in a cognate language (whether Germanic or Latinate), provides a basis for literacy in English, even if the spoken language remains difficult. Education also usually provides a guide to the complexity of modern societies and the way the written word threads through it, whether in understanding the news, the cultural content of the new society, or more mundane job and housing contracts. Education may also provide useful skills for employment, especially if that education mirrors current US employment needs. That tends to be most true of technical and scientific skills rather than the humanities. There are also more specific skills and abilities, such as sewing, which provided a route to a livelihood for many immigrants a century ago in the "needle trades," and still for some today. Other, more inchoate beliefs and orientations may help in the United States. Perhaps above all, the immigrant dream of success is conventionally built on hard work.

Such individual characteristics are supplemented by what is sometimes called "social capital." People do not generally live in isolation. They are connected to other people, and those connections make a difference. For migrants, the issues of human connection are complex since they move between different environments that often have different kinds of human connection. If people migrate with others—with their families, for example—they bring with them a crucial network that can pool efforts in productive ways in a new environment and shield them from the ravages of being adrift in an alien world, from being overly off balance from culture shock. Continuing connections to people in the country of origin can also be valuable in practical and emotional ways. These connections can also cause difficulties. The obligation to send remittances back to the country of origin may limit life in the United States: more jobs, longer working hours, less money to buy a house or support one's children's education. Probably the most crucial point for immigrants is the need to have a variety of connections and the ability to manage them proactively toward the challenges of a new environment and flexibly in ways that can evolve with the shifting trajectories of their lives. That variety of connections today often includes ties in the country of origin as well as the country of destination. Such a web of ties spanning both countries helps maintain the many transnational aspects of migrant lives.

Alone and together, immigrants move forward through their lives in a new, often unpredictable, and sometimes dangerous environment. The remainder of this chapter provides examples of the different trajectories of life for more recent immigrants. The examples are presented in pairs. They are not meant to be formal group profiles, although some profile-like information is included. Rather, the examples aim to introduce general patterns and variations among different immigrants. Note especially that the experience of individual immigrants, and the general national-origin groups with which they are associated, vary and evolve over time. There is no typical Cuban, Soviet, Cambodian, or Salvadoran immigrant, but the individual lives of immigrants are nevertheless influenced by their previous national contexts, as they are by their current context in the United States. As always, immigrants are moving through their lives simultaneously as they move across territory and into different economic, social, cultural, and political worlds.

PAIRED COMPARISON: CUBANS AND SOVIETS

Those coming to the United States from Cuba and the Soviet Union during the 1960s and 1970s illustrate the links among the historical conditions at the time of migration, the reasons for coming to the United States, and the challenges of creating new lives in the United States (see table 4.1). In both cases, the arrivals were considered refugees, reflecting the general post–World War II recognition of the right of people to flee communist systems and find refuge in the United States. America was still to be a haven for those fleeing tyranny.

The situations in the two cases were in some ways similar and in some ways different. In each case, for example, there was an interplay between immigration controls in the United States and emigration controls in the sending countries. Both Cuba and the Soviet Union carefully controlled emigration. Some people might flee clandestinely, but it was not easy, through sealed and guarded borders. What happened in both cases is that the communist governments would ease restrictions at some times and then the volume of those leaving would increase. The flows were thus not evenly paced but rather showed surges and ebbs. The situations were also parallel in being extremely political in terms of who would be allowed to leave their country of origin and who would be allowed to enter and stay in the United States. For the United States during the 1960s and 1970s, the general rule was to accept. That would change in 1980, when a sudden exodus from the Cuban port of Mariel strained US willingness to accept large numbers of Cubans.

Table 4.1. Cuban and Soviet admissions

	Cuba	USSR
1950s	73,221	453
1960s	202,030	2,329
1970s	256,497	28,132
1980s	132,552	33,311
1990s	159,037	433,427
2000s	271,742	167,152

Source: US Department of Homeland Security, *Yearbook of Immigration Statistics: 2015* (Washington, DC: US Department of Homeland Security, Office of Immigration Statistics, 2016).

Note: The definitions of the USSR and Russia have changed over time, so figures are not entirely consistent.

The notion of America as a haven from tyranny continues to be important to many Americans, as in Boise, Idaho, where a woman shows support for Syrian refugees (2015). (txking/Shutterstock.com)

In other ways, the cases were very different. Communist rule was well established in the Soviet Union. Those who were able to leave had experienced a full lifetime under that communist rule. Furthermore, those leaving were Jewish; indeed, that was the reason they were allowed to leave. Generally they had to profess an intention to go to Israel, and, once on the way, they could "break off" and shift toward the United States. The passage was thus complex, time consuming, and bureaucratic. As they waited in their home country, Soviet refugees lived under a shadow. This was not a refugee crisis in the usual sense of an immediate need to flee. Rather, it was a continuing series of harassments that extinguished hopes for their own futures and for the futures of their children. Those children, for example, were increasingly being excluded from educational and occupational opportunities. In the Cuban case, by contrast, the flows began with a crisis created by a revolution. Many Cubans fled even before the establishment of the new government under Fidel Castro, and many more during the early years. As exit controls in Cuba were established, flows diminished. Thereafter, the Cuban government would occasionally ease exit controls, and people would leave for the United States, often in large numbers. Sometimes flows would be normalized for a while, but then controls would again be eased, and outflows would surge, or controls would tighten, and outflows would ebb. For Cubans in the early years, the reasons for flight were often quite immediate: that life would be impossible under the new regime and that their lives might well be in jeopardy from imprisonment, if not death. Over time, their reasons for leaving tended to become a bit more like those of the Soviet refugees: a tightening noose of political control and economic decline. To live under such a system was unthinkable.

So, when they could, these Cuban and Soviet refugees came to the United States. Neither group was a cross-section of the countries from which they came. The Soviet case was explicitly constructed in terms of religion, and the Cuban case was largely one of class and political ideology—at least in the early years. But the two groups were also similar in many ways (see table 4.2). Their educational levels, for example, tended to be quite high, both for men and for women (especially so in the Soviet case). Their occupational skills were often quite good, whether managerial or technical. Their families were generally small and their marriages durable. They thus had in place a set of economic skills and social resources that they could use in adapting to the United States. To live in America was not always easy, but the reason for being in a new country was unambiguous and the hurdles eased by individual human capital and strong family ties.

Cubans and Soviets are also an interesting comparison in terms of the situation they found in the United States. Both had strong support from the federal government, including various kinds of financial support. They also had strong nongovernmental support. The Soviet Jewish refugees had the advantage of the highly professionalized Jewish agencies. The overall attention and support from the Hebrew Immigrant Aid Society was extensive and amplified by efforts of local Jewish congregations and social service agencies. The relationship between these agencies and the refugees was not always smooth. The Soviet Jews had long been deprived of opportunities for active religious engagement, and they often seemed all too secular to the US Jews. But that did not undermine the commitment of the American Jewish community to assist. Especially for refugees who lack their own personal connections to people in the United States, that kind of institutional support can be essential. In the Cuban case, there was also institutional support, much of it from the Catholic Church. But Cuba and the United States have a long relationship, and, prior to the Castro regime, there had been frequent flows back and forth between the two countries. Thus the Cuban arrivals often had personal acquaintance with the United States and often had personal contacts and family already in the United States. With the first flow of anti-Castro refugees, that ethnic base became far bigger and far more effective in mobilizing resources for new arrivals. Especially in Miami, which would ultimately become home to more than half of the United States' Cuban-origin population, this was not simply amorphous ethnic support but very effective linkages into a local economy that provided good opportunities in both professional work and skilled trades. That ethnic community also helped create a Spanish-language environment that did not require high levels of English proficiency.

Table 4.2. Selected characteristics of foreign-born Cubans and Soviets

		Other foreign-born
Average years of schooling		
Cubans entered in 1960–1964		
Men	11.6	10.6
Women	10.9	9.7
Cubans entered in 1965–1970		
Men	9.2	11.4
Women	8.6	10.1
Soviet Jews in New York City, 1975–1979		
Men	13.5	
Women	13.3	
Soviet Jews in Los Angeles, 1975–1979		
Men	15.3	
Women	14.2	
Occupational mobility of Cubans (% in administrative or managerial occupations)		
Entered in 1960–1964		
As of 1970	14.5	
As of 1980	20.9	
Entered in 1965–1970		
As of 1970	6.1	
As of 1980	8.7	

Sources: Guillermina Jasso and Mark R. Rosenzweig, *The New Chosen People: Immigrants in the United States* (New York: Russell-Sage Foundation, 1990), 367, 376; Steven J. Gold, "Soviet Jews in the United States," *American Jewish Yearbook* 94 (1994): 45, http://www.ajcarchives.org/AJC_DATA/Files/1994_3_SpecialArticles.pdf.

Note: These sources and years do not use fully consistent data, but the general patterns are still convincing.

There is one fundamental way, however, in which the two cases were quite different. Those leaving the Soviet Union were leaving a country that was oppressive to them on religious and ethnic grounds, and they tended not to look backward to it. Cubans in the United States, however, remained adamantly attached to their homeland and tended to label themselves as exiles rather than refugees or immigrants. With Cuba so close to their major core in southern Florida, the homeland was never far away, and any easing of border controls by Cuba would immediately result in large numbers of Cubans from the United States visiting their homeland to see their relatives. Despite all the attempts to keep the border in place, the Cuban imagination consistently demolished that border. In Cristina

García's 1992 novel, *Dreaming in Cuban*, for example, one sees constant international movements, whether to the United States, Europe, or Africa. The novel opens with an elderly woman standing guard on the northern shore of Cuba. She is guarding against any US attacks, and doing so for her beloved leader Castro. On the beach she sees a kind of radiance that "takes shape in the ether on the beach." Slowly, phantom like, her husband "emerges from the light and comes toward her, taller than the palms, walking on water in his white summer suit and Panama hat." It turns out that he has been in the United States and just died there. As García switches back and forth between Cubans in Cuba and Cubans in New York, and as the focal granddaughter herself moves back and forth between the two countries, one easily senses that being Cuban is an affair of the heart and spirit, not of one's actual or legal residence.[3]

The Cuban and Soviet cases have evolved in different ways over time. Cubans have continued to arrive, although after the disorder of the Mariel exodus in 1980 there has been a tendency to interdict unauthorized boats crossing from Cuba and instead institute a more orderly departure program—currently set at twenty thousand a year. The Mariel exodus and afterward have also tended to bring a broader cross-section of Cuban society and large numbers of people who do not have firsthand experience with American society or with capitalist societies in general. Furthermore, Cubans are now only a modest segment of the overall Hispanic population. Yet their dense concentration in Miami makes them a palpable economic and political presence similar to the largest groups in earlier American history, much like the Germans in colonial Philadelphia in the late 1700s or the Irish in Boston and New York in the latter part of the 1800s. In the Soviet case, the overall numbers have been far smaller, but the Soviet Jews remain important for assessing how best the United States can be a haven for refugees, especially religious ones, who may not exactly meet the formal international definition of refugees. In the case of Soviet Jews, special legal provisions were needed to continue to accept Soviet Jews as refugees, and a special amendment in 1990 made that possible.[4] But the amendment set in place a broader policy of accepting other persecuted religious minorities, whether Pentecostal Christians from the Soviet Union or Baha'is from Iran. That, too, is an important legacy: keeping alive the possibility for at least some people to escape religious persecution and find refuge in the United States.

PAIRED COMPARISON:
CAMBODIANS AND SALVADORANS

The migration of large numbers of Cambodians and Salvadorans to the United States has its roots in the instabilities in both countries during the 1970s (see table 4.3). In a coup in 1970, Norodom Sihanouk of Cambodia was deposed by a right-wing group more willing to cooperate with the United States in the ongoing conflict in Vietnam. As a result, a precariously peaceful society was shattered into factions and split between rural areas dominated by communist forces and an encircled urban core under the control of the rightist government. That urban core was swollen by large numbers of people fleeing the fighting in the hinterland. In 1975, as South Vietnam fell, the rightist government in Cambodia also collapsed. In a chilling reminder of how violent utopian revolutionary forces can be, virtually the entire population was moved out of the capital city of Phnom Penh into the countryside by the communist forces. Millions were killed either directly or by starvation, families were broken up, and all traces of supposedly corrupt Western ways were obliterated. To be literate, even to wear glasses, was sufficient cause to be executed. It was a holocaust, and, like the Jewish Holocaust of the Second World War, most people could not get out. A few Cambodians escaped in 1975, but the vast majority of people who would have fled simply could not. The borders were sealed. In 1979, however, the forces of the now-unified Socialist Republic of Vietnam invaded Cambodia, which had the effect of opening up the borders to the west into Thailand. The result was mass flight. It was chaotic, often resisted by the Thai government (including forced marches of refugees back through the minefields on the border), and complicated by the fact that those fleeing were now both the people oppressed by the communist forces and those communist forces themselves, now in flight from the Vietnamese.

Table 4.3. Cambodian and Salvadoran arrivals

	Cambodian	**Salvadoran**
Total population	162,086	1,260,721
%		
Since 2010	4.1	4.2
2000–2009	17.8	32.7
Before 2000	78.1	63.1

Source: US Census Bureau, combined 2011–2013 American Community Survey data, accessed through American Fact Finder, at https://factfinder.census.gov/faces/nav/jsf/pages/index.xhtml.

Note: Actual legal admissions do not include unauthorized Salvadoran arrivals, so American Community Survey data are used here to provide a better sense of population size.

In the case of El Salvador, the precipitating event was the election of 1972, marred by corruption, and resented by virtually all segments of the population. The result over the 1970s was an increasing polarization. Another governmental change in 1979 rapidly degenerated into a full-scale civil war. As in Cambodia, a rightist government was supported by the United States, which was reacting in part to the success of the leftist Sandinistas in neighboring Nicaragua. During the 1980s, the United States remained locked into a system supporting rightist governments against leftist guerillas in El Salvador while supporting rightist guerillas against a leftist government in Nicaragua. The resulting situation in El Salvador may not have matched the Cambodian case for sheer destruction, but conditions were nevertheless often deadly, and independent reports confirm that much of the carnage was by government forces and allied paramilitary groups. People in El Salvador were thus caught between the sides, under intense pressure to pick sides, and at risk if they picked the wrong side, seemed to pick the wrong side, or simply refused to pick a side. So they fled. They fled anywhere they could go, but the United States had particular appeal and one with which many Salvadorans were at least partly familiar.

The response in the United States to the two groups was very different. The Cambodians were part of an overall Southeast Asian refugee crisis that directly reflected US support for, and ultimate failure with, anticommunist governments. It was a painful defeat, but the US government was clear in its support of refugees fleeing the now-communist countries of Cambodia, Laos, and Vietnam. While there was hope that Cambodian refugees might one day be able to return under a new government, that possibility remained far in the future. So Cambodians were seen as potential refugees, and, based on reviews and interviews in refugee camps in Southeast Asia, many were accepted into the United States and arrived with their immigration papers in order. In the El Salvador case, by contrast, the US government saw people fleeing a government that the US government itself supported. That raised a dilemma: If these people were truly refugees, subject to persecution by the government in their own country, why would the United States be supporting such a government? So there was no before-the-fact consideration of refugee status for those fleeing El Salvador. If they wanted to come to the United States, the only path was the one of unauthorized migration, generally through Mexico and then across the border into the United States. Once in the United States, fleeing Salvadorans could try to claim asylum. The asylum process tends to be very legalistic and dependent on Department of State evaluations of conditions in the origin country. Not surprisingly, the applications of Salvadorans for asylum were routinely disapproved. During the 1980s, only about 3 percent were approved versus a far higher approval rate for Nicaraguan refugees fleeing the leftist Sandinistas. That is the politics of refugee status, and it can be a very rough politics.

The Cambodian and Salvadoran experiences in the United States thus developed based on very different categorizations and legal statuses. That difference would be crucial in people's lives, making it harder for those without full legal status to find work, housing, and services. But there were also two crucial similarities between Cambodians and Salvadorans. First, there was strong support outside government for both groups. As always in the United States, there were negative reactions, but the positive ones were vital. With Cambodians, the support at the private level was impressive. Sponsors, local groups, and churches all tried to help. The government may have provided the cash, but these organizations provided the in-kind support, the welcome, and perhaps above all the connections into mainstream American society. With Salvadorans, there was similar support, enhanced by the view of many people that the US government's position on Salvadorans was wrong, inconsistent with international refugee law, and inconsistent with the moral and spiritual underpinnings of American society. Thus began the Sanctuary Movement, in which individual churches and ultimately entire urban areas declared themselves sanctuaries for people they viewed explicitly as refugees. Predictably, the US government challenged this use of sanctuary and harassed the organizers but ultimately was not able to stop or punish them.

The second major element shared by Cambodians and Salvadorans fleeing to the United States was that, unlike the earlier Cuban and Soviet cases, these refugees were, by and large, not elites. Instead, they were quite ordinary urban and rural people, often with limited education. What they shared were the horrors of personal loss, of being the victims of a kind of institutionalized terrorism, of having suffered themselves, and of having witnessed the suffering, torture, and death of their friends and relatives. It is thus far harder to talk about the Cambodian or Salvadoran experiences in the United States as if they were just migrations across borders to live in a better place. For them, the "to live" part of migration was more primal and overrode more routine, day-to-day considerations. Nevertheless, there were also day-to-day considerations. For both groups, for example, there was little preparation for life in the United States or even for life in urbanized, industrial societies. Furthermore, the very trauma of the conditions that propelled them across borders tended to carry forward internally (as emotional dynamics) and externally (as ruptured family and community relationships).

Given their background, it is not surprising that information on Cambodians and Salvadorans in the United States presents a more mixed portrait than that for Cubans and Soviets (see table 4.4). There is clear progress for both groups: Cambodians and Salvadorans did find jobs, continued old and established new families, raised children who generally fared better economically than they did, and created community—on both secular and religious bases. But the jobs were often not very good ones, families were often truncated, children faced problems in poor schools in poor neighborhoods, and the communities were often quite short on resources. In cases like this, when the arriving immigrants are not manifestly "successful" in the United States, there is a tendency to focus instead on their children. These "second-generation immigrants" are, of course, not immigrants; they are Americans. Because they live their lives from the start in the US context, they do tend to do better in many ways. Yet there are problems for them as well and concern about whether the children are progressing into mainstream American society or regressing into an underclass of American society.

In view of the many difficulties Cambodians and Salvadorans have faced, it may be appropriate to question what should be considered "success" for new arrivals in the United States. Which of these paired stories—Cubans and Soviets versus Cambodians and Salvadorans—should be considered the true success—the laudable economic success of the early Cuban and Soviet arrivals or the more basic will to survive against obstacles of the Cambodians and Salvadorans? That question might be asked both about the people themselves and about the US policies that have shaped their arrival and new lives in the United States. Are US immigration and refugee policies shaped to help those most in need or those who are likely to adjust most successfully to US society?

Table 4.4. Selected characteristics of foreign-born Cambodians and Salvadorans

	Cambodian	Salvadoran	Native-born
Households			
Average household size	3.9	4.1	2.5
In family households (%)	86	85	64
Median household income (USD)	52,000	43,000	53,000
Households in poverty (%)	18	21	10
Speak only English at home (%)	8	5	89
Speak English very well (%)	33	30	98
Own a home (%)	56	41	66
Median value of home (USD)	215,000	177,000	170,000
Men			
Total population (%)	44	52	49
In labor force (%)	71	88	67
Median earnings (USD)	40,000	29,000	51,000
Married (%)	63	51	48
With BA or above (%)	17	6	29
In professional occupation (%)	24	8	34
Women			
Total population (%)	56	48	51
In labor force (%)	57	66	59
Median earnings (USD)	31,000	23,000	39,000
Married (%)	54	48	45
With BA or above (%)	11	7	29
In professional occupation (%)	20	11	41

Source: US Census Bureau, combined 2011–2013 American Community Survey data, accessed through American Fact Finder, at https://factfinder.census.gov/faces/nav/jsf/pages/index.xhtml.

Having stressed in this chapter the importance of understanding migration as a process by which people simultaneously maintain and refocus their lives, succeeding chapters will focus on three aspects of life in America that are especially crucial: work as an economic task as well as a personal vocation, in chapter 5; belief as a way to integrate the realities, hopes, and meanings of life, in chapter 6; and chapter 7's consideration of belonging as a path to connecting to others, both within and across racial, ethnic, class, cultural, spiritual, and national boundaries.

5

⌐⌐

To Work: Great Opportunities
but Heavy Costs

Whether or not their intent is to better themselves economically or simply to escape intolerable conditions in their home country, immigrants must work in America. Their experience at work ranges at least as widely as the native-born, from low-wage, erratic work that cannot fully support them and their families to the reasonable pay of technical and professional work, to not infrequent success as entrepreneurs ascending into the top financial tiers. An enormous volume of research exists on immigrant work, and the factors that hinder and facilitate it are well known. Above all, education and English-language competence facilitate initial employment, the durability of employment, and the ability to increase the quality and pay of employment over time. Good social connections with other immigrants and Americans can also help considerably. But, for first-generation immigrants, the obstacles can be significant and result in work that is—by the old formula—dirty, difficult, and dangerous. Perhaps for no one is that more true than for the many unauthorized migrants who have come to the United States in recent decades, often at the direct instigation of employers looking for the inexpensive, tractable, and often very good labor they provide.

The existing research on immigrant employment yields some general patterns that distinguish different national and ethnic groups, people of different backgrounds, and people in different areas of the United States. The research also indicates the different constellations of opportunities and obstacles that immigrants face in particular places at particular times. Yet the more important point may be the variation within those groups and in those specific places. The supposed success of some "model" immigrant groups often ignores the many within such groups who are left behind. Conversely, the concern over "problem" immigrant groups ignores the many successes within such groups. This chapter aims to sort out these issues of employment, including the way employment is far more than a simple economic aspect of life. Instead, it is one that often invokes people's highest personal aspirations. After discussion of the range in what immigrants work at, and some of the factors that influence that work, the chapter provides two paired comparisons. The first involves two very successful populations, Iranians and Indians, who have had the kind of educational and occupational backgrounds that are especially relevant to the current job market in the United States. The second compares two populations, Ecuadorans and Koreans, who have had to make more difficult adjustments to the US world of work.

THE NATURE OF WORK

Discussions of immigrants and work often begin with such economic indicators as labor-force participation rates (how many people are actually looking for work) and unemployment rates (how many people are looking for work but cannot find it). But the issue of work is far broader, deeper, and more interesting than such indicators. Some of that complexity can be seen in the very words we use. *Work* itself conveys a broad range of meanings in English. There is certainly "work" in the sense of having a job. But "to work at something" implies something broader, a serious effort to get something done. Thus one can work at a job, of course, but one can also work at other activities. One can even work at playing. But the play may turn into work, as playing pickup basketball leads to playing basketball at the professional level or playing an instrument leads to a job as a musician. People with paying jobs may likewise consider that their work is play. Interviews with firemen, who have a distinctly dangerous job, nevertheless included such statements as "We don't go to work; we go to play." The job, while dangerous, was somehow so meaningful and fulfilling that it was not "work" in the pejorative sense.[1]

So "work" can have many meanings, and, beyond the financial requirements to survive in a new country, it has a similar range of meanings for immigrants. Consider the implications of the words *occupation*, *vocation*, and *avocation*. An *occupation* is a kind of work that requires particular skills and may or may not produce very much money. A *vocation* is a bit more like a personal track that combines inherent skills and interests and, again, may or may not produce very much money. Finally, the word *avocation* provides a stronger sense that this is a personal commitment that, even if done for money, is not done for the purpose of money. Any full consideration of immigrants "working" in the United States must include all these different meanings. Human mobility is not solely drawn through a calculus of differential economic benefits. It has many sources and elements, ranging from the raw need to survive to the full development of a meaningful life, with all the economic, social, cultural, and spiritual domains that implies.

The question, then, is not so much "Are immigrants working?" or even "What are the jobs of immigrants?" but rather "What are immigrants actually working at?" The answer, of course, is that they are working at many things. Some are short-range and practical, mere tasks to be accomplished. Others are long-range and more holistic: a good life for oneself and one's children, one's community, and perhaps even the world at large. What immigrants happen to be working at, at any particular time, depends on their individual personal characteristics but is also conditioned by the two crucial attributes of age and gender. Age invokes the life course. For earlier immigrants, even childhood was a time to work, helping on the farm, in the store, and in industrial work and freelancing on the streets. In more recent times, that family work continues, but child-labor laws and school-attendance requirements tend to take children out of the domain of work and create a different educational world for them. With adulthood, however, they start to work in a formal, job-related way, and they are then included in all the vast data on labor-force participation and unemployment rates. Finally, with advanced age, there is a general expectation that people will be able to live without formal jobs, even though they may voluntarily continue to work for pay or for satisfaction or some combination of the two. With immigrants, the effects of age are often not quite the same as for the native-born: for example, immigrant children may face a more difficult time in school, their transition to adult work may be more erratic, and older people may lack the financial resources and work history that would permit some kind of self-supporting retirement.

The other factor that has a pervasive effect on what people work at is gender. Human societies distinguish between male and female. Many have other de facto genders, but the male/female binary remains dominant, and the delineation of appropriate roles between the two can often be very strict. Once people have children, that gender distinction has strong effects on what people are working at on both biological and social grounds: women have the children, nurse the children, and generally have parental priority during a child's early years—although with enormous variation across different cultures. The classic division of labor puts men as the workers outside the home and women as the internal sustainers of the home. This has changed drastically in the United States over the last two generations. The percentage of women looking for work in the sense of a job has more than doubled since 1950, while the rate for men has actually dropped. During the crucial years from twenty-five to thirty-four, when childcare is likely to be an important factor, only a third of women worked in 1950 versus more than 80 percent in 2015 (versus the male rate of 93 percent). Lower numbers of children have an important effect, but so do increasing employment opportunities for women. This becomes an important issue in migration studies, since whether immigrant women will place their efforts in or outside the home is highly variable and reflects a range of practical and cultural desires and expectations.

The effects of age and gender are especially important within families. People sometimes live alone but are usually part of some kind of household, which usually involves living with family. This affects how individuals allocate their effort, whether for gains in money or in quality of life. It also raises the question of how much of their individual effort is for the family and how much of the family's efforts are for the individuals. In a gender alignment that puts women at home and men more frequently outside the home, for example, the reasoning is that the woman's efforts at home are better for the family as a whole, particularly during children's younger years. Having two wage earners outside the home, by contrast, may slight parental roles in taking care of children yet provide a much more stable financial situation for the family. In earlier days, there was a similar decision to be made about children: should they go to school for their own future betterment, or should they go to work for the immediate improvement of the family's overall situation? In many immigrant households today there are similar decisions being made about the respective roles of husband versus wife, parent versus child. What should each of them be working at and for what short- and long-range purposes?

PATTERNS IN IMMIGRANT EMPLOYMENT

Despite these caveats about the many different things people may be working at, the issue of actual employment remains extremely important. How often and with what income are immigrants working? Overall, the most complete data show that the foreign-born in the United States are, compared to the native-born, more often in the labor force but with far lower financial rewards from employment. Sample data are provided in table 5.1. Specifically, the foreign-born have a labor-force participation rate of 67 percent (versus 63 percent for the native-born) but with only 29 percent in managerial and professional occupations (versus 38 percent for the native-born), with lower median yearly earnings ($48,000 for the foreign-born versus $53,000 for the native-born), and with a far higher percentage of their households living below the defined poverty line (18 percent for the foreign-born versus 10 percent for the native-born).

The data thus suggest an image of hard-working but underpaid immigrants that makes sense in terms of the long history of US immigration. Immigrants have often been good, reliable, inexpensive workers. The overall figures, however, mask considerable variation. For the five largest recent groups of immigrants, for example, household income for those from China, India, and the Philippines is well above the average for the native-born, is about the same as the native-born for those from Vietnam, and is well below the native-born average for those from Mexico (see table 5.2). Those differences by country of origin raise the question of why the economic situation of these groups is so different and what causes the variation among those groups. Part of the answer is that those who have arrived

Table 5.1. Economic status of foreign-born

	Foreign-born	Native-born
Labor-force participation rate	66.9	63.2
In professional work (%)	29.4	37.5
Median household income (USD)	47,753	52,910
Households in poverty (%)	18.2	10.4

Source: US Census Bureau, combined 2011–2013 American Community Survey data, accessed through American Fact Finder, at https://factfinder.census.gov/faces/nav/jsf/pages/index.xhtml.

Note: The American Community Survey data are used here solely to provide consistency with other tables. Numbers vary somewhat in different sources because of sampling and definitions.

more recently are in the early stages of what will be a better trajectory later on. An enormous amount of research has indicated how the economic status of immigrants improves over time as they adjust to the United States. Perhaps the most telling research has been on refugees who often arrive ill prepared for life in the United States and with heavy burdens of physical and emotional trauma. Their initial economic situation is often difficult, but research clearly shows progress over time.[2] General census data show a similar but more gradual improvement over time. Thus the economic profile of immigrants who have been in the country for longer is indeed better than that for more recent immigrants (see table 5.3 for illustrative data).

Table 5.2. Variation in economic status by major country of origin

	Median household income (USD)	In professional occupations (%)
Mexico	36,299	8.9
China	61,026	53.4
India	101,543	71.6
Philippines	81,871	42.6
Vietnam	56,713	29.0
Native-born	52,910	37.5
Foreign-born	47,753	29.4

Source: US Census Bureau, combined 2011–2013 American Community Survey data, accessed through American Fact Finder, at https://factfinder.census.gov/faces/nav/jsf/pages/index.xhtml.

Note: List of countries is by overall number of immigrants.

Table 5.3. Ratio of foreign-born to native-born earnings and earnings growth

	Foreign-born					
	Men			Women		
	At entry	After ten years	Increase	At entry	After ten years	Increase
Year of arrival						
1960–1964	1.00	1.04	1.08	1.08	1.06	0.96
1965–1969	0.83	0.80	0.94	1.18	1.07	0.83
1970–1974	0.72	0.86	1.42	1.03	1.05	1.04
1975–1979	0.68	0.79	1.40	1.08	0.96	0.77
1980–1981	0.54	0.75	2.09	0.81	0.94	1.34
1982–1983	0.60	0.92	2.56	0.76	0.97	1.66

Source: Harriet Orcutt Duleep and Daniel J. Dowhan, "Research on Immigrant Earnings," *Social Security Bulletin* 68, no. 1 (2008): 42, https://www.ssa.gov/policy/docs/ssb/v68n1/68n1p31.pdf.

Note: The text emphasizes the increase over time, but there is also a decrease in the starting point over the years. There is thus less increase for those who started with higher earnings and a greater increase for those who started with lower earnings.

For the children of immigrants, the starting point is generally higher than for their parents. They have been in a US educational system that provides better skills in terms of English-language usage and in the content of education. The major national data sources indicate those changes very clearly. Combining all the foreign-born, for example, about three-quarters have a high school diploma, compared with about 90 percent for the entire US population. But for the children of immigrants, that figure rises to a similar 90 percent. Percentages with a bachelor's degree also rise: from 30 percent for the foreign-born to 37 percent for their children. These figures are roughly the same for men and women. That increased education is seen in a range of higher-level jobs. Of the foreign-born, about 30 percent have jobs that are classified as professional or managerial. Of their children, about 40 percent have such jobs. Again, the figures are roughly similar for men and women. There are enormous variations that underlie these data, but they confirm the general expectation that more time in the United States is generally helpful for the foreign-born in economic terms and that their native-born children show further progress.[3]

Progress over time—whether individual or in terms of generations—is thus an important part of the immigrant story. But the starting point is indeed crucial. Consider the two essential background characteristics of English-language proficiency and education. A vast range of research has shown that, as would be expected, proficiency in English among new arrivals is highly valuable in finding employment. So is education, particularly if education in the country of origin overlaps with the content of US education. Almost all professional and managerial occupations require this combination of English and education. It is those occupations that make high earnings possible. Compare, for example, the median annual wages for jobs with different educational requirements: $25,000 for jobs with no educational requirement, $42,000 for jobs requiring a high school diploma, and $82,000 for jobs generally requiring a bachelor's degree.[4] Education and English are the key credentials for professional and managerial jobs and thus the key to maximize earnings. Those "new immigrants" who have already been working in the United States as H-1B temporary workers are in a particularly favorable situation. Not only are they qualified for higher-paying professional jobs, but they already have them. They may well be paid less than the native-born for the same work, but the earnings are probably better than they would be in their country of origin and certainly far better than those of their immigrant peers lacking that crucial "human capital" of English and education.

Employment at the lower end of the wage scale poses more problems. Work is usually more erratic even in relatively well-paying skilled-labor jobs. The job hazards from injury may also be significant, and benefits such as health insurance and retirement may be lacking or limited. Furthermore, many of these jobs are buried in layers of contracting and subcontracting, so there is no regular employer who can be held accountable for missing pay, unfairly docked expenses, or liability for injury or occupational disease exposure. Many immigrants remain trapped in such jobs. However, there are ways to improve one's prospects. Some

Immigrant seasonal farm workers in California's central valley (2015). (David Litman/Shutterstock.com)

Foreign ("alien") workers on the New York subway (c. 1910). (Everett Historical)

jobs have built-in upward mobility, or at least opportunities for advancement. Construction, for example, can yield entrance into supervisory work or more skilled trades (carpentry, bricklaying) that offer better wages. It may also be possible to move up the contracting/subcontracting ladder to become the head of a company, even if only a small one. Even a dead-end job that supports little more than survival may nevertheless yield time for improving education and skill

levels. It will, in any case, support one's children, who, with a better match to the
US labor market, will generally do better than the parents. The "moving up" part
of the immigrant story is often delayed a generation, with parents working tough
jobs to piece together the foundation for their children's future.

There are some basic strategies that immigrants can employ to leverage their
efforts. Above all, they must balance short- and long-term goals. The long-term
goal is often the children, but the decisions are not simply that everything should
be for the children. Instead, immigrants must make a careful assessment of when
children's future needs are most important and when the household's needs are
more important. When, for example, should parents' time and money be invested
in children's education, and when should children's time and money be invested
in the household? Sometimes both goals can be met simultaneously. For example,
if children continue to reside as adults with their parents, they can reduce their
own costs and also continue to help support the larger household. That can be
helpful on a variety of grounds, from sharing housecare to sharing childcare. It
can also be a very effective tool for accumulating capital to start a business or buy
a house. Another family strategy involves setting up a business that can benefit
from the labor of the family members and provide a flexible way for both the
adults and the children to balance the needs to work, learn, and take care of home
and family. Here again the ability to combine individual resources into a more
flexible group endeavor can make a crucial difference in immigrant adaptation
to a new environment.

OCCUPATIONS, VOCATIONS, AND AVOCATIONS

Understanding the immigrant world of work thus requires recognizing the general patterns in immigrant employment but also all the different strategies that
immigrants use and the ways their work reverberates as an occupation (what they
do on a regular basis), a vocation (a set of skills and aptitudes that they pursue),
and an avocation (a kind of professional or personal calling). Here some sampling
from literary accounts of immigrant life is helpful. Consider, first, the case of
the daughter in the previously discussed novel *Bread Givers*. She had seen in the
burnish of a doorknob a future life: not to go out into the street but into a small,
clean, quiet apartment. To live alone. But what kind of job could she do that
would yield that kind of life? The answer was teaching. Part of her reasoning was
quite practical: teaching is a job that is clean, stable, and honorable. But teaching
was also a way to keep alive her love of learning and of reading. So teaching was
neither simply a job nor just an occupation. It was a vocation for which she had
to train very hard as an immigrant outsider. Teaching was also an avocation—a
matter of the heart and spirit.

As another example, consider again the travails of Jurgis, the central figure in
Upton Sinclair's 1906 novel *The Jungle*. As the story opens, Jurgis has recently arrived in Chicago from Lithuania and has married his beloved Ona. The managers
of the Chicago meatpacking plants see in Jurgis the ideal worker: young, strong,

and as yet untarnished by labor activism. So Jurgis has no problem finding a job. He works hard, the pay is good, and he is able to provide for his family and even purchase a home—that derelict house with the new coat of paint and the impossible payment plan. Initially all seems well, but then Jurgis is injured, and there is no coverage for the injury. The plant keeps his job open for a while, since he is still potentially a good worker, but further injury puts him on the street. The dream begins to unravel. His wife must work, and, to keep her job, she must sleep with her boss. Meanwhile, Jurgis drifts from job to job. In summer, he vagabonds to the countryside, stunned by its quiet, its beauty, and its clean water. He readily finds work helping out on farms, but, as the weather cools, the work disappears, and he drifts back to the frenetic chaos that is Chicago. He loses the house, of course, and his wife Ona dies. Ultimately he finds work—and solace—as a labor organizer and as a manager for a building owned by a socialist.

This is the harsh side of work in America: valued as a young and strong laborer but jettisoned with age and injury. That harshness has characterized much of US immigration from the early days of slavery and indentured servants to the factories and sweatshops of the late 1800s and early 1900s and to today, when still manual agricultural and urban jobs remain the fate of many migrants. As a further problem, immigrant jobs often lie in contested social and political terrain. For example, the Greeks, a relatively new set of migrants at the end of the 1800s, took work where they could find it. One place was in the mines as strikebreakers when the regular miners were striking for decent pay, better working conditions, and an end to the requirement that they buy goods at rapacious company-store prices. So the Greeks were reviled by the regular miners, who were themselves often earlier immigrants. Yet the regular miners also had problems. Confronting the company also meant confronting the local political power structure and its law-enforcement agencies. So, while the Greeks might be hated as strikebreakers in one place, the regular Slavic immigrant miners in another place might be hated by the mining company and the political elite who controlled their conditions. Thus in Lattimer, Pennsylvania, occurred the massacre of miners described in the last chapter: shot, and mostly shot in the back.

These events highlight work as a struggle to survive, and they are a commonplace part of the immigrant story. But the immigrant struggle to not only survive but also prosper is a commonplace part of the immigrant story as well. Such immigrant success mirrors general success stories for American society overall. For example, the nearly one hundred books written by Horatio Alger during the latter part of the 1800s had a standard plot, beginning with a young boy at work with no one to help him. Through dint of constant effort, the boy gradually rises. Sometimes that success comes through some heroic act leading to recognition and an opportunity for a job. Many immigrants have achieved such success in ways that mirror the Horatio Alger formula. Many others have found ways to at least marginally improve their working conditions or find ways to balance employment with more meaningful personal activities. A perusal of immigrant autobiographies from the great wave of migration in the latter 1800s and early 1900s, for example, yields a range of such trajectories. Many involve setting up family businesses—laundries, bakeries, restaurants, garment shops, grocery stores. Many involve finding activities outside work—writing (poetry in particular), amateur theatrical groups, and many kinds of religious and community engagement.

A review of the autobiographies from one particular set of immigrants, from Finland, gives a sense of these varied trajectories. Edith Koivisto (born in Finland in 1888), for example, came to the United States to join her sister. As a student, Edith worked in a college office, in the library, and as a teacher in the correspondence classes. After graduation, she worked first as a baker's helper, then as a bookkeeper, then as a beautician. She earned extra money by sewing and selling goods and produce. Those were her day jobs. But she derived her greatest pleasure from writing for newspapers, writing her own plays, painting, and directing plays and choruses. Hers was a full life with an especially broad mix of occupations, vocations, and avocations. Helmi Mattson (born in 1885), as another example, attended business school in Finland. Her first move was to Canada to join her brother, but, through a variety of moves, she ended up in the United States. She worked as a maid before marriage but was a housewife thereafter. Beyond those jobs, she also pursued creative writing and poetry and served as the editor of a newspaper.[5]

Finnish men's autobiographies, and the discussion of male ancestors in the women's autobiographies, show a broader range of manual labor, including mining and lumbering, with comments about how physically damaging those jobs could be. But there are also cases of business success. Edward Aho (born in the United States to a father who immigrated in 1890) helped on the family farm when he was growing up. He then worked as a bookkeeper before opening his own store and finally becoming general manager of an insurance company. Francis Hanson's autobiography notes how his father (born in 1853) came to the United States in 1873 with his parents. He, too, had a sequence of jobs, starting as a miner and then switching to farming. Land was still readily available in Minnesota at that time. Later, however, he became a postmaster and served as clerk assessor and county commissioner. At one point, he also worked for a gas company in Minneapolis. His jobs thus ranged from exacting manual labor to more independent labor as a farmer and then to more white-collar jobs, although these may have been more as supplements to a core farming occupation. There is also a stronger political thread in some of the male accounts. Immigrants from Finland (as from the rest of Scandinavia) were often educated and politically active.[6]

These experiences of early Finnish immigrants suggest a range of opportunities in America and alertness on the part of immigrants about those options. There is optimism, although some of that may reflect the desire of autobiographical authors to tell a story that shows progress. Darker visions, however, also emerge. There are thus both options and constraints, which continue for immigrants today. The remainder of this chapter discusses, as in the last chapter, two paired sets of immigrant groups. The first pair, Iranians and Indians, suggests how a combination of education and English can propel immigrants toward the top of the economic range, especially when combined with strong social connections and cultural values. The second pair, Ecuadorans and Koreans, illustrates alternative employment strategies that can be used when the match between background characteristics and employment options in the United States is less immediately apparent.

PAIRED COMPARISON: IRANIANS AND INDIANS

In economic terms, Iranians and Indians have historically been among the most successful immigrants in the United States. They provide examples of how working can be as much a matter of prosperity as of mere survival, even for the first generation. The explanation is, in many ways, an easy one: both Indians and Iranians have tended to have exactly the education and language skills that can be most easily leveraged in the United States. But the Iranian and Indian migration histories are also complex and diverse and include outbreaks of hostility from the native-born US population. Success has been neither automatic nor easy.

For Iranians as well as Indians, the United States has not always been an obvious migration destination. There were few from either country in the early United States. Some Indians (mostly Sikhs) were brought in as agricultural labor on the West Coast in the latter 1800s, and a few Iranians arrived in the early 1900s. However, the numbers were very small in both cases, and the primary migration destinations for Iranians and Indians tended to be elsewhere. Iran, for example, was more oriented toward Europe, and India, as a former colony and Commonwealth member, was decidedly oriented toward the United Kingdom. The relative strength of the US economy after the Second World War, however, made the United States an increasing focus of business ties for the Iranians, and the prevalence of English as a de facto global language made the United States a logical migration option for the Indians. Increasing student migration to the United States was common for both groups.

Political conditions were also important. In the Iranian case, a new fundamentalist Islamic government—and especially the 1979 hostage taking of personnel at the US embassy—created a situation in which the United States granted refuge to Iranians who opposed the regime and were stranded in the United States, including the many Iranian foreign students. Most had ties to the former regime of the shah and thus feared return. In the Indian case, long democratic traditions and warming political relations with the United States made the continuing flow of students easy and congenial. In addition, Indians became the major group of high-tech workers under the H-1B program. Those two temporary statuses of student and high-tech worker were then, and remain today, major tracks leading to permanent residence in the United States.

The resulting admissions numbers for permanent residence are shown in table 5.4. Iranian admissions were modest in the 1950s and 1960s, escalated in the 1970s, jumped very sharply in the 1980s (reflecting the acceptance of Iranians stranded in the United States after the revolution), and declined thereafter. The

Indian admissions start at a lower level in the 1950s but escalate dramatically thereafter by decade: jumping to 148,000 in the 1970s after the implementation of the 1965 Hart-Celler Act, and continuing to nearly 600,000 in the first decade of this century. In recent years, India has been in a virtual tie with China as the second-most important country of origin for US immigrants, trailing only Mexico.

Table 5.4. Indian and Iranian admissions

	India	Iran
1950s	1,922	3,195
1960s	18,638	9,059
1970s	148,018	33,763
1980s	231,649	98,141
1990s	352,528	76,899
2000s	590,464	76,755

Source: US Department of Homeland Security, *Yearbook of Immigration Statistics: 2015* (Washington, DC: US Department of Homeland Security, Office of Immigration Statistics, 2016).

In their pursuit of survival and success through international migration, these two groups provide a glimpse of a very effective formula. That formula can be expressed in terms of four kinds of capital. The first, as noted earlier, is simply *capital.* Money helps. Money eases the journey, the initial settlement, and everything thereafter. Money for the children, for example, yields the best residences in the best school districts or the best of private schooling. The second kind of capital, also discussed earlier, is generally called *human capital.* That includes such characteristics as language ability and educational background but also encompasses the many other kinds of skills people may have picked up over the years. Experience with market-driven economic systems and interest-group politics, for example, can come in handy in the United States. The third kind is generally termed *social capital.* That refers to all the connections that people have, within the family, within some general kind of ethnic or religious community, and with broader society. Good connections are helpful as sources of information and assistance. Intuitively it makes sense that those connections ought to be broad as well as deep. Finally, the fourth kind is often called *cultural capital.* It includes all the values, beliefs, and symbols on which people can draw to create meaning out of the vagaries of life and to focus effort on particular goals. A belief in the value of hard work, for example, is helpful, as is a belief in mutual effort in a group setting—whether that of family or community.

Iranians and Indians match up well in terms of all four of these kinds of capital. Both have historically had access to financial resources. These generally are not destitute immigrants, but rather people who were well off in their origin countries. Many have had the funds to finance education or to establish businesses.

Both also have significant human capital. English-language proficiency is generally high, almost automatically for Indians and very frequently for Iranians. Educational levels are also high, and college degrees are common. Furthermore, the significant amount of US education for both Iranians and Indians has provided not only English and education but also exactly the kind of English and education needed in the United States. In terms of social capital, both groups are noted for strong family ties, including within the immediate family and with extended kin. Those extended ties can be crucial. It is usually better to seek information and assistance from kin than from strangers, especially in a new environment where—like Jurgis and his house—it is easy to be misled, cheated, or worse. Both groups also have significant broader communities created from national, regional, occupational, and religious ties. Finally, both groups have impressive cultural capital. They can draw on very ancient—and glorious—civilizations and can trace their descent from them. "Persia" continues to resonate among Iranians in the United States, and the many glories of India are re-created repeatedly in Indian life and contemporary culture. Those are cultures of excellence that permit some existential ease in facing life in a new place, including hostility from the native-born.

Not all of these kinds of capital can be fully analyzed with quantitative data, but there exist very good data on language and educational background that are very positive (see table 5.5).[7] The data are also very positive on current employment and income. For the Indian immigrants, household income is nearly double that for the US native-born overall, and the percentage of households in poverty is about half that for the native-born. The median earnings for both men and women are also higher than for the native-born, reflecting higher percentages of individuals with college degrees and working in professional occupations. The comparison of Iranians to the native-born is less sharp, but household earnings are somewhat higher than the native-born, and the same pattern of higher proportions of both men and women in professional jobs and with college degrees also holds.

This positive portrayal of Indian and Iranian immigrant success in the United States obscures a number of more complex issues. Some of these are positive and some negative. On the negative side, this overall portrait leaves out the many problems that people from both countries have faced in the United States. One such problem is that this package of capital, human capital, social capital, and cultural capital does not work out equally well for everybody. There are inevitably some people who do not fare as well. Both groups have also at times faced hostility from the native-born. Iranians were targeted at the time of the hostage episode as if they were somehow responsible—even though they were in opposition to the Iranian regime that took the hostages. Indians have also been targeted: they are often quite visible in how they dress, perhaps especially with the bindi as a physical marker on the foreheads of Hindus and Jains. Thus, although Indians and Iranians may well lie at the whiter end of the US color-line spectrum and the higher end of the US class spectrum, they have not escaped prejudice.

Table 5.5. Selected characteristics of foreign-born Indians and Iranians

	Indians	Iranians	Native-born
Households			
Average household size	3.1	2.6	2.5
In family households (%)	82	69	64
Median household income (USD)	102,000	59,000	53,000
Households in poverty (%)	4	12	10
Speak only English at home (%)	10	10	89
Speak English very well (%)	74	57	98
Own a home (%)	54	56	66
Median value of home (USD)	360,000	457,000	170,000
Men			
Total population (%)	52	51	49
In labor force (%)	84	73	67
Median earnings (USD)	85,000	70,000	51,000
Married (%)	76	65	48
With BA or above (%)	80	61	29
In professional occupation (%)	74	55	34
Women			
Total population (%)	48	49	51
In labor force (%)	56	54	59
Median earnings (USD)	63,000	51,000	39,000
Married (%)	79	58	45
With BA or above (%)	71	46	29
In professional occupation (%)	67	50	41

Source: US Census Bureau, combined 2011–2013 American Community Survey data, accessed through American Fact Finder, at https://factfinder.census.gov/faces/nav/jsf/pages/index.xhtml.

On the positive side, there are two especially interesting elements in both the Indian and the Iranian experiences. The first is that, while their success hinges on English proficiency, they are not "native English speakers" in the usual sense. Iranians are largely Farsi speaking; English is an additional language for them. Even for the Indians, English may be the common national language and what the educational system is based on, but the vast majority of Indians even in the United States speak a different language at home. This is English, then, as a part of a bilingual language package. Success may hinge on English-language proficiency, but it does not appear from these cases to hinge on English as people's only, or even primary, language.

The second interesting point is that, despite having a strong cultural heritage, Iran and India are very diverse societies. In the Iranian case, that diversity is most clearly seen in religion, and that religious variation is greater among the Iranians in the US than those in Iran. The Iranian population has deep roots in Baha'i, Christianity, and Judaism, as well as in (largely Shia) Islam. In the Indian case, diversity is seen especially in the language of choice at home, and the Indian population in the United States represents the home country in its wide range of languages, whether Hindi, Marathi, Telugu, Tamil, Urdu, Gujarati, or a host of others. There is also religious variation: Hinduism for the great majority but also Christianity and Islam. These two cases of relative economic success thus highlight predictable features of human and social capital but also suggest that such success does not require cultural or linguistic uniformity either among the arriving immigrants or between them and the US native-born. Keeping the old ways does not seem to preclude effective overall adaptation to the United States.

PAIRED COMPARISON: ECUADORANS AND KOREANS

While the United States may not originally have been a main destination for Iranians and Indians, for other countries there are more specific US connections that have created durable paths to the United States. Ecuador and South Korea provide examples of how such connections have evolved into substantial and continuing migration: sometimes permanent and sometimes temporary, sometimes fully legal and sometimes unauthorized. The two migrant groups also provide glimpses of the economic strategies that immigrants use when they do not have the kinds of language and educational background that translate as readily to the United States as has generally been true for Iranians and Indians.

In the Ecuadoran case, the initial link was economic: the production of so-called panama hats. The main business connection was to New York City. This established the link. Later, when Ecuadorans began to think of going overseas, often for education, New York became a logical destination. It was not, however, always the only or favored destination. In the early 1900s, the main destination was France, but France was soon replaced by the United States as the preferred destination, and, over time, a long sequence of economic difficulties in Ecuador pushed young, mostly male, Ecuadorans to find work overseas, largely in New York, whether legal or unauthorized. Such migration to the United States was often part of a series of moves—first from the countryside to the cities in Ecuador, then from Ecuadoran cities to the United States. Frequently they then returned to Ecuador. Much of this migration came from and through the southern highland city of Cuenca, so the connection was in many ways more place to place (Cuenca to New York) than country to country. One result is that the personal networks in both places, and along the path between, were very dense.

In the case of Korea, there are many points in time that might be used as the beginning of a special connection. One is with the arrival to Korea in 1884 and 1885 of the first American Presbyterian and Methodist missionaries. Korea would soon fall under the control of Japan (and was officially colonized in 1910), but both denominations flourished in Korea, providing spiritual solace during the years of Japanese rule and also a continuing connection to the United States. After the partition of Korea at the end of World War II, that connection would broaden and deepen into a strong military alliance, extensive economic interaction, and constant population flows: US military and business people to South Korea and people from South Korea to the United States for a range of educational, marital, and economic reasons. Although there were concentrations of Koreans in particular areas, especially Los Angeles and New York City, the overall numbers were far larger than for Ecuadorans, creating Korean clusters in many US localities.[8]

The data on admissions from these two countries show modest numbers in the 1950s and 1960s for both countries, growing thereafter, especially for Korea (see table 5.6). As for other Asian countries, the change in immigration laws in 1965 opened up migration possibilities that had not existed before. In the Ecuadoran case, the more modest increases indicate a far less populous country and the way the 1965 changes (as later amended) tended to formalize and limit entry from the western hemisphere. The numbers in the table are for legal admissions (as permanent-resident alien) and thus miss large numbers of unauthorized Ecuadoran migrants, estimated at about two hundred thousand. Those numbers also do not include the many Korean legal but temporary visitors, such as students, business people, and visiting relatives of US-based Koreans and their children. Some of those have overstayed their visas; the estimate for the number of unauthorized Korean migrants is also about two hundred thousand.

Both countries thus have generated a large number of people coming to the United States. How do they support themselves? In the Ecuadoran case, the basic human-capital profile is relatively low (see table 5.7). This is a population with limited formal education and limited English-language ability. However, the population is heavily concentrated in the New York City area, with well over half of the Ecuadoran-origin population there. Indeed, Ecuadorans are the third-largest Latin American population in the city. That suggests that there is

Table 5.6. Ecuadoran and Korean admissions

	Ecuador	Korea
1950s	8,574	4,845
1960s	34,107	27,048
1970s	47,464	241,192
1980s	48,015	322,708
1990s	81,358	179,770
2000s	107,977	209,758

Source: US Department of Homeland Security, *Yearbook of Immigration Statistics: 2015* (Washington, DC: US Department of Homeland Security, Office of Immigration Statistics, 2016).

a great deal of social capital arrayed at both origin and destination. Since there is a significant unauthorized component of the population, there is also a need for some caution in where people work. The result is a reliance on jobs in the service sector, especially jobs that are behind the scenes and that are gained through trusted personal networks. For men, this is often restaurant work; for women, domestic work. The pay is not very good, and the work can be erratic, but jobs are available, and people know how to find them through personal contacts. Furthermore, the very density of Ecuadoran settlement creates at least some business opportunities, especially in Queens, the focus of the Ecuadoran

Table 5.7. Selected characteristics of foreign-born Ecuadorans and Koreans

	Ecuadoran	Korean	Native-born
Households			
Average household size	3.7	2.7	2.5
In family households (%)	81	71	64
Median household income (USD)	48,000	54,000	53,000
Households in poverty (%)	17	12	10
Speak only English at home (%)	5	16	89
Speak English very well (%)	37	46	98
Own a home (%)	39	47	66
Median value of home (USD)	260,000	365,000	170,000
Men			
Total population (%)	52	43	49
In labor force (%)	83	72	67
Median earnings (USD)	32,000	51,000	51,000
Married (%)	55	65	48
With BA or above (%)	15	59	29
In professional occupation (%)	15	50	34
Women			
Total population (%)	48	57	51
In labor force (%)	61	51	59
Median earnings (USD)	27,000	41,000	39,000
Married (%)	52	62	45
With BA or above (%)	17	46	29
In professional occupation (%)	21	43	41

Source: US Census Bureau, combined 2011–2013 American Community Survey data, accessed through American Fact Finder, at https://factfinder.census.gov/faces/nav/jsf/pages/index.xhtml.

community. The income from these different sources can be pieced together into effective household strategies. The long-range prospects, however, are not very good, and it is clear that Ecuadorans are often torn about whether to stay in the United States or return to Ecuador. One indication of dissatisfaction with the United States is the rapidity with which Ecuadorans shifted their migration in other directions in the 1990s. At that time, economic growth in the European Union was strong, and in Spain the cultural environment and language were congenial. Within a few years Spain was about even with the United States as a migrant destination. Then the Spanish economy collapsed, and many Ecuadoran migrants returned to Ecuador or focused again on the United States. The United States may not have been an ideal destination for Ecuadorans, but it turned out to be a far more reliable one than Spain.

In the Korean case, strong national and religious connections have yielded migrants with generally high educational levels and extensive exposure to English. That English exposure occurs in the Korean educational system (both regular school and after-school private classes) and through extensive educational migration to the United States and other anglophone countries at the high school and college levels. Furthermore, Korean migrants often come to the United States with significant financial resources from personal and family savings. So, at first glance, their situation might seem similar to that of Indians, another well-educated, English-exposed population. However, there are mismatches among Korean immigrants, on both the educational and language sides. In terms of education, many Koreans have degrees that are not readily translatable to the US context. English exposure, in turn, has often not yielded true English fluency. Additionally, Korean and English are extraordinarily different in their phonetic and grammatical structures. So this set of migrants has some constraints in terms of employment. The data in table 5.7 show Koreans with a far higher percentage of college graduates than the native-born but with only about the same earnings as the native-born. However, social and cultural capital are considerable and highly applicable to the United States. Family ties are strong, and Korean Christian congregations are fervent on both spiritual and social grounds. Furthermore, the cultural valuation of hard work and education produce a US-relevant trajectory: hard work now to produce well-educated, English-proficient children.

Despite their relatively high educational profile, Koreans were effectively blocked from many professional and managerial job options. However, there was another alternative—self-employment—and here Koreans have shown very high levels of entrepreneurship. They were able to manage the technical details of running a business, family assistance could keep costs down, and such a business was a culturally acceptable way of establishing themselves in the community. Furthermore, their dense community ties, especially through churches, provided a useful network for broader business dealings. What is most interesting about the Korean case is that their entrepreneurship was not, by and large, based on any business experience before coming to the United States, much less any specific experience in their new US niches of convenience stores and greengrocers. Self-employment, often in an unknown business, was a new line of work that helped maximize their social and cultural capital when their human capital was less immediately transferable to the US context.

The general implication of the Ecuadoran and Korean cases is that, when the fit between the background characteristics of immigrants and the demands of the US labor market is not a good match, immigrants create transitional adjustments that maximize what capital they do have to help overcome their lack of other kinds of capital. In the process they may find a very good economic niche that is not being filled by other people. But what are those transitional adjustments transitions to? For that question, there is no definitive answer. As with many earlier immigrants, America can be a final home, a transition back to the origin country, or one anchor in a continuing back-and-forth transnational life. Ecuadorans have often returned from the United States to Ecuador and have often continued to move back and forth. With Korea's economic transformation, that back-and-forth pattern is also becoming more common. In retirement, for example, Koreans in the United States may return to buy an apartment in South Korea since the government there has created special economic zones in which they can easily do that. Even Koreans adopted by US families often return to Korea seeking their biological and cultural heritage. There they find, among other things, that it is just as hard for adult English speakers to learn Korean as it is for adult Korean speakers to learn English.

Overall these two paired examples—Indians and Iranians, Ecuadorans and Koreans—suggest some of the ways in which immigrants adjust to the United States in terms of the work that they do, learning ways to maximize the different kinds of capital they bring with them in response to the opportunities and constraints of the US economic system. Yet those economic adjustments—work in the sense of a job—are only part of a broader set of goals on which they are working, many of which are long term and many of which are far more than merely economic. Their movement across space as migrants is intertwined with their movement through life. That dual movement hinges ultimately on what they believe and how their beliefs endure, develop, and change as they move. That is the topic of the next chapter.

6

⌒⌒

To Believe: Hopes, Dreams, and Commitments

The reasons why people move are varied and complex. Their decisions to move may reflect very pragmatic concerns (marriage, a better job) but also reflect deep beliefs, whether about the moral value of political liberty or the spiritual need for freedom of worship. Life in the United States has both a practical side and a more spiritual one. What is the nature and meaning of life in a new land, and what changes does that require from one's native land? For some immigrants, there is a sharp cleavage between old and new lives: ways of behavior, relations with family and neighbors, basic political views, and reverence for the spirit are all challenged. That may lead to loss of faith but also to heightened faith or perhaps conversion. For other immigrants, there are easier bridges between the old and new: Christians may find a home in American churches (whether as part of the same congregation or as a separate one sharing the same physical facilities); Jews tend to find an active and welcoming (though sometimes a bit directive) religious community; Muslims, Buddhists, and Hindus now find a range of mosques and temples in most US cities. These issues of meaning are not, however, limited to formal religion. Those with a strong belief in political freedom and human rights may treasure life in a country that reveres those values more than the countries from which they come. Those who seek the freedom of artistic creation may also find a haven in America.

This chapter begins with a general discussion of the classic economic model of migration and some of the factors it overlooks, especially the complexity and multiplicity of meanings that migration has to people. The chapter continues with the level of commitment people have to their beliefs and then sketches the general vectors of belief, whether religious, political, or more personal. The sequencing in the discussion—level of commitment first and kind of commitment

This Buddhist temple in Los Angeles dates from 1905. (Tupungato/Shutterstock.com)

second—highlights how important the sheer force of belief is in the prearrival and postarrival journeys of migrants. The force of one's convictions may be more crucial to migration than the exact content of those convictions. As usual, the latter part of the chapter provides two paired case examples. The first pair includes Catholics from two major origin countries for current US immigrants: Mexico and Vietnam.[1] For both, religion has helped provide a social and spiritual framework for migration to the United States and for life in a new country. The second pair involves a contrast between European Muslims and African Christians, specifically those coming from Bosnia and Sudan, respectively.

THE MANY MEANINGS OF MIGRATION

Classic discussions of migration often posit a scenario in which people decide whether to move based on a variety of push-and-pull factors. Those factors may involve either basic survival or some overall improvement in the quality of life. That kind of analysis works best in situations in which migration is a major change in people's lives and is relatively permanent. That kind of analysis also works especially well in the US case, since the opportunities, particularly economic opportunities, tend to be greater there than in other countries. Once people migrate to the United States, they have many reasons to stay, because the opportunities are both greater than in the countries from which they come and greater than in the alternative countries to which they might go. So the classic immigration model—leave there, come here, and stay—often seems to work quite well as a way to understand US immigration.

The meaning of migration in this classic scenario tends to lie with the way migrants make rational decisions to deliberately seek some kind of economic improvement. However, the situation of migrants is more complex than that simple scenario. One reason is that many migrants do not actually make decisions about whether to move. Migration is often forced. That is true, of course, of that vast initial migration of slaves to the United States. But it is also true of many people in seemingly more voluntary, decision-based migration. Children, for example, might be consulted on a family's move, but the younger ones are simply uprooted. Even adult children may be more directed by their parents to move than making the decision themselves. Wives, depending on the culture, may also be relatively removed from the decision to move. Thus, in most cases, there are "tied movers" whose reasons to move have more to do with their attachments to other people than with their own decision about the relative merits of moving to a new place. Thus the package of dreams, fears, gains, and losses for any move is likely to vary among the people involved—and between them and those who are left behind. Migration may mean different things even to people who travel together.

Another reason that the meaning of migration varies is that there is often not a single point at which a decision is made. Instead—as we know from a broader consideration of human mobility—people are likely to make a series of moves in their lives, and it is difficult to assess which of those moves may be the most crucial. For example, if a student comes to the United States, returns to the home country, then returns to the United States on a temporary work visa, then applies for permanent resident status, and, after receiving that status, later applies for citizenship, what is the actual decision point? Migration is so intertwined with so many crucial moments in people's lives that it may be hard to identify a single core decision point. Perhaps the explanation lies even beyond that person's own life. Perhaps an older sibling attended university in the United States. Or perhaps the parents made a decision early on that their children would go to primary and secondary schools that emphasized English because that would give their children a better chance of going to the United States later on for university education.

The classic scenario's emphasis on rational decisions about economic opportunities may also obscure the broader beliefs, values, goals, and commitments of migrants. Migration is not necessarily a move for a better life in economic terms but often, instead, a move for a proper and meaningful life. What is proper and meaningful may vary among those considering moving, among those actually moving, and also between the migrants and those they encounter in a new environment. The earlier discussion of Cubans provides one example. Some Cubans fled, and some did not. Even close relatives found themselves making different decisions. Those who fled to the United States were generally classified as refugees.[2] In the prevailing Christianity of the United States, *refuge* implies a new place that is permanent. Flight is to a new promised land. That model meshes well with the idea of people fleeing from a (godless) communist regime to the United States. The Cubans, by contrast, tended to label themselves *exiles*. An exile is indeed in refuge somewhere else but not in a new promised land that claims full attention and devotion. Instead, an exile aims to return; moving to the United States is only one stage in a longer itinerary. There were thus sharp differences in the meaning of migration among Cubans in Cuba and between Cubans in the United States and the people who welcomed them. Many of those coming to the United States today are on a similar multistage journey that will end in a return home. Others are forging lives that balance the attachments and opportunities of the United States and those of their origin countries. Their journeys back and forth between the two countries continue over time, both in body and in spirit. The meaning of migration shifts accordingly.

There are thus many meanings to migration before, during, and after the fact. Some of those meanings are indeed economic, but many challenge the classic economic scenario of moving from there to here and staying. These other meanings of migration derive from broader and deeper resonances of human hopes and dreams. The variation among these meanings may be caused by individual differences even among sets of people—like families—who move together and may be amplified or reduced over time as people move through their lives. The great difficulty in migration and mobility studies is how to understand people's movement through their lives as their paths lead from place to place. That understanding must be rooted in people's own experience of their lives. Sometimes their lived experience can be pieced together from their own accounts. Sometimes it can be seen through in-depth outsider accounts (by anthropologists, for example). Sometimes it is made manifest in the arts, perhaps especially literature. Sometimes, however, it can be inferred not from discussion of what people say they believe and how they say they decided on migration but from the raw conviction with which migrants act to pursue their moves to, and lives in, the United States.

EVEN TO THE DEATH

Sometimes migrants flee death itself, and sometimes they also confront death on their journeys, even knowing before the fact how risky the journey may be. Those confrontations with risk illuminate the strength of the beliefs and commitments that propel people along their journeys. Two examples, one from early colonial history and one from current times, help show the strength of the motivations to move and thus how migration is often more an elemental necessity than simply an economic option. The first example returns to the early Massachusetts colony; the second example concerns contemporary undocumented crossing of the Mexico–United States border, especially by children fleeing violence farther south in Central America.

The early Massachusetts colony represented the efforts of a set of coreligionists to create a better life in a new and freer environment. That better life was a matter of religion, not economics. They wished to live according to their conscience, which, in their case, meant according to God's will. The freedom they gained in Massachusetts from interference in their religious life, however, did not mean that individuals had the right to go against the leadership of the colony. It was not long before intolerance crystallized. As a case in point, Mary Dyer arrived in the colony with her husband in 1635, just as the turmoil over the individualistic views of people like Anne Hutchinson was reaching its peak. Dyer was "of a comely stature and countenance, of a piercing knowledge in many things, of a wonderful sweet and pleasant discourse, so fit for great affairs."[3] She and her husband were soon strong supporters of Anne Hutchinson, whose views were unacceptable to the colony's leaders. In 1637 Hutchinson was expelled, and her followers, including Mary Dyer and her husband, went to join Roger Williams in what is now Rhode Island.

Until that point, Mary Dyer was simply one of many new colonists caught in this paradox of religious freedom for the group but lack of religious freedom for the individual. But Mary Dyer's case had an additional twist. In 1651 she returned to England. There she was exposed to a new kind of religion that emphasized the individual conscience of each believer. That must have been especially appealing to her, given the group control she had seen in the Massachusetts colony. Furthermore, the views of this group, the Quakers, included a role for women as preachers. That, too, must have been appealing. Dyer was soon swayed to Quakerism and, in her conversion, determined to return to Massachusetts to spread this new and, to her, better understanding of the human connection to God. In 1656 she arrived and was soon in trouble again with the colony authorities. Brought before the governor, she and two other Quakers were judged guilty for their views but, even more damaging, judged guilty for having returned to the colony with views that they themselves knew were heretical. Dyer was challenging the social order and its official hierarchy. After questioning Dyer and the others, the governor judged that "we have made many laws and endeavored in several ways to keep you from among us, but neither whipping nor imprisonment, nor cutting off ears, nor banishment upon pain of death will keep you from among us. We desire not your death." But death it was to be, and Mary Dyer was sent off to be "hanged till you be dead." Dyer's reply: "The will of the Lord be done . . . and joyfully I go." There was, however, a last-minute reprieve when she was taken to the hanging tree the next week. But it was only a delay, because, after being banished once more, she returned yet again, and yet again she was sentenced to death. This time the sentence was carried out. She spoke eloquently of her purpose as she faced death and concluded, "I came to do the will of my Father, and in obedience to his will I stand even to the death."[4]

Mary Dyer's life and death underscore several key themes in the immigrant experience in America. One is the vacillating coexistence of currents of freedom and repression in the colonies and in the United States. Another is the continuing nature of migration. Even in these early times, the journey from Europe to America was not a simple from "there" to "here." It often involved a return to Europe and sometimes a back-and-forth between the two. Dyer's personal connections were not lost because of her move to the colonies. She had friends with whom to stay when she returned to England, and their connections to this new Quakerism transformed her life and her understanding of it. Her sequential moves across land and sea were thus intertwined with her own personal and spiritual development. The crucial element in her martyrdom, however, was her willingness to sacrifice life itself. That, too, is a core theme in American history, whether it is in a religious pursuit, as in Dyer's case, or in the civic, political sense of Patrick Henry's "Give me liberty or give me death"—a notion even more suc- cinctly phrased on New Hampshire license plates today as "Live free or die." This is not migration simply for a better and more secure life but migration as one part of a life that is lived for a larger purpose. That kind of life requires risks that may extend even to the death.[5]

The risks in migration show up in many ways. One might remember those Slavic miners whose pursuit of union demands for fair pay resulted in their being shot—and largely in the back. Such attacks against immigrants are also reminders that contesting the system has its costs. But risk is everywhere in the processes of migration, and the risks are sometimes very high. As a contempo- rary example, it is helpful to look again at the Mexico–United States border. Many Mexicans cross it in fully legal fashion. Many cross it illegally. They do so for numerous reasons. Sometimes the explanation "for a better life" may make sense. At other times it is probably fairer to say that it is not "for a better life" but simply "for a life." One of the effects of NAFTA, for example, was to reduce barriers to US agricultural exports to Mexico. On the Mexican side of the border, that undermined the economic feasibility of small farms, putting those former farmers in the position not of finding a better life but of finding a life that could replace the life they had lost. For such reasons there is continued pressure on the border from the Mexican side, even though declining birth rates in Mexico are simultaneously reducing that pressure.

Whatever the case, over the last two decades the risk in trying to cross that border has increased. Lacking legal authorization, a cat-and-mouse game de- velops. As the US fortifies sections of the border, those trying to cross it either match technology (ladders over and tunnels under walls) or find unguarded parts of the border. Those unguarded parts of the border are where the risk changes from inconvenience (being caught and returned) to danger. Migrants die in those unguarded, deserted, and dangerous areas. They die from a combination of exposure, inadequate preparation (not enough water), and betrayal by their guides. They are also often abused even if they do survive. So there is risk, even to the death. There is also a dysfunctional interaction of perspectives between the migrants and those trying to control the border. On the US side, policy and program people often think their job is to make it harder to cross the border. The implicit thinking seems to be that, if the border becomes harder to cross, then people will cross it less frequently. If the border becomes very dangerous to cross, then people may not cross it at all. Studies on the migrant side, however, show a different logic. For many migrants, the issue is not to adjust their behavior in terms of increased risk but simply to accept that increased risk. If it takes more times to successfully cross the border, then they make more efforts. If there is a chance of death, then they accept the risk.[6] The question for the migrants—or at least for many of them—is not whether to cross. They must cross, sometimes to find a life on the other side, sometimes to return to a life in the United States that they have already established, and often to be with the people they love. Migration, in this case, is not just going to a new life or returning to a former life but also reconnecting with life, with family, and with home.

These border-crossing risks have become even more of a concern as children began fleeing the catastrophic collapse in security in Central America. That situation developed, at least in part, from a combination of internal problems since the civil wars that erupted at the beginning of the 1980s and a continuing return of people from the United States who had been involved in gang activity, especially among Salvadorans. The result has been a recognition in El Salvador, and neighboring Honduras, that children do not have the possibility of a normal life in their home countries. Homicide rates in these countries, for example, are among the highest in the world, running from ten to twenty times the rate in the United States—and the US rate is itself high for an industrialized country. Pressure for young males to join gangs increases their future risks, but not joining may expose them to immediate danger. So children, and often their mothers, have fled. They take an arduous path into Mexico, through Mexico (about two thousand miles, depending on the route), and then across the newly dangerous US border. US authorities have had a mixed reaction—sympathetic, to some extent, but deeply concerned about potentially large inflows of immigrants. Whatever the public-policy response, however, it is clear from research that these new migrants—whom humanitarian organizations view as refugees—know the risks they face. Surveys in Honduras, for example, show very large majorities recognizing that migrants face prejudice in the United States, that deportations are on the rise, and that border crossings are increasingly difficult. They flee through known dangers and toward a United States that has its own dangers. But they flee away from the even greater dangers in Central America.[7] That these are children whose lives are being risked makes the situation more poignant. The risks are real, including possible death. That vulnerability of children in transit is also a common theme in US immigration history. Attempts to take children out of harm's way have sometimes resulted in tragedy. The memories of a ship sinking while carrying British children being brought to the United States during World War II, and the airplane crash out of Saigon during Operation Babylift in 1975, remain warnings that attempts to save children may cost them their lives.

These examples of the willingness to face death itself reflect the strength of the commitments that people have to go somewhere else, whether to bear witness to their beliefs, to reach new and better lives, to return to existing lives, or to salvage for their children the hope of decent future lives. That fervency of belief in the need to move is a core issue in understanding US immigration. It is also recognized in parts of US immigration policy. There is recognition of the force of circumstances in refugee and asylum policy, and there are also special immigration categories for people who may not meet the regular refugee standard but whose need to be in the United States is high. For example, special immigration channels exist for people who have worked for the United States as interpreters in Iraq. There are also temporary statuses such as TPS (temporary protected status), a presidential determination that people from certain countries cannot at the moment return safely to those countries. Another element of US immigration and naturalization policy tests directly the degree of personal commitment of immigrants. For those legal-resident aliens willing to serve in the US Armed Forces, which requires a commitment to serve even to death, the path to full citizenship is shortened. Here is a situation in which proving one's commitment through accepting risk is recognized and rewarded.

VECTORS OF BELIEF

The strength of migrant commitments raises the related question of the nature of those commitments. Much of the conventional discussion of US immigration is phrased in terms of the search for a better life. The discussion in this chapter, by contrast, looks to the need to maintain life as a first step and then to develop a life that is sustainable for oneself and one's children in practical, emotional, and spiritual ways. Migration is not simply an option but often an elemental necessity. The nature of this elemental necessity varies for different migrants and can be generally divided into religious, political, and economic vectors. Some general comments on each of these follow below, but note that these vectors are likely to be mixed together in different combinations for different migrants and that the list is not meant to be exclusionary.

The concept of America as a place of religious freedom is foundational, whether for those early Pilgrims in Massachusetts, the many Catholics who sought religious freedom in an often-unsympathetic Protestant country, Jews (despite the frequent hostility to them), and the many ranges of religious beliefs and practice since then. For many immigrants, freedom of religion has been crucial to their migration. In other cases, its effect on the decision to immigrate has been more indirect. For the Irish Catholics of the famine years, for example, it was indeed the famine that propelled them onto the famine ships and then to the United States. But that famine was created by a system of economic oppression of those Catholics by largely Protestant landlords. So religion—as is often the case—is found at the root of issues that may seem on the surface to be more political or economic. For the Vietnamese Catholics fleeing a collapsing Republic of South Vietnam in 1975, religion was part of the reason for flight but connected with the experience of being a recognizable, and relatively privileged, political minority. For many of those fleeing Iraq after the US intervention in the early 2000s, flight reflected the loss of the previous social framework in which religious minorities could live in peace among the largely Muslim population. Their reasons to leave were less about their particular religion than about being members of religious minorities.

The United States has thus functioned as a haven for all kinds of religious groups from all kinds of places, including, for example, both Christians from Muslim countries and Muslims from Christian countries.

Religion as a vector of commitment often lies at the core of why people migrate. It also functions as a vector of commitment in a new life in the United States. It remains a touchstone for how people organize their lives in a new environment. Sometimes religion must be rebuilt by the migrants themselves. The efforts of migrants to build churches, mosques, temples, and gurdwaras—and to construct in their homes memorials and shrines to ancestors and other spirits—are a staple of the immigrant experience. Sometimes religion also provides a useful connecting point to the United States. Migrants can thus join existing US congregations or develop their own religious worship by sharing physical structures with existing religious organizations. Sometimes, however, religion creates divides between newcomers and native-born. One result may be the need for dialogue to try to understand differences—for example, Abrahamic dialogues among the Jewish, Christian, and Muslim "People of the Book." Such attempts are quite traditionally American, very reminiscent of the ecumenical efforts among Catholics, Jews, and Protestants in the mid- and late 1900s. One of the grounds for cooperation is that the United States remains a very religious country by the standards of the industrialized world. Immigrants who believe religion is important are among a native-born population who share their belief that the vector of religious commitment and community is indeed vital—even when the details of their religions are different.[8]

Religion is not the only core vector of belief among immigrants to the United States. The founders of the country had a vision of a republic that would be a haven for those who opposed the tyranny of authoritarian governments. The United States has been a beacon for people seeking political freedom from early colonial days, through those like the German Forty-Eighters discussed in chapter 1, who brought their progressive politics with them, to more recent immigrants—especially refugees—for whom the liberty in the American system is its greatest virtue. For many migrants, that vision of America as a land of political freedom has become an organizing principle for life in the United States. The people who have found refuge in the United States from communist regimes provide one example. In both the Cuban and the Vietnamese cases, those coming to the United States had been allied at least implicitly with the US struggle against communism and were at considerable risk from the communist regimes that took control in each country. Migration, for them, was a political statement about who they were and what they believed in. That political statement became a central theme in their adjustment to the United States. Both groups maintained strong public positions against the communist regimes in Cuba and Vietnam and were often influential in swaying US government policy. Both groups tended to vote Republican (at least compared to the general Hispanic and Asian populations) and quickly mobilized against any people who advocated for better relations with the Cuban and Vietnamese governments. Fidel Castro for Cuba and Ho Chi Minh for Vietnam were vilified by the refugees. A picture of either one in a public setting in the United States would draw retribution. Vietnamese students on college campuses were even able to keep the current Vietnamese national flag from being flown on global-diversity days, despite the coexistence on campuses of foreign students from Vietnam. Instead, they would parade the flag of the former Republic of South Vietnam.

Political beliefs remain crucial today as motives for migration and as guides to life in the United States. The exact notions of liberty that new migrants hold may vary—from relatively liberal to the staunchly conservative, anticommunist stance of Cubans and Vietnamese. These political commitments may fade among the children of the original immigrants, but the political vector of belief remains important and often overlaps economic considerations. The liberty to voice an opinion, for example, is linked to the liberty to make money. The United States as a land of political freedom and economic opportunity is a strong and appealing package for those who find themselves at risk because of political turmoil and economic constriction. That combination, for example, helps explain many of the ebbs and flows of Mexican migration into the United States, rising in times of political turmoil and economic constriction and ebbing in times of political stability and economic improvement.

Despite its overlap with political issues, economics still deserves consideration on its own as a vector of belief and commitment for migrants both before and after migration. There are, after all, many ways in which the explanation of migration as a search for a better life makes sense, and makes sense in quite economic terms. The way those economic options work tends to differ between people, on the one hand, with professional and technical skills and those, on the other, whose work lies in more manual or service occupations. Current migration to the United States tends to be split between migrants with extensive education and professional training and those largely without such education and skills. For those with relatively high educational and professional status, migrating to the United States resembles the classic model of the rational assessment of economic alternatives and how it might improve their current or future situation. For those lacking education and professional skills, there is also a clear economic calculus in the comparison of wages: an hour's work in the United States may pay as much as a day's work at home. The monetary differential is generally higher for low-wage than high-salary immigrants. However, the actual migration process for low-wage migrants is harder, more dangerous, and more unpredictable—including the possibility of deportation after successful arrival. For both groups, then, an economic calculation may indeed be the crucial vector of commitment, but the nature of that calculation varies in terms of its rewards as well as its costs.

Some migrants may be easily categorized as religious, political, or economic in their motivations for migration. For most migrants, however, these three vectors are likely to be intermixed with a broader range of personal beliefs. One crucial additional factor is that migrants are often moving to places where they already have some personal connections, so their core belief may be about the need to be with those people, whether from obligation, desire, or simply continuity in their lives. If others close to them move, for example, they may feel the need to do so as well. That is another kind of belief—a belief in the importance of living within a core community, which itself may have developed for a variety of religious, political, economic, or simply cultural reasons. The crucial point is that people's destinies as migrants exist in tandem with their lives as people and within the web of meaning that is in part inherited from the past, in part derived from the new environment, and in part born anew out of the beliefs, commitments, and dreams that migrants hold as individuals and as members of social groups and networks.

The two paired case examples that follow focus on religious affiliation among four very different migrant groups. Formal religion is not the only crucial vector of belief, but, since religion is so often at the core of people's beliefs and commitments, it is emphasized here. But note that in all these cases religion is intertwined with political, economic, and cultural strands in the fabric of people's lives. The first pair involves Mexican and Vietnamese Catholics whose similarity in religious beliefs and rituals rises out of very different historical roots. The second pair contrasts Sudanese Christians and Bosnian Muslims, for whom the mix of national, ethnic, religious, and racial identities is especially complex.

Shiite Muslims in the Ashura festival in Los Angeles (2012). (betto rodrigues/ Shutterstock.com)

PAIRED COMPARISON: MEXICAN AND VIETNAMESE CATHOLICS

Mexicans are, by far, the largest set of migrants coming to the United States in the post–World War II era. They arrive in a variety of ways, with a variety of legal statuses. Mexicans dominate the number of legal admissions to permanent-resident status. Those numbers are supplemented by large numbers of Mexicans in various temporary statuses (workers, students, visitors) and a large unauthorized population (see table 6.1 for Mexican and Vietnamese admissions). US Census Bureau numbers, which include both legal and unauthorized migrants, suggest a population of nearly twelve million foreign-born Mexicans in the United States out of a total of some forty-one million foreign-born people overall. Those from Vietnam, by contrast, are a much smaller group but, at about 1.2 million, still a major immigrant group. In terms of current economic status, Vietnamese generally approximate the native-born in terms of earnings, while Mexicans fare less well in terms of earnings (see table 6.2). It is also worth noting the large size of households among both Mexicans and Vietnamese.

The two groups have very different histories. Mexicans have long been crossing the US border and also had the border cross them in the mid-1800s. Their labor remains highly valued, especially in the agricultural sector in California and the Southwest. Their cross-border movement has often been informal but also at times directly managed by the Mexican and US governments. Many would argue that the recent surge in unauthorized migration from Mexico is simply a return to those more informal days, including the recruitment of undocumented workers by employers who value their labor for its quality—and, of course, its low cost in terms of wages and benefits. Through all those different informal and formal mechanisms, however, Mexican migration can be seen largely as labor migration that is, somewhat paradoxically, both highly valued and underpaid.

The Vietnamese case is different. The historical connections between Vietnam and the United States were almost nonexistent until the Second World War, when Vietnamese revolutionaries became useful partners for a United States seeking to rescue pilots shot down during attacks on the Japanese in southern

Table 6.1. Mexican and Vietnamese admissions

	Mexico	Vietnam
1950s	273,847	290
1960s	441,824	2,949
1970s	621,218	121,716
1980s	1,009,586	200,632
1990s	2,757,418	275,379
2000s	1,704,166	289,616

Source: US Department of Homeland Security, *Yearbook of Immigration Statistics: 2015* (Washington, DC: US Department of Homeland Security, Office of Immigration Statistics, 2016).

Table 6.2. Selected characteristics of foreign-born Mexicans and Vietnamese

	Mexican	Vietnamese	Native-born
Households			
Average household size	4.3	3.6	2.5
In family households (%)	86	84	64
Median household income (USD)	36,000	57,000	53,000
Households in poverty (%)	30	14	10
Speak only English at home (%)	4	7	89
Speak English very well (%)	30	33	98
Own a home (%)	45	67	66
Median value of home (USD)	115,000	252,000	170,000
Men			
Total population (%)	53	47	49
In labor force (%)	84	74	67
Median earnings (USD)	27,000	42,000	51,000
Married (%)	59	67	48
With BA or above (%)	5	26	29
In professional occupation (%)	7	32	34
Women			
Total population (%)	47	53	51
In labor force (%)	53	63	59
Median earnings (USD)	22,000	32,000	39,000
Married (%)	57	62	45
With BA or above (%)	6	22	29
In professional occupation (%)	12	26	41

Source: US Census Bureau, combined 2011–2013 American Community Survey data, accessed through American Fact Finder, at https://factfinder.census.gov/faces/nav/jsf/pages/index.xhtml.

China. With the collapse of French colonial authority in Vietnam in the early 1950s, the United States become the major supporter of anticommunist forces and, in 1954, of a new Republic of South Vietnam. As a result, there was increasing movement of Vietnamese and Americans back and forth for political, business, and military reasons. When the US-supported government of the Republic of South Vietnam collapsed in 1975, the United States became a haven for fleeing Vietnamese, particularly those who had been most tied to the United States either politically or personally. So the heart of the Vietnamese migration was political, although later followed by increasing levels of family-based migration.

These two different migrations share one crucial feature: the importance of Catholicism. Catholicism is the dominant religion in Mexico and among both foreign- and native-born Mexican Americans—mainly, though not exclusively, Roman Catholicism.[9] So being Catholic is not, in itself, a particular *reason* for migration. Mexicans are Catholics in a Catholic nation. However, Catholicism is a vital *context* for the processes of migration to, and life in, the United States. Catholicism is, after all, a very migration-friendly religion. It is hard to visit specifically Roman Catholic churches or organizations, for example, without seeing the enjoinder to "welcome the stranger," often on a poster or flyer with a picture of the pope. The current pope, Francis, has been even stronger on this issue than his predecessors. His first homily after ascending to the papacy in 2013 was delivered on Lampedusa, an Italian island that is a major transit point for refugees and migrants crossing the Mediterranean from northern Africa. Francis has been especially clear that the dictum to welcome the stranger applies to all people, whether or not they are recognized by the official migration policies of recipient countries.

Catholicism also provides some hope of divine help and companionship in crossing dangerous borders. Thus Mexican Catholics—like many other Latin American migrants—pray in Mexico before their departure and convey their thanks after arrival at shrines in the United States that may receive thousands of visitors a week. The border crossing is thus wrapped within a spiritual environment of meaning and potential assistance. Catholicism also turns out to be a useful spiritual and communal context within the United States. Although Catholicism existed in the early American colonies, it was the great waves of migration in the 1800s and early 1900s that solidified its importance, especially with the Irish and Italians. The current Catholic Church not only is supportive of migration but also has its very roots in immigration. Having separate services and even parishes for migrant groups is a natural part of its mission. Mexican Catholics thus have in their religion a supportive spiritual context for their migration and for their lives in the United States.

The situation for Vietnamese Catholics has some similarities but also many differences. Perhaps most important, Catholicism has been a minority religion in Vietnam, and Catholics have often been persecuted there. The persecutions in the early part of the 1800s were particularly vicious and were the basis for the eventual canonization of 117 martyrs by Pope John Paul II in 1988. The situation of Catholics in Vietnam improved during French colonialism but then declined as communist forces took control, initially in the northern part of the country. After partition between communists in the north and anticommunists in the south in 1954, many Catholics fled south. They were never a large part of the Vietnamese population, well below 10 percent of the population in southern Vietnam even after the arrival of those fleeing the north. Many of them, however, became very prominent in the South Vietnamese government. Catholics thus had multiple reasons for fleeing when that government collapsed in 1975: they were at risk as a religious minority under a communist government, at risk for retribution for having been part of the now-fallen South Vietnamese government, and at risk for having previously fled from communist control in the north.

Despite its distinctive history as a minority religion in Vietnam, Catholicism has provided many of the same resources to Vietnamese refugees in the United States as it has for Mexicans. Perhaps three-tenths of the Vietnamese refugees in the United States are Catholic, enough to support separate Vietnamese services and even parishes in some places. New Orleans provides one example. There Vietnamese Catholics have been able to create an environment very much like the one they had known in Vietnam. They grew gardens under somewhat similar tropical conditions, could put their skills to use in fishing, and could create a community around their local Catholic parish. Here was a strong immigrant community with shared cultural values and a shared religious framework of belief and action. That would serve them well in the wake of Hurricane Katrina, when Vietnamese Catholics were among the first to reclaim damaged parts of the city. As they reclaimed their community, they also had to engage in a protracted political battle with the city to avoid having all the wreckage from the storm placed in one huge dump right next to where they lived. For them, as for the Mexicans, a cohesive ethnic community with a solid religious core has been an invaluable asset in confronting the challenges of life in the United States.

PAIRED COMPARISON: AFRICAN CHRISTIANS AND EUROPEAN MUSLIMS

Immigrants to the United States have diverse religious origins. They have also often been religious groups who were at risk in the countries from which they came. Their religious experience was thus crucial in their decisions to move, the exact paths of their movement, and their subsequent lives in the United States. As two examples of the interplay of religion and migration, consider Christians from southern Sudan and Muslims from Bosnia.[10] Both were religious minorities in countries controlled by people of other religions: Christians in a Muslim-controlled Sudan, and Muslims in a communist but also Christian Yugoslavia. As Sudan fell into increasingly bitter civil war in the 1980s, and as Yugoslavia crumbled in the early 1990s, the situation of Bosnian Muslims and Sudanese Christians became more tenuous. For many of them, flight away from the conflicts became more appealing and more necessary. Large numbers surged into neighboring areas, and both Bosnians and Sudanese turned up increasingly among refugee arrivals to the United States (see table 6.3 for overall arrivals and table 6.4 for some basic characteristics).

In the United States, both groups received assistance from the government and from the many private organizations and individuals committed to refugee resettlement. However, in both cases, exactly how the refugees should be identified was not always clear. The Sudanese Christian refugees, for example, were

Table 6.3. Bosnian and Sudanese arrivals

	Bosnian	Sudanese
Total population	119,549	42,857
%		
Since 2010	2	11
2000–2009	28	51
Before 2000	70	38

Source: US Census Bureau, combined 2011–2013 American Community Survey data, accessed through American Fact Finder, at https://factfinder.census.gov/faces/nav/jsf/pages/index.xhtml.

Note: These figures are for country of origin, and they thus include, especially for Sudan, people other than those discussed in the text.

Table 6.4. Selected characteristics of foreign-born Bosnians and Sudanese

	Bosnian	Sudanese	Native-born
Households			
Average household size	3.2	3.7	2.5
In family households (%)	82	73	64
Median household income (USD)	57,000	32,000	53,000
Households in poverty (%)	9	41	10
Speak only English at home (%)	5	10	89
Speak English very well (%)	52	59	98
Own a home (%)	62	25	66
Median value of home (USD)	144,000	170,000	170,000
Men			
Total population (%)	51	58	49
Percent in labor force	83	84	67
Median earnings (USD)	40,000	32,000	51,000
Married (%)	61	50	48
With BA or above (%)	19	34	29
In professional occupation (%)	18	22	34
Women			
Total population (%)	49	42	51
In labor force (%)	73	62	59
Median earnings (USD)	29,000	26,000	39,000
Married (%)	60	57	45
With BA or above (%)	19	37	29
In professional occupation (%)	23	32	41

Source: US Census Bureau, combined 2011–2013 American Community Survey data, accessed through American Fact Finder, at https://factfinder.census.gov/faces/nav/jsf/pages/index.xhtml.

from the south of the country and in tribal terms were mostly Nuer and Dinka. They also tended to be a largely male population, since it was the males who were able to escape the conflict, survive the long treks to places of refuge, and endure often-lengthy stays in refugee camps in Africa. These were the "lost boys" who received widespread attention in the media.[11] They were clearly not representative of Sudan as a whole in either religious or ethnic terms, and their difference was the reason for their flight. However, other refugees and immigrants from Sudan were coming to the United States, many of them Muslim and from the northern part of the country. There was thus potential confusion among the Americans engaging with newcomers from Sudan and among the people from Sudan themselves in how they should present themselves. In government surveys, for example, answers to questions about ethnic identity varied. People from Sudan did not always identify themselves as "Sudanese." Rather, some of them identified as tribal groups (such as Dinka), others identified themselves as "black," and yet others did indeed identify themselves ethnically as "Sudanese." The nature of ethnic identity was thus highly variable and challenged by competing national, regional, religious, ethnic, and racial categories.

In the Bosnian case, there was a similar complexity of national, regional, religious, ethnic, and racial categories. As Yugoslavia shattered into components, the meaning of *nation* rapidly changed. In what is now Bosnia and Herzegovina, the split was especially sharp, leaving Bosnians and Serbs in a brutal confrontation based on different cultural heritages and political goals. That difference also reflected the long history of the two religions in an area of southeastern Europe that was sometimes under Christian control from the west and sometimes under Islamic control from the east. Here again was a set of people whose personal and group histories, both recent and very long term, defied common American expectations about what they would be like and what they would look like. They, too, showed some ambiguity about their identities. Coming in after the collapse of Yugoslavia, "Yugoslav" was not an option as an identity label. In national terms, they might be "Bosnian," and some of them identified themselves that way. But there were other options. Some said they were "Muslim" as their key identifier. The greater number, however, settled on "Bosnian Muslim" as the proper label. It was the combination of place of origin and religion that created a meaningful identity—not just from Bosnia and not just Muslim but people of a particular religion (Islam) from a particular place (Bosnia). However, there were other options that some chose for themselves. One was simply "white"—a way of stressing that they were not stereotypical Muslims. Another response was nonresponse. In surveys, there are often people who do not answer particular questions either because they do not understand the question or because they do not like the implications of the question. In these particular surveys it was people from Bosnia who often chose not to respond about their ethnic identity. They noted that they came from Bosnia but did not elaborate on whether that made them Bosnian or Muslim or Bosnian Muslim or just white. They simply did not respond.

However they identified themselves, religion was indeed a crucial factor for both groups in their background, in their flight from their country of origin, and in their personal identities. It also affected their adjustment to the United States. Religion can cause complexity, but it can also yield options. For the south Sudanese Christians, one major option lay precisely in their Christianity. The Sudanese were often Protestant with existing ties to the mission work of US religious organizations and congregations. That gave these refugees an existing link to a central facet of American society—and one inclined to support newcomers as an issue of humanitarian commitment. Religion opened doors in a very personal way. It also helped lay the basis for extensive and positive media coverage. The story of escape was almost biblical in its travails and was consonant with Christian notions of flight to a promised land. The "lost boys" had, in a way, been found, and there lay a great symbolic connection.

In the Bosnian case, by contrast, religion was not a strong connector to American society. American Muslims are involved in outreach to newcomers, but their resources are far fewer than for Christians or Jews. Furthermore, there is public hostility toward Muslims that sometimes surges into fear and rejection. The Bosnians, however, were hardly the regular American stereotype of Muslims. They were white and European. Here, then, lay a different option—to stress the racial and historical connections to the still-paramount European origins of the United States rather than the religious issues that were actually more the basis of why they had left Bosnia. The result can be seen in much of the research on Bosnians after arrival in the United States. Religion remains vital to the internal lives and connections of the Bosnians, but it is a very specific Bosnian version of Islam that in many ways separates them from other Muslims. Bosnians create their own mosques that reflect their own particular history and religious traditions. For the outward connections, other factors are needed. There Bosnians interact more on the basis of racial and historical similarities to the mainstream US population. They are, in effect, invisible as they go about their daily lives. That can be a great benefit when they look for work and when they look for housing. Ironically, their very invisibility leaves them open to hearing virulent American views on Islam. Nobody thinks to stereotype them as Muslims; they assume the reverse and thus feel free to vent their dislike of Muslims in front of Bosnian Muslims.

The two cases of Sudanese Christians and Bosnian Muslims suggest the complexity of religion as a factor in migration and its frequent interconnection with political and economic issues. In particular, religion is both a system of personal belief and a way of interacting with other people. The cases also suggest that religion can work in multiple ways as a bridge to other people—although sometimes quite differently for connections among one's own people versus connections to the broader American society. That, in turn, raises what has long been one of the core concerns of both immigrants and the native-born: How do immigrants come to belong in America? How do they, reinvoking the concerns of Benjamin Franklin, George Washington, and Thomas Jefferson, assimilate to life in the United States?

7

⌒

To Belong: Assimilation, Adaptation, and Accommodation

Much of the discussion of immigrants in the United States has focused on how they are drawn—or not drawn—into American society. The exact nature of that process is, however, unclear and variable. The complexity of the process is reflected in the nuances of the words people use: *adaptation* invokes a basic human ability to synchronize with new environments; *acculturation* invokes internal changes in how people view the world; *integration* implies newcomers become fully functioning members of the host society and its institutions; and *assimilation* tends to imply that newcomers are fully incorporated into American society in both action and belief. Other words tend to emphasize the reciprocal nature of immigration: *accommodation* and *adjustment*, for example, can be used from the perspective of the migrants or that of the host society. These words suggest that, as immigrants adapt to their new American localities, those localities, and the people in them, are also adapting to the immigrants. However defined, this process is sometimes smooth, positive, and rapid; sometimes it is rough, negative, and slow—with even the children, grandchildren, and further descendants of immigrants remaining on the periphery of American life and institutions.

This chapter begins with an overview of key issues in immigrant/host interaction and then continues by examining the personal and individual aspects of how people belong and to what they belong. The discussion continues with a review of the basic generational patterns that have, over time, brought the children and grandchildren of immigrants more closely into American society. For this chapter, the usual set of paired comparisons at the end focuses on particular national-origin groups in particular US cities, thus aiming to bring the discussion more to the local level at which people actually live. The two sets are Mexicans in Los Angeles versus Cubans in Miami, and Yucatecans in Dallas versus Koreans in Washington, DC.

VECTORS OF BELONGING

Among the many debates about the nature of immigrant destinies in America, the most venerable word is doubtless *assimilation*. It is the word that several of the republic's founders used as they considered the benefits and costs of accepting new arrivals in a new country. We see, perhaps especially with George Washington, an enduring commitment to the idea of the United States as an asylum for those fleeing religious and political oppression. We also see the enduring concern that these new arrivals should respect the rules of their new republic and recognize its purposes. Finally, we see a concern that the sheer numbers of arrivals from a particular place may undermine their acceptance of American ways. In the usage of the Founding Fathers, this "assimilation" is also clearly something that immigrants must do. They must either already share the same values or change themselves to share those values. Assimilation in that usage is thus a purposive, intentioned process of learning and accepting the rules that underlie the US republic.

The usage of the word *assimilation* has changed over time, and there have been many other words used to describe this process of immigrant belonging in a new country. Several crucial issues underlie how these different words—or even the single word *assimilation*—are used. One is the relative roles of the newcomers and those they join. Is it, as the Founding Fathers seemed to believe, something that the newcomers do, or is it something that the receiving society does to them? If the responsibility is on the newcomers, how do they adjust to changing circumstances and to people around them who may have very different beliefs? Do they indeed acculturate to US society, taking on its values for themselves? Or do they find ways to extend their own values to cover this new situation? If the responsibility lies with the receiving society, how does that work? The word *absorption*, for example, is sometimes used in the immigration literature to indicate that newcomers are so fully brought into the receiving society that they do not exist in any significantly separate way—other than perhaps a few traditional cultural markers. The word *Americanization* also emphasizes the receiving society's role in orienting newcomers, and there have been periodic public efforts in the United States to develop formal Americanization programs for newcomers. There is also a middle ground. A word like *accommodation*, for example, works very well to describe a situation in which both immigrants and the receiving society are changing as each makes an accommodation to the other.

Another crucial question about immigrant/host interactions is whether the process is about individuals or groups. The distinction helps explain some of the Founding Fathers' uncertainty about immigration—perhaps especially Benjamin Franklin's concerns about the Germans. His concern was that large sets of people from the same national, cultural, and linguistic origins may tend to remain apart from the overall society, thus limiting the possibility of individuals' adjustment to the rules of the republic. Much of the contemporary discussion of assimilation follows that tendency to focus on groups. How are the Vietnamese assimilating?

Does the large number of Cubans in Miami help or hinder their assimilation? Can groups with very different cultural traditions ever be fully incorporated into US society? That group focus may make sense in general discussions about immigration, but it elides two fundamental points. First, life itself is experienced through the thoughts and feelings of individuals—no matter how tightly enmeshed in social relationships. So the focus on group processes may obscure the experience of individuals. Second, the designation of the groups is often fundamentally flawed. Immigrants from a single national origin are often very heterogeneous. Overall national labels like "Syrian," for example, quickly decompose into smaller sets of people who vary by religion, class, political orientation, and such life-course distinctions as age and sex, gender and generation.

Exactly who is doing what in this relationship between newcomers and hosts is thus not exactly clear, which helps explain why the current debates about immigration are so volatile and often unproductive. One further complicating factor is that the actual list of beliefs, values, and behavior to which newcomers are supposed to conform is often unclear. Sometimes the list seems to be a complete inventory of everything that "normal" Americans do. For the Founding Fathers, the list was more specific. They were creating a new kind of republic, and, based on their concern that this republic survive, they believed it was vital that newcomers share a commitment to the central elements of that new republic. But they were also explicit that newcomers did not have to share other, more cultural, values. Above all, this new republic was to provide full freedom of religion and carefully separate religion from civic life. Thus even today the US census does not inquire about religion. So the continuing question is what immigrants must adhere to in the United States from the point of view of their hosts. What must they adhere to in terms of their own goals for their lives? What ways of belonging in the United States strike a balance that permits mutual accommodation?

PERSONAL TRANSITIONS

As people move, whether across a national border or not, they encounter much that is new. They may also, however, find much that is familiar. Indeed, their new place may not be so new. Many migrants are returning to places that they already know and often reuniting with people with whom they are already connected. So whether and how they belong raises a broad range of questions. Is this issue of belonging about the most immediate social groups, like the family? Is it about the actual physical and social environment of the specific localities in which people live? Is it about the major organizations and institutions in which newcomers interact with others, particularly work settings, schools, and religious organizations? Is it about the overall cultural and social scheme of the new country and its beliefs, values, and behaviors? Or is it about a much shorter, practical list of obligations like work, pay taxes, and obey the law?

In this mix of family, locality, institution, and culture, the ways that newcomers belong are varied. Some kinds of belonging are quite primal. Consider again the case of noncitizens who join the US military and, as one result, have a shortened route to citizenship. They have indicated that they are willing to risk their lives for a new country, thus certifying their level of commitment. Should they die in the national service, they will have demonstrated not only how primal is their attachment but also how primal is the connection of their parents to the United States. They become Gold Star families. Both the fallen soldier and the bereft parents belong in a very basic, blood-based way to the United States. They know it, and, with rare exceptions, that primal belonging to America is recognized by Americans in general. There are other primal—or near primal—ways in which newcomers can belong to American society. Many of these involve family connections. It is understood by all, and enshrined in American law, that parents and children of US citizens truly do belong in America. So do foreign-born wives and husbands.[1]

Other kinds of belonging are more prosaic, changeable, and subject to dispute. Immigrants who bring clear economic benefits, for example, are generally acknowledged to rightfully belong. If they are well off, they will usually have little difficulty staying in the United States on long-term temporary statuses and probably can convert fairly easily to permanent resident-alien status. If they are not well off, their situation is more precarious. There has long been a tendency to turn against those who may have made vital contributions to the United States but whose continued presence is opposed by at least some people. Thus in the late 1800s there was a sharp turn against the Chinese who had provided invaluable labor, including building the western section of the transcontinental railroad. Likewise in the late 1900s there was a sharp turn against the Mexicans who had for over a century provided the labor that made the United States a world-leading agricultural producer. In both the Chinese and the Mexican cases, these workers had, at least in part, been actively recruited by American employers, so they were indeed wanted—but their belonging was contested once the immediate need for their labor disappeared. For these two groups and for many other migrants, the issue of belonging is likely to remain uncertain as they weigh their own desires to stay or go against shifting circumstances in the United States.

Sometimes belonging is questioned when the cultural, social, or religious background of immigrants differs significantly from US norms. In such cases, the immigrants themselves may be uncertain about their own belonging. Legal status can also be a crucial factor. Yet, even with unauthorized migrants, many Americans look for additional evidence on which to assess whether these people belong. The case of unauthorized migrant children helps illustrate the grounds of that debate. Many Americans—the majority, according to most polls—think that those who came as undocumented children but have demonstrated themselves to be "good Americans" do indeed belong in America, even if still legally unauthorized. That argument is often made in terms of education. Thus unauthorized migrants who complete high school in the United States, and are in that sense fully American, should have their legal status adjusted. They should be allowed into universities and should receive in-state tuition rates. At the federal level, a range of bills (such as the original DREAM Act of 2001) has been proposed to make that happen. However, all have failed to pass in Congress. The unauthorized migrants' demonstration of their Americanness through beliefs, values, behavior, and education has thus not, at least to the US Congress, demonstrated a sufficiently primal belonging to justify providing them legal status. Theirs is a strong case for belonging, but it remains contested.

The issues of belonging are also experienced on a more routine daily basis as newcomers interact with those around them in their neighborhoods and in local places of business, recreation, education, religion, and politics. Depending on where the newcomers live, those interactions involve different kinds of people, sometimes newcomers like them, sometimes newcomers very much unlike them, sometimes native-born people who are very different from them, and sometimes native-born people with whom they share important attributes. Similarities of language, beliefs, and behavior generally make those interactions easier; differences make them more difficult. The world in which the newcomers live may physically resemble the world from which they came, or it may be very different. Newcomers who are adjusting both from one country to another and from a rural to urban lifestyle, for example, often face particular difficulties. There are also extensive debates about whether immigrant life among similar people of similar origins eases the adjustment of immigrants. A strong ethnic community has advantages, both cultural and economic. An ethnically based religious congregation, for example, can help maintain core beliefs. The ethnic community can also be a strong source of economic cooperation and business opportunity. Yet life

Cuban cigar store in Miami (2016). (littleny/iStock.com)

largely within an ethnic community can have long-term disadvantages. Its effects can be pernicious if it keeps newcomers from accessing mainstream society or puts their children in poorly funded inner-city schools. Ambivalence about the effects of a strong ethnic community often appears in American public attitudes about immigrants, that long-held fear that clannish immigrant communities represent a dangerous separation from American society—and even a threat to it. Immigrants, by that view, do not truly belong to America when their daily lives do not intersect with those of Americans.

The routine daily issues of belonging are complicated by the diversity among immigrants and among Americans generally. Gender roles provide an example, with often very sharp differences in the roles of men and women within and outside the family. The way people are categorized by race, ethnicity, religion, and national origin may also pose problems. The 2016 US presidential-election process saw particularly sharp aspersions against Muslims in terms of religion, and Syrians in terms of national and regional origins. But perhaps nowhere is the problem of American categorizations more acute than with the American notion of race. Despite the consistent debunking of race as a meaningful scientific category, the American history of immigration with its dual stream of free migrants from Europe and slave migrants from Africa created a sharply bifurcated racial structure that endures to the present. The many recent migrants from Africa and the Caribbean face acute difficulties in navigating these US racial categories. In cultural terms they may share little with the descendants of those early African arrivals, but they are almost always connected to them in the views of both black and white Americans. Sometimes the results are deadly: police shootings or public attacks on "blacks" turn out to have victimized immigrants who have struggled to *not* be a part of entrenched US attitudes about the importance of skin color.

The complexity of dealing with American racial, ethnic, and national categories is well conveyed by Chimamanda Ngozi Adichie in her novel *Americanah*. As the novel begins, the protagonist is considering returning to her home country. Ifemelu has done well in the United States. She is, after all, Nigerian, and Nigerian immigrants are among the best-educated and most successful recent immigrant groups in America. She is an accomplished academic and quite satisfied with her current boyfriend. Yet she is drawn to return to Nigeria. Meanwhile, Ifemelu's daily life in America is complicated by racial, national, and regional issues. She has to navigate through a maze in which the meaning of her black skin shifts in different contexts. From situation to situation, she has to decide what her response will be to others. She must be vigilant in looking for clues in people's appearance and in their words. That helps explain her decision to return to Nigeria, since, within this daily maze, "layer after layer of discontent had settled in her."[2]

On one particular day, early on in the novel, Ifemelu's tasks are simple: get a cab, and go to a hair salon. The cab driver is black. She worries that he is Nigerian and will be angered that she, a woman, has been the more successful Nigerian in America. She exhales in relief when the driver speaks—he is Caribbean. At the salon, a woman smiles at her; she, too, is African, and her smile, in its "warm knowingness," welcomes a fellow African. She is not just "black" in an American racial sense. Her hairdresser is also African, from Senegal, and she treats Ifemelu as if she were in Africa rather than in America, abandoning the niceties of American customer service for the more direct ways of an African marketplace. Ifemelu finds this a bit difficult, so she tries to strategize how to limit conversation during the many hours it will take to have her hair braided. Ultimately, however, the two women find a middle ground, discussing whether Ifemelu is Yoruba or Igbo. In that discussion, the hairdresser can put her own experience to work, judging why Ifemelu might be one or the other based on her physical appearance. Both are safe here from being confused with native-born blacks, either by whites or by blacks. Both can communicate within an understanding that they are truly African, although with roots now in two continents.

Ifemelu's navigation of daily events illuminates how cultural frameworks used by immigrants and native-born Americans often slide across each other in misunderstanding and confusion. Immigrants, after all, have roots in multiple places and futures that may involve multiple places. So they may belong in the United States by some criteria but not necessarily by all. That is something the native-born often find hard to understand and accept. Here the situation of immigrants and their children diverges. If they are born in the United States, or arrive in the United States at a young age, these children grow into, rather than simply adapt to, life in the United States.

GENERATIONAL PATTERNS

The experiences of the children of immigrants are very different from those of their parents. If the children are born in the United States, their legal status is automatic, and they are exposed to the United States, its people, and its institutions from birth. Consequently, they have sometimes been labeled the "first generation" because they are indeed the first generation to be part of the fabric of American life from birth. But they are also still very much their parents' children and exposed to country-of-origin language, values, beliefs, and traditions through their parents, often through some kind of ethnic community, and often through continued interaction—whether in-person or virtual—with their countries of origin. For that reason they are more commonly labeled today as the "second generation."

This sequencing of immigrant groups by generation is very common in discussions about immigrant assimilation and is often used by immigrants and their descendants. Japanese, for example, explicitly use "first generation," "second generation," "third generation" (*issei, nisei, sansei*), and beyond to designate their distance from the first arrivals. According to that kind of generational grid, the first generation has continuing connections to the home country, maintains home-country beliefs and traditions, is often forced to accept marginal jobs, and aims for a better future for the next generation. The second generation is more fully acculturated and competent in the new country, often drifts from country-of-origin values and beliefs, loses full linguistic competence in the country-of-origin language (although often with some continuing conversational ability), and may often move out to live away from others of the same ancestry. That second generation is often portrayed as living in two worlds, trying to craft a path that incorporates both their parents' ways and those they confront in American society generally. The third generation, according to this standard generational grid, is fully acculturated to the United States, no longer trying to live between two worlds, and has better education, higher earnings, and better housing in better school districts. That generational sequence is also reflected in increasing interaction with other segments of American society, including more intermarriage with other groups. This is assimilation in the classic group sense. Over time immigrant groups through their descendants become a fully enmeshed part of American life. They are just Americans who, like other Americans, have immigrant ancestors.

These generational patterns have much validity in considering American history and in considering contemporary American society. Linguistic change (more English, less country-of-origin language), educational improvement, economic advances, and intermarriage all continue to generally move in the expected direction in a multigenerational process. In particular, the concern that immigrants might never really learn English remains as unjustified now as it was in earlier centuries.[3] However, these generational patterns are not inevitable and reflect aspects of the American experience with immigration that may be less true today than in the past. Three factors deserve particular attention: the degree of difference between the immigrants and American society at time of arrival, the degree to which ties to country-of-origin ("transnational" ties) continue after arrival, and the degree to which immigration from particular countries continues over time with a constant flow of new arrivals.

The basic generational model presumes that there is indeed some gap between life in the country of origin and life in the United States, that this gap needs to be overcome, and that the gap is so wide that it will probably require a multigenerational process. Many immigrants, however, are not very different at all. The origins of the original colonists in England provided a ready bridge for later arrivals who came from England. The American Revolution brought a division from England, but it was one of political loyalties, not cultural background. That ability of people from the United Kingdom to move quite seamlessly into US society largely continues today. A similarly smooth transition also characterizes the many migrants—both temporary and permanent—from Canada, Australia, and New Zealand. But there are also many other contemporary immigrants who come from middle-class backgrounds, with good education and good English, who must navigate only a modest gap from US ways. They are, in effect, preadapted to the United States. So the generational sequence makes far less sense for such people. In such cases, the second and third generations may actually be worse off economically than the first generation.

On the other hand, a greater gap between country-of-origin and US social and cultural patterns may extend the standard three-generational sequence over more generations—or, at worst, make it impossible to ever fully belong in the United States and thus to never have the full range of belonging's opportunities. That gap may be sharpened by perceived racial difference. The generational pattern can be especially perverse for immigrants from Africa and the Caribbean who are assessed as "black" according to US racial categories. Well-educated first-generation immigrants may find their children absorbed into an American racial and class system that undermines the very opportunities for which they came to America.

The basic generational pattern is also affected by the degree to which ties with the country of origin are maintained. After all, migration across a national border does not necessarily imply a complete transfer of one's life to a new environment. From the very earliest days of the colonies, it has been possible to move back and forth. As transportation across the ocean to Europe became quicker and cheaper, more people could afford to make the passage both to the United States and back again. The first regular steam-powered crossing was (by most accounts) in 1838 by the *Great Western*, cutting the crossing time from a month or more under sail to under twenty days by steam. By around 1900, the crossing could be done in five days. Subsequent air travel and its decreasing cost have made back-and-forth movement still quicker and cheaper. Communication also has become easier. Letters have always passed back and forth between the United States and Europe. Those letters maintained relationships and served as a channel along which further journeys were planned. They, too, became faster and more reliable by steam, and then by plane. Books and newspapers also moved faster, as did the advertising about the United States as a migrant destination and how to get there.[4] While people have long been able to maintain transnational ties, today it is far easier, far cheaper, and available to far more people. For many children of immigrants, communication and visits to the home country are a normal part of life.[5]

The final problem with the basic generational pattern is that the starting point is often not very clear. If a married couple immigrates together, then they are first generation together, their children are second generation, their children's children are third generation, and so on. That is, however, only the case if the second generation marries second generation and the third generation marries third generation. This straightforward generational succession has often occurred in US history and thus is well established as a common point of reference in discussions of immigration history. That has been, however, more an accident of history than an inevitable sociological pattern. In such classic cases as the Japanese and Italians, there was indeed a period at which immigration greatly expanded, but then a time at which that immigration was almost completely shut off. In both cases, a set of people with similar experiences all came at roughly the same time. They were a cohort. At other times, however—and especially today—there is no cutoff to immigration flows. For most country-of-origin groups, new arrivals join now-established first-generation immigrants, the children of those immigrants (the second generation), and possibly the grandchildren of earlier arrivals (the third generation). There is no inevitable synchronization of these generations. Everything is churning. First generation is mixed with second generation, and often with third or subsequent generations.

This churning has some interesting effects. Consider the case of intermarriage. If a second-generation Vietnamese American marries someone from Vietnam—which happens often—then what generation are their children? What if a second-generation immigrant from Taiwan marries a new immigrant from mainland China or a fifth-generation Japanese American or a new Canadian immigrant who may or may not have some Asian ancestry? Consider also the kind of churning that occurs in many contemporary American universities, which often include various kinds of people from the same ancestry. The universities likely have immigrant students from at least such major origin countries as India, Korea, Mexico, the Philippines, and Vietnam. They will also probably have students of those ancestries who are native-born US citizens and who, at least in the Mexican case, may have very long lines of US-citizen ancestors. Finally, the universities are also likely to have foreign students coming directly from those countries on temporary educational visas. Sometimes the social lines between the groups of students are clear and interaction across the lines limited—especially if there is a linguistic divide. But often the lines start to blur. Some of those foreign students have relatives who are legal immigrants in the United States or who are native-born citizens. The long-range intention of those foreign students may well be to stay in the United States. Conversely, some of those immigrant and native-born students may be angling for a job back in the home country or at least a professional track that will keep them in motion between multiple countries. In both these cases of intermarriage and interaction in higher education, the exact nexus of belonging is variable and conditional. The ordered generational sequence of the classic assimilation model may still apply in many ways to many US immigrants, but it is far from being the only trajectory in the overall story of US immigration.

Overall, then, the issue of belonging remains complex for immigrants to the United States. Some may fit in easily, others with more difficulty. Linguistic, cultural, and educational similarity will ease the process; differences in those areas will make it more difficult. Sometimes fitting in will be a task accomplished by the first generation; often it will take the cumulative efforts of multiple generations. The issue of belonging extends beyond assimilation in the classic immigration model, requiring a consideration of all the social groups, networks, institutions, and nations to which people belong in at least some ways. Understanding how those processes of belonging evolve for particular immigrants also requires attention to the specific locales in which they live. The two pairs of case examples that conclude this chapter turn to such locales, dealing first with two dominant migrant groups (Mexican and Cubans) in two very immigrant-oriented cities (Los Angeles and Miami), and then with two smaller migrant groups (Yucatecans and Koreans) in less immigrant-oriented cities (Dallas and Washington, DC).

PAIRED COMPARISON: MEXICANS IN LOS ANGELES
AND CUBANS IN MIAMI

Many factors affect the ways in which immigrants belong in America. One of the most important involves the specific places in which they live. Those places are the context within which they live their lives, find their work, pursue their beliefs, and nest the many ways in which they belong, whether to their own families and compatriots or to the people and institutions of American society. Much of their lives is based in local neighborhoods and institutions. However, the broader locales are also important. They provide the general framework within which these more individual connections take place. For immigrants today, those places are generally cities. Although some migrants continue to move through rural areas and smaller towns, the bulk of immigrants, like the bulk of Americans, live in cities.

Some of those cities are very large and have very large foreign-born populations (see table 7.1). As in earlier US immigration, even today New York remains a vital gateway to America—now through JFK Airport rather than through Ellis Island. The proportion of the foreign-born in New York is one of the highest in the country, the range of groups is impressive, and the foreign-born often end up

Table 7.1. Major metropolitan areas with the highest percent foreign-born

Standard Metropolitan Statistical Area (SMSA)	%
Miami–Fort Lauderdale–West Palm Beach, FL	38.9
San Jose–Sunnyvale–Santa Clara, CA	37.2
Los Angeles–Long Beach–Anaheim, CA	33.7
San Francisco–Oakland–Hayward, CA	30.0
New York–Newark–Jersey City, NY–NJ–PA	28.6
San Diego–Carlsbad, CA	23.5
Houston–The Woodlands–Sugar Land, TX	22.7
Washington–Arlington–Alexandria, DC–VA–MD–WV	22.1
Las Vegas–Henderson–Paradise, NV	21.9
Riverside–San Bernardino–Ontario, CA	21.7
Sacramento–Roseville–Arden-Arcade, CA	18.1
Chicago–Naperville–Elgin, IL–IN–WI	17.8
Dallas–Fort Worth–Arlington, TX	17.7
Boston–Cambridge–Newton, MA–NH	17.3
Seattle–Tacoma–Bellevue, WA	17.3

Source: US Census Bureau, combined 2011–2015 American Community Survey data, accessed through American Fact Finder, at https://factfinder.census.gov/faces/nav/jsf/pages/index.xhtml.

Note: Figures refer to standard metropolitan statistical areas (SMSAs). Only those with a population greater than one million are included in this list.

in exactly the same neighborhoods populated by immigrants a century ago. But other major cities also have large numbers of the foreign-born, and some of them have not only a large number of immigrants but also a large number of immigrants from a single source country. Such cities provide a context for immigrant belonging that raises again the question of whether very extensive ethnic communities are a help or hindrance in the incorporation of immigrants into American life and in the incorporation of American beliefs and values into immigrant life. Two stand out: Los Angeles for Mexicans and Miami for Cubans.

The Los Angeles metropolitan area is second only to New York City in overall population, with approximately thirteen million people. Of those, about 4.5 million are foreign-born. In Los Angeles, then, about one in three persons is foreign-born. The range of groups is impressive, including both Latin Americans and Asians from many different countries. Of groups already discussed in previous chapters, for example, there are large numbers of Salvadorans, Koreans, and Iranians—indeed, two alternate labels for Los Angeles are Irangeles and Tehrangeles. Other previously discussed groups are largely missing: Indians and Cubans are few in number; their destinies lie more on the East Coast. Not surprisingly, the largest foreign-born group in Los Angeles, only about a two-hour drive from the Mexican border, is from Mexico (see table 7.2). There are about 1.7 million foreign-born Mexican Angelinos. If their US-born children are included, the numbers are far higher.

Compared to both the overall foreign-born population and the native-born population of Los Angeles, the Mexican-born population has a relatively modest socioeconomic profile (see table 7.3). Only about a third are high school graduates, well below the Los Angeles average, and English-language ability is also relatively low. Earnings and overall household income are low, homeownership rates are low, and poverty rates are correspondingly high. This is very much a working-class population and one that is struggling in economic terms. On the other hand, the Mexican-born population in Los Angeles shows very strong family connections. Households are relatively large, the percentage of people who are married is much higher than for the native-born, and the percentage of people living in family households is high. Furthermore, they are not alone in their struggles. There are, after all, 1.7 million people who make this a virtual city of Mexican-born migrants. The situation is reminiscent of earlier immigrants from places like Ireland and Italy; they were so numerous in cities like New York and Boston that they could create their own economic, social, political, and cultural framework within which to craft their own sense of belonging to America.

One crucial question is whether such a buffer—especially of a very large ethnic community—is help or hindrance in the long run. For this group, the long run is clearly a generational one, based on the hope that the children can improve on their parents' economic situation. The data remain inconclusive as to whether they can do so. Studies of the children of these Mexican-born

Table 7.2. Major foreign-born populations in Los Angeles and Miami

	Population
Los Angeles	
Mexico	1,718,000
China	318,000
Philippines	295,000
El Salvador	282,000
Vietnam	238,000
Korea	225,000
Guatemala	189,000
Iran	136,000
India	84,000
Armenia	63,000
Total foreign-born	**4,436,000**
Miami	
Cuba	734,000
Haiti	213,000
Colombia	166,000
Jamaica	137,000
Nicaragua	93,000
Venezuela	77,000
Mexico	66,000
Dominican Republic	63,000
Peru	63,000
Honduras	62,000
Total foreign-born	**2,279,000**

Source: US Census Bureau, combined 2011–2015 American Community Survey data, accessed through American Fact Finder, at https://factfinder.census.gov/faces/nav/jsf/pages/index.xhtml.

migrants show that they do indeed have competence in English, so they are not linguistically isolated from the rest of American society, even though they may also use Spanish much of the time. Educational levels are far higher among the children than among the parents, although still low compared to American society in general. But problems remain for that later generation, particularly high levels of high school dropouts and, some believe, a worrisome level of gang membership.

Table 7.3. Selected characteristics of foreign-born Mexicans in Los Angeles

	Mexican-born	Foreign-born	Native-born
Households			
Average household size	4.6	3.7	2.6
Median household income (USD)	40,000	48,000	67,000
Households in poverty (%)	27	19	8
In family households (%)	89	80	60
Individuals			
Speak English very well (%)	28	40	95
In labor force (%)	61	60	57
≥ high school diploma (%)	39	63	92
≥ college diploma (%)	5	25	37

Source: US Census Bureau, combined 2011–2013 American Community Survey data, accessed through American Fact Finder, at https://factfinder.census.gov/faces/nav/jsf/pages/index.xhtml.

Note: Foreign-born and native-born figures are also for the Los Angeles area only.

The situation of Cubans in Miami provides a different perspective on the implications of a very large ethnic community. The greater Miami metropolis has approximately six million people. Well over a third are foreign-born, and, much like in Los Angeles, about a third of that third are from one particular national-origin group: Cubans. The previous discussion of early-arriving Cubans, with strong family solidarity and high levels of employment, suggested a positive situation reflected in the frequent references to the "Cuban success story" in the United States. Over time, with additional arrivals from a broader range of social backgrounds, that portrait is less uniformly positive (see table 7.4). Recent data suggest that, compared to other groups, the Cuban-born in Miami do not stand out in terms of educational background or current economic activities. They are about average for the foreign-born. However, the Cuban-born population is aging. In terms of generational succession, the more important question may be how their children are doing.

Fortunately, there is quite detailed research on the experience of these second-generation Cubans in Miami.[6] In terms of school achievement, for example, the data suggest relative success, but the degree of success does not appear to match that implied by the frequent emphases on the way Cubans have transformed Miami, the way that transformation helped Cubans find and develop better economic opportunities, and the way strong social and political ties among Cubans created coherent families and a strongly supportive ethnic community—and ethnic economy. To simplify a rather long story of statistical analysis, the Cuban story turns out to be two stories. One is not unlike the Mexican experience in

Table 7.4. Selected characteristics of foreign-born Cubans in Miami

	Cuban-born	Foreign-born	Native-born
Households			
Average household size	3.1	3.2	2.5
Median household income (USD)	34,000	40,000	54,000
Households in poverty (%)	18	18	10
In family households (%)	71	72	58
Individuals			
Speak English very well (%)	35	48	96
In labor force (%)	58	65	62
≥ high school diploma (%)	73	77	91
≥ college diploma (%)	19	24	34

Source: US Census Bureau, combined 2011–2013 American Community Survey data, accessed through American Fact Finder, at https://factfinder.census.gov/faces/nav/jsf/pages/index.xhtml.

Note: Foreign-born and native-born figures are also for the Miami area only.

Los Angeles—a major immigrant group in a very immigrant city, but one that is struggling in economic and social terms, with a somewhat uncertain generational trajectory: children are doing better than their parents in some areas but not in all. The other story, however, is very much the original story of Cuban success, with parents working together and working hard to produce a decent life for themselves and a better life for high-performing children. That second story, again to simplify, hinges on parents who have worked hard enough and been successful enough to put their children in private schools. To put the contrast starkly between these two different Cuban-immigrant stories, the private-school second generation has prospered; the public-school second generation has struggled.[7]

The cases of Mexicans in Los Angeles and Cubans in Miami have some common features. Being a dominant immigrant group in an immigrant-oriented city has some advantages and some disadvantages. Low incomes may keep people in poor neighborhoods with poor schools. There lies potential doom for the hope of generational improvement in socioeconomic status. Yet those dense immigrant neighborhoods may also provide a social and cultural buffer as well as economic opportunities. In belonging to those neighborhoods, immigrants belong to the wider American society in some ways but do not belong in others. That mix of kinds of belonging may yield, as it has in the past, an eventual merging of the descendants of immigrants into the overall fabric of American life, or it may leave them, as it also has sometimes in the past, with continuing ambivalence about life in America and about whether the American promise of opportunity truly applies to them.

Immigration-labor rally in Los Angeles, 2015. (Ken Wolter/Shutterstock.com)

PAIRED COMPARISON: YUCATECANS IN DALLAS
AND KOREANS IN WASHINGTON, DC

The situation of very large national-origin groups in major immigrant-destination cities helps illustrate the context within which people assess how they belong to America and how that is shaped through connections with similar people from similar origins—what is usually just called the ethnic community. Many immigrants, however, belong to less numerically dominant groups and are in cities, towns, or rural areas where the overall effects of immigration are more muted. There are many variations: some cities (Pittsburgh, Saint Louis, Indianapolis, Birmingham) still have a percentage of the foreign-born well below the national average.[8] As two examples of situations somewhat in the middle, consider Yucatecans in Dallas and Koreans in Washington, DC.

The Dallas–Fort Worth metropolitan area is about 15 percent foreign-born, less than half the percentage for the Los Angeles and Miami areas already discussed—although the percentage in the city of Dallas itself is much higher. As with Los Angeles and Miami, there is one very dominant country of origin: Mexicans account for about half of the foreign-born population in the Dallas area (see table 7.5). The statistical profile of the Mexicans in Dallas is roughly similar to that of Mexicans in Los Angeles, with relatively low socioeconomic background, large family households, high levels of employment, but relatively low incomes. Again, this is a family-based, hard-working, but economically struggling population. Hidden within those overall numbers for Mexican-origin migrants are some more specific histories of particular people from particular places in Mexico. One involves migrants from the Yucatán Peninsula. By country of origin, they are indeed Mexican, but in terms of cultural and social background they are Mayan. Their experiences, in some ways, reflect the same border-crossing dynamics as other Mexicans. In other ways, however, they mirror more closely the experiences of indigenous groups from other Latin American countries, particularly the indigenous groups who make up a major segment of Guatemalan migrants in the United States.

Table 7.5. Major foreign-born populations in Dallas and Washington, DC

	Population
Dallas	
Mexico	610,000
India	84,000
Vietnam	57,000
El Salvador	49,000
China	36,000
Korea	24,000
Philippines	22,000
Honduras	19,000
Nigeria	18,000
Canada	14,000
Pakistan	14,000
Guatemala	14,000
Total foreign-born	**1,207,000**
Washington, DC	
El Salvador	180,000
India	90,000
China	69,000
Korea	60,000
Philippines	50,000
Mexico	49,000
Vietnam	49,000
Guatemala	45,000
Ethiopia	43,000
Peru	37,000
Total foreign-born	**1,316,000**

Source: US Census Bureau, combined 2011–2015 American Community Survey data, accessed through American Fact Finder, at https://factfinder.census.gov/faces/nav/jsf/pages/index.xhtml.

These Yucatecan Maya were for many years not part of the migrant flows from Mexico to the United States. The Yucatán is far removed from the Mexico–United States border, and only the completion of the Mexican railroad system brought them within the orbit of Mexico–United States interactions. The creation of a resort community in Cancún in the 1970s also served to integrate the Yucatecans into a more cosmopolitan economy, alerting them to employment options farther away. The Yucatecans were then increasingly drawn into the flow of Mexicans across the border into the United States. Some found their way to Dallas and were soon followed by family and friends.[9] Gradually, a Yucatecan Maya community formed in Dallas, relatively concentrated in a few housing projects. Ethnic contacts helped them find and sustain jobs in the service sector, particularly in restaurants for men and domestic service for women. Those personal connections have been especially important, since many of the Yucatecans are undocumented.

With Yucatecans having relatively low wages and often uncertain legal status, their commitment to life in America—and therefore to America overall—has remained uncertain and variable. Should they stay, or should they go? Is life in Dallas on the path to permanent life in the United States or on the path to life back in the Yucatán? That decision is not simply an individual one. Most Yucatecan adults are married, and the decision is thus a conjugal one. The context of that conjugal decision is affected by various factors. One is legal status. If a couple is legally in the United States, then staying in the United States often makes sense. If they are not legal and have little hope of becoming legal, then return is likely to remain a stronger option. One complicating factor is that husbands and wives may have different legal statuses, making joint decisions more difficult. Furthermore, husbands and wives may not live together regularly, with one in Dallas and the other back home in the Yucatán.

Children also affect the decision. Citizen children born in Dallas may push the decision toward staying. Children born in the Yucatán, by contrast, may push the decision toward life in the Yucatán. Indeed, those children may still live there, perhaps with one of the parents or perhaps with grandparents. In the Yucatecan case, the overall issue of belonging is not easily, quickly, or permanently resolvable. This is a case in which lives are lived across borders. Border controls make it harder for the undocumented members of the community to move back and forth, but the evidence suggests Yucatecans continue to do so anyway. That willingness to accept the many risks of unauthorized border crossings shows a high degree of commitment to both the United States and the Yucatán.

As another example, consider Washington, DC, and its Korean-origin population. The DC metropolitan area, like the Dallas metropolitan area, has a percentage of foreign-born well above the national average but well below such cities as Los Angeles and Miami. In the case of DC, there is no dominant country of origin (see again table 7.5). The only country of origin represented by over one hundred thousand people is El Salvador. This is a different kind of metropolitan context, with no clear dominance of particular groups—or even particular regions of origin. The number of Koreans in the area is just a fraction of that in Los Angeles (see again table 7.2), and the overall profile is slightly different. Furthermore, depending on their particular economic status, time of arrival, and family situation, Koreans are spread out across a trijurisdictional area (Washington, Maryland, Virginia) that provides a wide range of economic options, neighborhoods, and schools. That issue of schools is crucial, since Koreans, like other East Asians, are strongly interested in education and often fierce in their pursuit of education for their children.

Koreans in the Washington, DC, area are on a number of rather different migration tracks. Some are quite traditional immigrants, firmly committed to the United States, although with abiding attachments to traditional Korean culture and considerable pride in how successful South Korea has become. Their experience suggests the classic generational pattern, as the first generation struggles with English and a somewhat forbidding job market that gives only partial rewards for their educational background. The second generation, in turn, has complete facility with English, American culture, and how the US economic system works. But there are also more recent arrivals from Korea in the DC area who are working on still other migration tracks. For example, Korean high-skilled and professional workers who are now in the United States on temporary visas are reassessing whether careers in South Korea might now be more attractive than those in the United States or whether working for a Korean company (like Samsung) is wiser in the long term than working for an American company.

Another migration track involves students from Korea. Parents in South Korea face quandaries about the education of their children. The Korean educational system is highly stratified and often oppressive in its demands on students. Also, despite much effort, the system does not produce a level of English competence that many parents feel is essential for success. So parents are interested in the possibility of an American education. One possibility is a US college education, but by college age their children may be too old to pick up true fluency in English. Another possibility is to send children to the United States when they are younger, place them in a good American high school, and let them move from there into the US university system. As a result, among Koreans in the DC area are many children studying at US schools in preparation for US colleges. Sometimes they are alone, but usually they are with a relative. Often that relative is one of their parents, usually the mother. So a Korean couple, in pursuit of a child's education, is split between a working father in Korea and a caretaking mother in the United States. There are strains on members of the family, but perhaps especially on the father—often characterized as a "goose father," a *gireogi appa*, as he flies back and forth to see his family, and sometimes even as a "dead seagull," exhausted and bereft from his lonely efforts to support a family with whom he does not even live. As Krys Lee writes of one of these fathers in her short-story collection *Drifting House*, he had "relinquished so many possible selves to rescue his children from Korea's university-exam hell and his wife from the crippling anxiety of the education disease."[10]

Both the Yucatecan and the Korean cases provide insight into the way specific locales affect immigrant life. In Dallas, there are enough Yucatecans to create a viable ethnic community but also a broader and larger Mexican community within which they can move with some familiarity. They are, after all, also Mexican by nationality and experience, even though quite distinct in their history and culture. Dallas thus provides a doubly buffered environment that is especially helpful for those with mixed legal status: a smaller Yucatecan community nested within a much larger Mexican community. In Washington, DC, the influence of locale is more varied. There are areas of dense Korean businesses and residences, but Koreans are spread very broadly across the three political jurisdictions (Maryland, Virginia, and the District itself) that offer quite different employment, housing, and educational options. Here is an array of multiple options through which Koreans can decide how closely they want to live with how many other Koreans and how they want to triangulate employment, housing, and educational options. Their decisions will pull them in different directions—with those *gireogi* families, for example, moving directly toward good school districts with modest housing costs.

More broadly, however, the Korean and Yucatecan cases underline the complexity of the goals that migrants have and their level of commitment to them. Those commitments interact with the contexts in which people live and shift in relevance as migrants move through daily life in American locales and also between the different worlds of the United States, on the one hand, and Korea or Mexico, on the other. The increasing speed of travel and the pervasiveness of instantaneous communication can ease the transnational divides but cannot erase them. These two cases also bring full circle the discussion in part II of this book about the lived experiences of migrants. Their lives are far more complex, far more individualistic, and far more unpredictable than might be indicated by classic discussions of US immigration emphasizing predictable generational sequences. Those classic discussions also tend to focus on the overall question of whether newcomers assimilate rather than the more fruitful (and certainly more interesting) consideration of all the different ways migrants adjust, adapt, accommodate, and, perhaps, in the long run, do indeed Americanize—just as American society itself is being redefined as it adjusts, adapts, and accommodates to these newcomers.

Epilogue: Beyond Immigration

A CENTENNIAL CHOICE

Much about contemporary immigration raises anew the hopes and fears expressed a century ago about the role of immigration in US society. There were those at that time who saw the country not simply as one part of the world but also as a unique place in which all the people of the world could come together, with freedom and opportunity, to become more fully what they could be. This was a melting pot not just for the newcomers but also for everyone in the country, whether old or new.[1] In 1915, for example, Horace Kallen expressed concern that, if the United States failed to keep its doors open to the new migrants, the result might be a country slipping back into a caste system. In continued immigration, Kallen saw how the outlines of a "great and truly democratic commonwealth become discernible." The common language would, of course, be English, and the basic structure of government would continue to be the existing republican model, but each nationality would be able to express "its emotional and voluntary life in its own language, in its own inevitable aesthetic and intellectual forms." Kallen's metaphor for this process was a symphony.[2]

The following year, Randolph Bourne discussed his idea of a "transnational America" that could serve as a model of better world integration by itself being a model of how the integration of diversity could take place. "Only America," Bourne wrote, can lead in that effort by its "liberty of opportunity."[3] His notion of *transnational* was rather different from the contemporary use of the term. Today the term usually refers to the ways people's lives span national borders, maintaining connections in multiple societies and often moving back and forth between them. For Bourne, however, it was the singular nature of the United States as a country, as a place, and as an environment that was crucial. Only in that singular

American environment was true diversity possible. For him, it was *America* that was transnational, not the people. There is an echo in his ideas of that original notion from the birth of the republic that the United States is indeed a haven for all and that its virtue as a haven is in the provision of liberty for political, economic, and religious quests.

The more diverse and integrated world that both Kallen and Bourne espoused a century ago would also be, they thought, a safer world. It was not so much whether the world would be in interaction but what path that interaction would take. Both Kallen and Bourne were, after all, writing on the eve of the First World War, which would indeed be a globally integrating experience, though hardly the one they were seeking. They were also writing as the gates of US immigration were beginning to swing shut. Today, a century later, the United States is at a similar point, subject to great insecurities at home and abroad and facing a similar choice: on the one hand, to accept the influx of diversity as an occasion for renewing American society and expanding it out to the world or, on the other hand, to reject that diversity and rejuvenation in favor of turning inward. That choice was explicit in the 2016 US presidential election. The result, which gave the popular vote to one candidate and the electoral-college victory to another, suggests that the choice remains a sorely contested one in the United States today.

THE WIDER WORLD

Immigration has become an issue of contention not only in the United States but also in many other countries. As in the United States, the pressure points are often refugees and unauthorized migrants. The surge of Syrian refugees into Europe in 2015 and 2016, for example, reverberated throughout European politics. Some governments, like those in Poland and Hungary, took strong stands against efforts to distribute refugees among EU countries. Even countries that chose to open their borders, like Germany, experienced surges in anti-immigrant public opinion as a result. In Austria, it took two elections to vote in a new president. In both cases the anti-immigration candidate lost, but the votes were very close each time. There were other immigration issues as well. In the United Kingdom, concern about migrants legally arriving from other EU countries was a major factor in its "Brexit" vote to leave the European Union. In this case, the objection was to immigrants who were fully legal and who, according to most research, had largely positive economic effects.

By mid-2017, the net trend in this cultural and political battle over immigration was not entirely clear. In the United States, the new president and a Republican-controlled Congress had taken some practical action against refugees and unauthorized migrants, particularly by constricting entry of refugees and proposing to extend the sections of the border with Mexico that have an actual wall. In Europe, elections in the Netherlands and France demonstrated the strength of anti-immigration sentiment, but the net result in both the Netherlands and France was a victory for centrist approaches to government. For migrants

Protesters against the Brexit vote. Young adults often supported the European Union, but their voting levels were relatively low (2016). (mellis/Shutterstock.com)

worldwide, the developments in 2017 were generally negative—and especially so for refugees. Fewer opportunities for resettlement combined with inadequate funding of UN refugee programs left millions of refugees stranded in a precarious limbo—with especially high numbers of those from the Middle East stranded both in the Middle East itself and on uncertain passage routes to Europe. There were some brighter spots, however. For example, Canada continued its commitment to refugee issues, having pledged late in 2015 to accept some twenty-five thousand Syrian refugees. Even in comparison with similar support of Syrian refugees by then–US president Barack Obama, the Canadian effort was proportionately twenty-five times that of the United States. For Canadians, the choice about the benefits and costs of immigration was decidedly in favor of including newcomers, with all their diversity and all their challenges.

THE HEAT AND THE HAZE

Much of the contentiousness in the debates over immigration rises from the heat of debate. Immigration raises complex issues with multiple possible approaches. It is a set of policy issues about which differences of opinion can be expected. At the overall level, the numbers admitted make a difference, perhaps especially when there are sharp changes in the characteristics of those arriving. Despite the benefits of immigration, people and institutions that must adjust to increased numbers and increased diversity bear some negative effects. Such predictable policy debates, however, have escalated into heated cultural and political battles, replete with appeals to America's history as land of refuge and land of opportunity, on the one hand, and dire warnings about the dangers of increased insecurity, the loss of cultural values, the loss of jobs, and simply the loss of control, on the other. The potential of a moderated middle ground is thus lost. That loss is perhaps clearest in the cases of those who were brought, unauthorized, to the United States as children and have been here since. The bipartisan support for them seen in the initial DREAM legislative proposal of 2001 has long since disappeared.

In addition to the heat of the battle, there is also much haze. As this book has suggested, the seemingly simple topic of "immigration" turns out to be a complex set of issues about a variety of people who may or may not be immigrants in the common sense of the word (or even in the formal legal sense). It is sometimes difficult for the public even to grasp the basic numbers of contemporary immigration. As two examples, consider the frequently erroneous estimates of the number of immigrants and the number of Muslims in North American and European countries.[4] Consider first the discrepancy between the public's estimates of the number of immigrants and the actual numbers of immigrants (see table E.1). As it happens, the discrepancy is highest in Russia and the United States. In both countries people on average estimate the percentage of immigrants in the population at 19 percentage points higher than it actually is. In the US case, the public estimate is that the foreign-born are 33 percent of the total national population when they are actually only 14 percent. But the Russian and US discrepancies are

Table E.1. Estimates of immigrants as percent of total population in receiving countries

	Perceived	Actual	Difference
Russia	27	8	19
United States	33	14	19
Canada	39	21	18
Italy	26	9	17
Serbia	22	6	16
France	26	12	14
Germany	26	12	14
Belgium	24	10	14
Netherlands	25	12	13
Great Britain	25	13	12
Hungary	15	5	10

Source: Ipsos, "Perils of Perception 2015," 2015, https://www.ipsos.com/ipsos-mori/en-uk/perils-perception-2015?language_content_entity=en-uk.

Note: The table is ordered by the degree of difference between real and perceived numbers.

not significantly higher than many other countries'. The case of Great Britain deserves a special comment: The data presented here suggest the British discrepancy in estimating immigrant numbers is not greatly different than in other countries. Yet other data show how wrong the British public has been about the *origins* of its immigrants. Specifically, the public thinks a far higher number are from the European Union than is actually the case. That miscalculation figured prominently in the Brexit vote.

Similar discrepancies appear between public estimates and actual numbers of Muslims in North American and European countries (see table E.2). These data are especially important because Muslims are, in the public debates, often associated with the most problematic parts of immigration. Again, the differences between the perceived and actual numbers vary, this time with France at the top of the list for the greatest discrepancy. France is a country in which concerns about Islam have been very high. The French, for example, have long been agonizing over whether head scarves (much less veils) should be allowed in public settings, such as schools. In the French case, the actual percentage of Muslims in the total population is about 7.5 percent, but the French public estimates it at more than 30 percent. In terms of the discrepancy between perceptions and realities of Muslims, the United States is further down the list, with a 16-percentage-point difference between the public's estimate and the actual figure. But in the US case, the actual percentage of Muslims is very low, at about 1 percent, so Americans are overestimating the number of Muslims by a factor of seventeen. Such divergence suggests a very dense haze limiting people's ability to see even the population

Table E.2. Estimates of Muslims as percent of total population

	Perceived	Actual	Difference
France	31.0	7.5	23.5
Italy	20.0	3.7	16.3
Germany	21.0	5.0	16.0
Belgium	23.0	7.0	16.0
United States	17.0	1.0	16.0
Russia	24.0	10.0	14.0
Canada	17.0	3.2	13.8
Sweden	17.0	4.6	12.4
Netherlands	19.0	6.0	13.0
Spain	14.0	2.1	11.9
Denmark	15.0	4.1	10.9
Great Britain	15.0	4.8	10.2

Source: Ipsos, "The Perils of Perception 2016," 2016, https://perils.ipsos.com.

Note: The table is ordered by the degree of difference between real and perceived numbers.

size of particular groups of people—whether immigrants or Muslims—much less what their actual effects on US society might be. Haze is perhaps too thin a metaphor; smog might be a better one—dense, thick, hard to see, hard to breathe, and extremely frustrating to anyone hoping for rational consideration of what the options are for managing migration in the contemporary world.

PEOPLE ON THE MOVE

Despite the heat and the haze of migration policies and politics, migrants continue to move for many reasons along many paths. Those movements may be temporary, permanent, or recurring. They may involve only a few places or an ever-widening set of routes and destinations. The United States may not have the highest level of foreign-born or a particularly high proportion of its own people who move out to other countries, whether on a temporary, permanent, or recurring basis. Yet the United States remains a vital point on the world map of human mobility because of its sheer size, economic opportunities, political liberties, and cultural influence. It has benefited greatly from those arriving, whether as temporary workers, students, or visitors or as longer-term immigrants—whatever their particular legal statuses and future trajectories. The demographic, economic, scientific, and cultural bonuses have been invaluable. Furthermore, the United States continues to draw the very best of migrants, whether it is the excellence in manual labor vital to such sectors as agricultural and construction, the professional skills that sustain sectors like health care and information technology, or the entrepreneurial talent that has helped fuel American scientific discovery, innovation, and invention.

Because of this long experience with immigration, the United States has often been viewed as *the* land of immigration. The United States is not, however, the most immigrant-based society today. Australia, Canada, and New Zealand have far higher proportions of foreign-born, and many European countries, like Britain, Spain, and France, now match the United States in percentages of foreign-born residents. Nor, perhaps, are immigrants as committed to permanent life in America as they once were. Return is now a far easier and quicker option, whether for a short time or in the long term, whether for oneself or one's children. These changes raise the question of whether the United States is indeed the same kind of immigrant nation it was in the past or whether it is being integrated into a more open and fluid system of transnational human mobility. Whatever the case, the lived experiences of America's immigrants will continue to provide rich insight into the dynamics of US society and the dynamics of a world in which human mobility is on the rise. That enhanced mobility will bring benefits and challenges for those who move and for those who do not. It will also bring benefits and challenges to the countries to, from, and through which migrant trajectories are constructed across space and through time.

Timeline

US Immigration Contexts, Events, and Legislation

This timeline began as an inventory of key immigration-related legislation in the United States and then expanded to include something of the context in which that legislation emerged—both in terms of US events and those world events that most directly affected the US situation. There are some limitations: (1) colonial law and regulation are not included—unfortunate, since the different colonies tried out very different immigration strategies; (2) this is United States based, so the broader stories of migration to and around the rest of the Americas, much less global migration, receive short shrift; and (3) the discussions of the laws are themselves quite abridged. For better detail, see especially Michael C. LeMay and Elliott Robert Barkan, *U.S. Immigration and Naturalization Laws and Issues: A Documentary History* (Westport, CT: Greenwood, 1999). Most online listings are quite cursory, and the solid chronology of immigration legislation that used to appear in the annual statistical yearbooks of the Immigration and Naturalization Service are not being updated.

Year	World events	US events	US legislation
1776		Declaration of Independence written.	Declaration includes criticism of Britain for undermining migration to the colonies.
1788		Constitution ratified; Washington elected first president.	Constitution specifies there will be no migration controls until 1808 but Congress can provide uniform rules for naturalization.
1790			Naturalization Act of 1790 establishes rules for naturalization but is limited to white persons.
1795			Naturalization Act of 1795 establishes five-year period for naturalization but is limited to white aliens of good moral character.
1798	Napoleon's campaigns extend to Switzerland and Egypt.	Concern in US about French expansion under Napoleon.	Series of laws (Alien Friends Act, Alien Enemies Act, Naturalization Act) lays out provisions for expulsion, monitoring passenger lists, and extends wait for naturalization to 14 years. Includes criminal sanctions for anyone criticizing US government.
1800		Thomas Jefferson elected president; election seen partly as referendum on restrictions on immigrants under prior administration of John Adams.	
1802	Treaty of Amiens ends war between France and UK.		Naturalization Act of 1802 returns naturalization waiting period to 5 years.

Year	World events	US events	US legislation
1808			Act Prohibiting Importation of Slaves takes effect (20 years earlier, Constitution had set 1808 as earliest possible date for migration controls).
1819	SS *Savannah* crosses Atlantic using partial steam power; voyage takes 29 days.		Steerage Act requires passenger lists from all arriving ships and sets general standards for transportation of immigrants on those ships.
1838	SS *Great Western* built; voyages now routinely under 20 days.		
1848	Europe undergoes series of revolutions; potato famine sharpens in Ireland.		
1849		Gold rush in California draws migrants, including thousands from China, over next decades.	
1852		Nativist "Know Nothing" party has resounding success in several state and local elections.	
1855			Passenger Act codifies requirements on ships transporting migrants, including separate reporting for temporary and permanent migrants.
1858	First transatlantic telegraph-cable communications are made.		

Year	World events	US events	US legislation
1864		Civil War creates serious civilian labor shortages.	Legislation sets up system for controlling and encouraging immigration; repealed in 1868.
1868			14th Amendment ratified: defines citizenship as automatic by birth (or by naturalization).
1870			Naturalization Act of 1870 extends naturalization to persons of African origin.
1871	Unification of Germany gives rise to anti-Catholic sentiment and law.	German emigration shifts from Protestant toward Catholic.	
1875			Page Act excludes certain types of people, including criminals, prostitutes, and involuntary "coolie" labor from China.
1881	Major anti-Jewish pogroms occur in Russia. Waves of such pogroms continue into early 1900s.		
1882	SS *Alaska* reduces Atlantic crossing to under a week.		Chinese Exclusion Act suspends Chinese labor migration for 10 years, provides for deportation, and bars Chinese from naturalization; Immigration Act of 1882 broadens exclusion to include those likely to become public charge.
1885			Legislation outlaws most contract labor; control expanded in 1888.

Year	World events	US events	US legislation
1891			Immigration Act of 1891 establishes Bureau of Immigration, expands list of excludable people, and provides for inspection of arriving people.
1892		Ellis Island opens as processing center for immigrants in New York City.	Geary Act extends prohibition of most Chinese migrants.
1898			In *United States v. Wong Kim Ark*, Supreme Court rules children born in US to parents ineligible for citizenship still retain birthright citizenship guaranteed by 14th Amendment.
1901		President William McKinley assassinated by Leon Frank Czolgosz, US–born but Polish-origin anarchist.	
1903			Immigration Act of 1903 codifies existing law, expands list of excludable conditions (including political opinion), and expands time after arrival during which deportation is possible.
1905		Number of annual admissions exceeds 1 million for first time.	
1906			Naturalization Act of 1906 establishes clearer procedures but also introduces English-language competence as requirement for naturalization.

Year	World events	US events	US legislation
1907			Immigration Act of 1907 codifies existing law, adds new reasons for exclusion (e.g., physical and mental defects, moral turpitude), requires declaration of whether intent is to stay temporarily or permanently, and sets up Joint Immigration Commission (which becomes known as Dillingham Commission).
1910		Angel Island opens as processing center for immigrants in San Francisco.	
1914	Outbreak of World War I (assassination of Archduke Franz Ferdinand of Austria in Sarajevo).		
1917	Russian Revolution occurs.	US joins Allied effort against Germany in World War I.	Immigration Act of 1917 excludes illiterate arrivals, creates "barred zone" in Asia-Pacific region from which no one is admissible, and increases without any limitation period in which those admitted can be deported for certain serious offenses.
1918	World War I ends.		Entry and Departure Controls Act authorizes president to control entry and departure of anyone considered threat to public safety.

Year	World events	US events	US legislation
1921			"First Quota Act" (Emergency Quota Act) caps annual arrivals at 350,000 with any individual country capped at 3% of its national-origin population as of 1910.
1923			In *United States v. Bhagat Singh Thind*, Supreme Court rules Indians are not white and therefore any prior granted citizenship can be rescinded; white-only restriction on naturalization dates from Naturalization Act of 1795.
1924			"Second Quota Act" (Johnson-Reed Act) reduces total immigration quota to 164,667, with any individual country capped at 2% of its national-origin population as of 1890 (with some adjustments after 1927); preference within quota system is partly family and partly labor, but immediate family (spouses and unmarried children under 18) and those from western hemisphere not counted against quota; legislation also solidifies meaning of *immigrant* and defines all coming for temporary purposes as *nonimmigrants*.

Year	World events	US events	US legislation
1928	*Graf Zeppelin* makes first commercial air crossing of Atlantic.		
1929		Stock market crash signals beginning of Great Depression.	
1933		US immigration reaches lowest point in history: 23,000 arrivals.	
1939	World War II begins (German invasion of Poland); first commercial transatlantic flight is made by Boeing, from Newfoundland to Ireland.		
1941		US joins Allied effort in World War II (after Japanese attack Pearl Harbor).	
1942			Executive Order 9066 authorizes movement of Japanese Americans away from the West Coast and into internment camps.
1943		World War II creates labor shortages (thus need for Mexican workers) and also need to recognize China as ally (thus repeal of Chinese exclusion).	Legislation establishes formal temporary-worker program for Mexicans—so-called Bracero Program—which lasts until 1962; separate legislation repeals Chinese exclusion, but new quota is only 105 persons per year.
1945	World War II ends.		War Brides Act waives restrictions on admitting foreign wives of US military personnel (later laws address gaps in law and extend admission to fiancé(e)s of service personnel).

Year	World events	US events	US legislation
1946		US immigration exceeds 100,000 for first time since 1931.	
1948	Europe still slow to recover from World War II; millions displaced.		Displaced Persons Act allows 206,000 people to enter; number later increased to 415,000.
1952			McCarran-Walter Act codifies immigration law and makes several crucial changes: removes all racial grounds for exclusion; eliminates differential clauses regarding men versus women; revises national origins–quota formula, but with only a minimum quota of 100 and continuing caps on Asian immigration; establishes annual alien address–reporting system; greatly expands different kinds of temporary ("nonimmigrant") statuses.
1953			Refugee Relief Act allows 215,000 admissions outside regular quota system.
1954	Beginning of Senate hearings conducted by Senator Joseph McCarthy (televised with McCarthy's inevitable question, "Are you now or have you ever been a member of the Communist Party?").		Legislation provides for expatriation of anyone convicted of conspiring against US government.

Year	World events	US events	US legislation
1956	First transatlantic telephone-cable communications established; failed uprising occurs in Hungary.	President Eisenhower commits US to supporting resettlement of Hungarian refugees.	
1957			Refugee-Escapee Act provides slots outside quota system for refugees, including provisions for family members.
1958	First commercial transatlantic jet flight made.		Legislation provides for settlement and adjustment of status of Hungarian refugees (who had already been paroled into US).
1959	Fidel Castro confirmed new Cuban head of state.	Flows of Cuban refugees to US escalate.	
1960		President Eisenhower establishes program support for Cuban refugees in Miami; support echoed by incoming president John F. Kennedy.	
1962			Migration and Refugee Assistance Act provides support for refugee resettlement; so-called Bracero Program ends.

Year	World events	US events	US legislation
1965			Immigration and Nationality Act (Hart-Celler Act) provides major reconfiguration of US immigration law by abolishing national origins–quota system; establishing preference system that includes both family and labor factors; placing immediate family outside quota system; and setting overall caps of 170,000 for eastern hemisphere and 120,000 for western hemisphere. For eastern hemisphere only, there is a single-country cap of 20,000 (different treatment of western hemisphere later amended).
1966			Cuban Adjustment Act provides permanent resident status for Cubans who reach US.
1970		Percent foreign-born reaches lowest point in US history.	
1975	Communist forces take firm control in Cambodia, Laos, and Vietnam.	US accepts refugees fleeing those new governments.	Indochina Migration and Refugee Assistance Act provides support for refugee intake and resettlement in US.

Year	World events	US events	US legislation
1980	Fidel Castro opens port of Mariel for anyone wishing to leave Cuba.	Ronald Reagan elected president; he comes to support anticommunist rebels and governments in Central America, escalating flows of people especially from El Salvador. Sudden flows of Cubans from Mariel joined by significant outflows from Haiti (flows occur after and outside provisions of Refugee Act).	Refugee Act brings US into conformity with UN refugee definition, sets normal flow number of 50,000/year (based on presidential consultation with Congress), and establishes comprehensive resettlement system; Refugee Assistance Act provides assistance for Cuban and Haitian arrivals officially termed "entrants" rather than refugees but who receive same services and assistance as refugees.
1982			In *Plyler v. Doe*, Supreme Court rules undocumented immigrant children cannot be denied education.
1986			Immigration Reform and Control Act (IRCA) creates 2 separate legalization tracks (one based on 4 years' residence, the other on shorter-term agricultural labor), establishes system of employer sanction to reduce unauthorized migration in future, increases border enforcement, and makes general adjustments to immigration law.
1989	Berlin Wall falls; collapse of Soviet Union radically changes migration patterns within Europe and from Europe to US.	US immigration exceeds 1 million for first time since 1914.	

Year	World events	US events	US legislation
1990			Immigration Act of 1990 provides major reworking of immigration policy, including new flexible ceilings and expanded "diversity" program for people from countries underrepresented in prior flows; also creates temporary protected status for those who cannot currently return to their home countries.
1993			North American Free Trade Agreement (NAFTA) Implementation Act, which expands previous agreement only with Canada, facilitates temporary entry of workers and professionals—as well as changes dynamics of migration with Mexico in general.
1996			Several crucial pieces of legislation limit access of permanent-resident aliens to various kinds of government assistance and enhance safeguards against potential terrorists (Antiterrorism and Effective Death Penalty Act, Personal Responsibility and Work Opportunity Reconciliation Act, and Illegal Immigration Reform and Immigrant Responsibility Act).

Year	World events	US events	US legislation
1997			Nicaraguan Adjustment and Central America Relief Act (NACARA) permits several national-origin groups expedited processing and also reduces more negative effects of 1996 laws noted above on use of services.
1998			Haitian Refugee Immigration Fairness Act (HRIFA) extends some of the same options to Haitians provided in previous year through NACARA.
2001		Terrorist attacks committed on New York City and Pentagon.	Patriot Act tightens screening of various categories of migrants both at border and internally (full title is Uniting and Strengthening America by Providing Appropriate Tools Required to Intercept and Obstruct Terrorism Act).
2002			Homeland Security Act moves immigration management into new Department of Homeland Security.
2005			REAL ID Act tightens and expands procedures for inadmissible and deportable persons.
2006			Secure Fence Act authorizes expansion of control over border with Mexico, both for wall itself and for overall technology to monitor border.

Year	World events	US events	US legislation
2012			President Obama authorizes Deferred Action for Childhood Arrivals (DACA), providing work authorization and exemption from deportation for unauthorized migrants who arrived before age 16 and before 2007.
2014			President Obama authorizes Deferred Action for Parents of Americans and Lawful Permanent Residents (DAPA), providing work authorization and exemption from deportation for unauthorized migrant parents.
2015	Syrian refugee crisis strains European capacity and reveals fault lines within EU; Canada responds positively to Syrian crisis under new prime minister Justin Trudeau.		
2016	UK votes to leave EU ("Brexit") in part over concerns about immigration.	US election cycle shows very strong antirefugee and anti-immigrant sentiment among Republican candidates and voters.	In *United States v. Texas*, evenly divided Supreme Court fails to sustain DAPA (see above).
2017		Donald Trump inaugurated president; Republican majorities elected to both chambers of Congress. Trump and his party espouse sharp stands against refugees and unauthorized migrants.	

Notes

CHAPTER 1

1. Recent research has tended to push the arrival of humans in the Americas further back in time. For updates on the latest research, two useful websites are Smithsonian.com and ScienceDaily.com. Note, in particular, their reports in early 2017 on the work of Jacques Cinq-Mars and Lauriane Bourgeon (with Ariane Burke and Thomas Higham). See Lorraine Boissoneault, "Humans May Have Arrived in North America 10,000 Years Earlier than We Thought," Smithsonian.com, January 31, 2017, updated February 1, 2017, http://www.smithsonianmag.com/science-nature/humans-may-have-arrived-north-america-10000-years-earlier-we-thought-180961957/; and see Université de Montréal, "First Humans Arrived in North America a Lot Earlier than Believed," ScienceDaily, January 16, 2017, http://www.sciencedaily.com/releases/2017/01/170116091428.htm.

2. This was the so-called Seven Years' War, which is referred to in American history as the French and Indian War, although French Canadians tend to refer to it as the War of the Conquest. The years are generally noted as 1756–1763, but hostilities actually broke out in 1753 when French troops invaded the Ohio Valley.

3. For example, the Declaration of Independence itself declares that the king "has endeavoured to prevent the population of these States; for that purpose obstructing the Laws for Naturalization of Foreigners; refusing to pass others to encourage their migrations hither, and raising the conditions of new Appropriations of Lands."

4. There has been enormous debate about population numbers for Native Americans both before and after conquest. The sharp downward trajectory,

however, is universal. For a recent attempt to sort out the numbers and the causes, see Catherine M. Cameron, Paul Kelton, and Alan C. Swedlund, eds., *Beyond Germs: Native Depopulation in North America* (Tucson: University of Arizona Press, 2016).

5. George Washington, letter to Francis Adrian Van der Kemp, May 28, 1788. Available online from Founders Online, the National Archives, at https://founders.archives.gov/documents/Washington/04-06-02-0266.

6. Thomas Jefferson, "Proclamation Inviting Mercenary Troops in the British Service to Desert," February 2, 1781. Available online from Founders Online, the National Archives, at https://founders.archives.gov/documents/Jefferson/01-04-02-0622.

7. Benjamin Franklin, letter to Peter Collinson, May 9, 1753. Available online from Founders Online, the National Archives, at https://founders.archives.gov/documents/Franklin/01-04-02-0173.

8. Emphasis original. Benjamin Franklin, "Observations concerning the Increase of Mankind," first published in 1751 and reprinted at various times thereafter. Available online from Founders Online, the National Archives, at https://founders.archives.gov/documents/Franklin/01-04-02-0080.

9. George Washington, letter to John Adams, November 15, 1794. Available online from Founders Online, the National Archives, at https://founders.archives.gov/documents/Washington/05-17-02-0112.

10. Thomas Jefferson, *Notes on the State of Virginia*, 1781, chapter (query) 8, available online at http://xroads.virginia.edu/~hyper/jefferson/ch08.html.

11. Benjamin Franklin, "Information to Those Who Would Remove to America," March 1784. Available online from Founders Online, the National Archives, at https://founders.archives.gov/documents/Franklin/01-41-02-0391.

12. Thomas Jefferson, "Proclamation Inviting Mercenary Troops in the British Service to Desert," February 2, 1781. Available online from Founders Online, the National Archives, at https://founders.archives.gov/documents/Jefferson/01-04-02-0622.

13. George Washington, letter to Joshua Holmes, "To the Members of the Volunteer Associations & Other Inhabitants of the Kingdom of Ireland Who Have Lately Arrived in the City of New York," December 2, 1783. Available online from Founders Online, the National Archives, at https://founders.archives.gov/documents/Washington/99-01-02-12127.

14. Note that legislation regarding immigration is presented in greater detail in the timeline at the end of this book.

15. More specifically, 1790 legislation created a two-year waiting period before citizenship, which was extended to five years in 1795. This was extended to fourteen years in 1798, but that law was rescinded, and the waiting returned to five years—and remains so today. In the early laws, naturalization was limited to "free white persons."

16. I am not including the full tables here, but they are readily available as the first table in every year's *Yearbook of Immigration Statistics*, available online

on the US Department of Homeland Security's website, at https://www.dhs.gov/immigration-statistics/yearbook.

17. Mischa Honeck, *We Are the Revolutionists: German-Speaking Immigrants and American Abolitionists after 1848* (Athens: University of Georgia Press, 2011), 71.

18. There was an additional relatively small purchase of land from Mexico in 1853. The Gadsden Purchase added about thirty thousand square miles to the southern boundaries of the current states of New Mexico and Arizona.

19. The legislation did not actually end Chinese immigration, but it did severely limit it. Wives of those already in the United States could still enter, as could the children of those already in the United States. There was clearly some strategic use of these mechanisms by the Chinese.

20. The source is a letter from Roosevelt in 1919 to the American Defense Society but echoes his earlier views. The letter is held by the Manuscript Division of the Library of Congress and can be viewed online at http://www.snopes.com/politics/graphics/troosevelt.pdf.

CHAPTER 2

1. Germany, as a long-established source of migrants to the United States, fared rather well under the restrictive immigration caps of the 1920s. What was most appalling to refugee advocates was that the United States would not use even these available slots to help in this clear refugee crisis.

2. Supporters did manage to have the landing outside Germany, and a variety of countries agreed to accept the refugees (Belgium, Holland, France, and Great Britain) rather than have them returned to Germany. Yet three of those four countries would soon fall to Germany, and an exhaustive look at records indicates that, except for those who went to Great Britain, nearly half lost their lives by the end of the war. See Sarah A. Ogilvie and Scott Miller, *Refuge Denied: The "St. Louis" Passengers and the Holocaust* (Madison: University of Wisconsin Press, 2006).

3. Harry S. Truman, "Statement and Directive by the President on Immigration to the United States of Certain Displaced Persons and Refugees in Europe," December 22, 1945. Available online from the Harry S. Truman Library and Museum, at https://www.trumanlibrary.org/publicpapers/viewpapers.php?pid=515.

4. Harry S. Truman, "Statement by the President upon Signing the Displaced Persons Act," June 25, 1948. Available online from the Harry S. Truman Library and Museum, at https://www.trumanlibrary.org/publicpapers/viewpapers.php?pid=1688.

5. Dwight D. Eisenhower, "Statement by the President concerning Hungarian Refugees," January 1, 1957. Available online from the American Presidency Project, at http://www.presidency.ucsb.edu/ws/?pid=10800.

6. Dwight D. Eisenhower, "Statement by the President on Releasing a Report on Cuban Refugee Problems," January 18, 1961. Available online from the American Presidency Project, at http://www.presidency.ucsb.edu/ws/?pid=12097.

7. John F. Kennedy, "Letter to Secretary Ribicoff Requesting Him to Undertake Direction of Cuban Refugee Activities," January 27, 1961. Available online from the American Presidency Project, at http://www.presidency.ucsb.edu/ws/?pid=8544.

8. That legislation, the Cuban Adjustment Act of 1966, does not explicitly use the term *refugee*, though these people are routinely called "Cuban refugees" and the rationale for their automatic legality is based on consideration of them as refugees. Congressional committees, for example, routinely had the word *refugee* in their titles, and it was these committees that oversaw programs for them, including of the Cuban Refugee Program in the US Department of Health and Human Services.

9. Again, this is partly an issue of terminology. If we consider the many immigrants in the 1800s and early 1900s who were refugees in a normal, nonlegal sense (i.e., they had to flee), then this number of 167,000 is not comparatively so large.

10. The number might be as high as 60 percent depending on the calculation. But, as will be discussed in chapter 3, the issues of who has physically arrived in the United States and who has legally become a permanent resident are *not* the same. Nevertheless, since the annual number of legal immigrants was around a half million for the decade surrounding 1980, the comparison seems appropriate.

11. Quoted from John F. Kennedy, *A Nation of Immigrants*, rev. ed. (New York: Harper Perennial, 2008), 32 and 36.

12. Ibid., 45.

13. Ibid., 50.

14. John F. Kennedy, "Letter to the President of the Senate and to the Speaker of the House on Revision of the Immigration Laws," July 23, 1963. Available online from the American Presidency Project, at http://www.presidency.ucsb.edu/ws/?pid=9355.

15. Lyndon B. Johnson, "Remarks at the Signing of the Immigration Bill, Liberty Island, New York," October 3, 1965. Available online from the American Presidency Project, at http://www.presidency.ucsb.edu/ws/?pid=27292.

16. Note that the analysis shifts somewhat if we compare more recent decades with that of the 1960s, when the legislation was actually passed. The sharp drop in European arrivals and the sharp increase in Asian arrivals are still clear, although reduced. The western hemisphere figures show less overall change, reflecting the long US relationship with the Americas.

17. Note that the totals for 1989–1991 are aberrant. They reflect the special amnesty provisions of the 1986 Immigration Reform and Control Act (IRCA), which is discussed later in the chapter.

18. Their presence was even stronger in Hawaii, which was independent until 1898.

19. Again, see the timeline at the end of this book for more detailed discussion of immigration legislation.

20. The data come from the summary report of the Dillingham Commission, *Reports of the Immigration Commission* (Washington, DC: Government Printing Office, 1910), available online at https://archive.org/details/reportsofimmigra01 unitrich.

21. The oath is very clear that other allegiances are not acceptable—specifically, "that I absolutely and entirely renounce and abjure all allegiance and fidelity to any foreign prince, potentate, state, or sovereignty of whom or which I have heretofore been a subject or citizen." Technically, then, dual citizenship is not available to naturalized citizens even though it is often acceptable to the country of origin and quite allowable for persons born in the United States who may have US citizenship by virtue of that birth but also another citizenship through their parents.

CHAPTER 3

1. As one example, recent suggestions to legalize the undocumented are opposed by some people on social and cultural grounds but are also opposed by other people who would prefer a continued flow of undocumented workers and the benefits they provide as flexible, low-wage labor. When the undocumented are legalized, after all, they tend to move on to better-paying and more secure jobs, creating another round of demand for new undocumented workers.

2. It is, however, the case that immigrant hard work is sometimes counted as a factor against them, an unfair advantage they possess over the native-born. This often happens in the educational arena, especially at the university level, where hard-working immigrants, and sometimes simply hard-working foreign students, are seen as taking opportunities and even admissions slots away from the native-born.

3. Those comments by Trump were later used in the legal challenges to his executive orders of early 2017 barring arrivals from designated countries and reducing the refugee-resettlement program by about half.

4. There are also difficulties in the United States because of the allocation of rights and responsibilities among the federal, state, and local levels. In particular, the costs of immigration are borne in varying ways by those different levels of government. For both refugees and unauthorized migrants, there are costs, and, since these are not fully reimbursed by the federal government, there is a frequent complaint that the federal government makes the decisions while states and localities must absorb the costs.

5. See in particular Pew Research Center, "Chapter 4: U.S. Public Has Mixed Views of Immigrants and Immigration," *Modern Immigration Wave Brings 59 Million to U.S., Driving Population Growth and Change through 2065*, September 28, 2015, http://www.pewhispanic.org/2015/09/28/chapter-4-u-s-public-has -mixed-views-of-immigrants-and-immigration/.

6. Note that, because of these immediate relatives, the remaining more planned, controlled, and controllable parts of US immigration thus account for only the bare majority of all admissions.

7. Cubans, for example, were long able to establish legal residence simply by reaching the United States. That special status under the Cuban Adjustment Act of 1966 was based on US support for Cubans as refugees from communism. That special status was effectively revoked in early 2017 by President Obama, reflecting the restoration of US diplomatic relations with Cuba in 2015 and Obama's own visit there in 2016.

8. The Refugee Act of 1980, spurred by late senator Edward Kennedy, aimed to reconcile US refugee law with international law and practice, particularly the definition of *refugee* used in the UN Refugee Convention of 1951. That definition specifies that a refugee is someone who has fled across a national border because of a well-founded fear of persecution, not simply because of generalized violence or disorder. Among other issues, the Refugee Act of 1980 provides a reminder that US immigration law is often interwoven with America's stance in the wider world and a commitment to shoulder a fair share of the world's migration problems.

9. Somewhat ironically, given US history, the Irish were one of the groups for whom the program was designed. Although they have a very major place in American immigration history, there were relatively few recent Irish immigrants. They thus did not have the kind of immediate family connections that would merit admission as family members.

10. These counts are from US Department of Homeland Security, *2015 Yearbook of Immigration Statistics*, Office of Immigration Statistics, December 2016, https://www.dhs.gov/sites/default/files/publications/Yearbook_Immigration _Statistics_2015.pdf. Note that counts of foreign students depend on the sources. Counts from the Student and Exchange Visitor Information System (SEVIS) show current status, and those from DHS's yearbook show admissions. SEVIS data show far lower numbers of Canadian and Mexican students because they do not include data on exchange programs.

11. In the US case, for example, Mexicans crossing the border can expect to earn about as much each hour in the United States as they might each day in Mexico.

12. Technically it is not the European Union but the countries that accepted provisions of the Schengen Agreement, first signed in 1985 and in effect in 1995. Most EU countries have joined but not all (e.g., Romania, Bulgaria, and Croatia). Also, a few non-EU members have joined.

13. More generally, Europe now has a web of overlapping agreements. Most countries are formally part of the European Union, agree to its largely open-border process as laid out in the Schengen Agreement, and use the euro. But that is not true of all countries: some are in the EU but do not use the euro. In addition, some countries are outside the EU but nevertheless follow EU trade agreements and allow free passage of workers from the EU.

CHAPTER 4

1. In 1989, another Chinese man was murdered because he was assumed to be responsible for the deaths of Americans in Vietnam. Again, there was not only violence but also a fundamental confusion between race and nationality.

2. Anzia Yezierska, *Bread Givers: A Novel* (originally Garden City, NY: Doubleday, Page and Company, 1925). The quotations are from the online version of the book, so page numbers are not available. But a text search will yield the quotations and their contexts.

3. Cristina García, *Dreaming in Cuban: A Novel* (New York: Ballantine Books, 1992), 5.

4. The Lautenberg Amendment was originally passed in 1990 and has been repassed every year since—otherwise it would expire. It gives the US president discretion to define as refugees certain people who may not necessarily meet the formal refugee definition in US law. It was originally focused on Soviet Jewish refugees but has been used for a variety of religious minorities and other groups since then.

CHAPTER 5

1. See particularly the special 1999 issue of the *Anthropology of Work Review* (vol. 9, no. 2), on the work of Miriam Lee Kaprow. See especially Miriam Lee Kaprow, "The Last, Best Work: Firefighters in the Fire Department of New York," *Anthropology of Work Review* 9, no. 2 (1999): 5–26, doi: 10.1111/j.1548 -1417.1999.tb00619.x.

2. Much of this data is reviewed in the detailed endnotes to my previous work on refugees in the United States: David W. Haines, *Safe Haven? A History of Refugees in America* (Sterling, VA: Kumarian Press, 2010).

3. For the actual data, see the standard data sets from the US Census Bureau, specifically the decennial census for the most accurate population numbers, the American Community Survey for more detailed population characteristics, and the Current Population Survey for basic social and economic trends. For a gateway to more detailed information on these sources, see the US Census Bureau's website at https://www.census.gov/topics/population/foreign-born/surveys-programs.html.

4. For example, see the Bureau of Labor Statistics, *Occupational Employment and Wages—May 2016*, news release, US Department of Labor, March 31, 2017, https://www.bls.gov/news.release/pdf/ocwage.pdf.

5. These examples come from the University of Minnesota's Immigration History Research Center and its extensive collection and annotation of immigrant autobiographies from various places (see the IHRC's searchable archives at https://www.lib.umn.edu/ihrca/). Given the extent of Scandinavian migration to Minnesota, the center is especially valuable for people from Finland, as well as from Norway and Sweden. See in particular "Edit Koivisto Papers,"

http://archives.lib.umn.edu/repositories/6/resources/4085; and "Helmi Dagmar Mattson Papers," http://archives.lib.umn.edu/repositories/6/resources/4267.

6. See Immigration History Research Center, "Edward Aho Papers," University of Minnesota, http://archives.lib.umn.edu/repositories/6/resources/3863. And see also Nanette Dobrosky, *A Guide to the Microfilm Edition of Research Collections in Amierican Immigration, Part 1: Manuscript Autobiographies from the Immigration History Research Center* (Saint Paul, MN: Immigration History Center, 1988), 43–44.

7. These comments, and the comparative material in the tables, come from the US Census Bureau, since its work is so inclusive, is conducted at regular intervals, and is largely standardized. As a general warning, however, the data on the foreign-born are based only on samples (from the American Community Survey, not the decennial census itself). Furthermore, there are some oddities in the categories that reflect US systems of categorization. Much of what are national and ethnic categories, for example, are characterized as race. Furthermore, much important data is left out. As a matter of public policy, for example, the census does not ask about religion, even though religion is crucial to both immigrant origins and immigrant destinies.

8. The links within the Korean community, and between it and mainstream American society, have often reflected those early Presbyterian and Methodist ties. Christians remain a minority in South Korea but are generally assumed to be a significant majority of the Koreans in the United States. Since the US Census Bureau does not collect data on religion, however, it is difficult to be exact on the numbers.

CHAPTER 6

1. The discussion here of Catholicism is largely in terms of Roman Catholicism. That is adequate for the Vietnamese case, but it obscures the existence of many different kinds of Catholicism in Mexico, as in the United States. Similar problems exist for such other generic labels as *Muslim, Buddhist,* and *Protestant,* which include enormous variation in terms of both practice and belief. For simplicity, I have kept to such generic labels in this text but at the risk of oversimplifying the very specific kinds of belief and practice, and the defined religious communities, that are perhaps even more important in migration than in more settled life. The same problem exists for the discussion later of people whom I term *Christians* from southern Sudan who are a mix of Catholics and Protestants—and a varied set of Protestants at that.

2. They were considered refugees even though the law that provided permanent residency to them, the Cuban Adjustment Act of 1966, was explicitly about Cubans and did *not* use the word *refugees.*

3. There are several published biographies of Mary Dyer but also several extensive accounts online, including a solid Wikipedia entry. See *Wikipedia,* s.v.

"Mary Dyer," last modified May 12, 2017, https://en.wikipedia.org/wiki/Mary_Dyer. For more detail on her life and interactions with other Puritan dissenters, such as Roger Williams and Anne Hutchinson, see Ruth Talbot Plimpton, *Mary Dyer: Biography of a Rebel Quaker* (Wellesley, MA: Branden Publishing Co., 1994).

4. Horatio Rogers, *Mary Dyer* (Providence, RI: Preston & Rounds, 1896), 31, 41, 44, and 61.

5. Patrick Henry, speech of March 23, 1755, online at http://avalon.law.yale.edu/18th_century/patrick.asp.

6. See particularly Jason De León, *The Land of Open Graves: Living and Dying on the Migrant Trail*, with photographs by Michael Wells (Berkeley: University of California Press, 2015).

7. The data on Honduran perspectives come from Jonathan T. Hiskey, Abby Córdova, Diana Orcés, and Mary Fran Malone, "Understanding the Central American Refugee Crisis: Why They Are Fleeing and How U.S. Policies Are Failing to Deter Them," American Immigration Council, February 1, 2016, https://www.americanimmigrationcouncil.org/research/understanding-central-american-refugee-crisis.

8. The Pew Research Center provides very useful data on religion in the United States. While the data suggest that institutional membership in formal religions is declining in the United States, that decline is partly counterbalanced by the religiosity of immigrants and, in any case, is far less precipitous than in other European societies—or even Canada. Furthermore, there is some indication that a more general spirituality, less attached to formal organizations, is actually rising. See, for example, David Masci and Michael Lipka, "Americans May Be Getting Less Religious, but Feelings of Spirituality Are on the Rise," Pew Research Center, January 20, 2016, http://www.pewresearch.org/fact-tank/2016/01/21/americans-spirituality/.

9. Catholicism is not, however, universal. For Mexico, more than 80 percent are Catholic, with less than 10 percent Protestant. These percentages are different among Mexican Americans, with a lower percentage Catholic (barely 60 percent) and a higher percentage Protestant (nearly 20 percent). Some of the difference represents conversion after arrival in the United States. See the Pew Research Center for very good attention to the intersection of religion and migration. Note as well the earlier point about the many different streams of Catholicism in Mexico, a warning that applies as well to Protestantism.

10. The Republic of South Sudan achieved independence from Sudan in 2011—and has since been embroiled in political turmoil and civil war. For the period during which most Sudanese refugees came to the United States, however, it was still part of Sudan and thus is referred to in the text as "southern Sudan."

11. The term *lost boys* originated by aid workers as a reference to Peter Pan—specifically to the boys who created and maintained their own society without adults. The same reference had been used decades earlier for the many Cuban children moved from communist Cuba to the United States without their parents—although that program was Hispanicized to Pedro Pan.

CHAPTER 7

1. Not all family connections are viewed as so primal. In US law, for example, siblings are recognized as core relatives, like parents and children. This has been contested with the argument that within US culture siblings are not so primal, but for many foreign cultures they are. Attempts to downgrade sibling ties have, up to this point, failed.

2. Chimamanda Ngozi Adichie, *Americanah* (New York: Knopf, 2013), 7.

3. In recent years, this concern has mostly focused on Spanish-speaking immigrants who live in large concentrations in cities like Los Angeles. Even there, however, research suggests that the second generation does indeed move to primary use of English while maintaining conversational ability in Spanish.

4. Such advertising was sometimes banned by the government, but the proscription was rarely enforced.

5. As one example, an important option for immigrant parents who see their children adapting all too well to American youth culture is to send them back for a while to the home country of origin.

6. The discussion that follows is drawn from Alejandro Portes and Rubén G. Rumbaut, *Legacies: The Story of the Immigrant Second Generation* (Berkeley: University of California Press, 2001). It is an extensive longitudinal study, from which I am drawing this one specific issue about Cubans and schooling in Miami.

7. Sociologists often use the term *segmented assimilation* to describe how people's adaptation to the United States is affected by the particular settings in which they find themselves. For an early review of the topic, see Min Zhou, "Segmented Assimilation: Issues, Controversies, and Recent Research on the New Second Generation," *International Migration Review* 31, no. 4 (Winter 1997): 975–1008.

8. There is also, of course, still migration to largely rural areas, especially for agriculture and food processing, and sometimes to smaller towns. The percentages of the foreign-born in those places can be very high, even though the foreign-born in those places do not account for a very large percentage of the US foreign-born overall.

9. The discussion of Yucatecans in Dallas follows that of anthropologist Rachel H. Adler in her *Yucatecans in Dallas: Breaching the Border, Bridging the Distance*, 2nd ed. (N.p.: Routledge, 2007).

10. The quotation is from page 75 of the story "The Goose Father," in Krys Lee's collection *Drifting House* (New York: Penguin, 2013).

EPILOGUE

1. The use of the word *melting* to convey the way that new Americans blended from diverse origins goes back nearly to the birth of the republic. The specific metaphor of "the melting pot" gained prominence from the 1908 play

of the same name by Israel Zangwill. Perhaps the most contentious part of the metaphor is whether it applies to an original fusion of the American people or a continuing process of renewal.

2. Horace M. Kallen, "Democracy versus the Melting-Pot: A Study of American Nationality," *The Nation*, February 25, 1915, text available at http://www .expo98.msu.edu/people/Kallen.htm.

3. Randolph S. Bourne, "Trans-national America," *Atlantic Monthly* 118 (July 1916): 86–97, https://www.theatlantic.com/magazine/archive/1916/07/trans-national-america/304838/.

4. In the case of immigrants, there are some potential points of confusion regarding who exactly is an immigrant, since there are also many temporary workers and visitors in any country at any particular time. In that sense, much of the confusion is understandable.

Further Sources

The following provides a chapter-by-chapter list of key sources that can be used to expand the often very abbreviated discussions in this very introductory book. I have tried to emphasize sources that are readable as well as reliable.

INTRODUCTION: HUMANITY ON THE MOVE

The increasing emphasis on migration as one example of a broader range of human mobility can be seen in various disciplines, but perhaps the most important issue is continuing to look at—as this text suggests—the way people are moving across territory at the same time that they are moving through their lives. Their physical mobility is thus also their personal, social, economic, and cultural mobility. For examples of that broad understanding of mobility, see my own introductory anthropology text, David W. Haines, *An Introduction to Sociocultural Anthropology: Adaptations, Structures, Meanings*, 2nd ed. (Boulder: University Press of Colorado, 2017); or see texts that take mobility from particular disciplines—for example, Margaret Grieco and John Urry, eds., *Mobilities: New Perspectives on Transport and Society* (London: Routledge, 2016); Mark Wilson, Aharon Kellerman, and Kenneth E. Corey, *Global Information Society: Technology, Knowledge, and Mobility* (Lanham, MD: Rowman & Littlefield, 2013); or Tim Cresswell and Peter Merriman, eds., *Geographies of Mobilities: Practices, Spaces, Subjects* (Aldershot: Ashgate, 2012). A useful set of disciplinary perspectives on migration is provided in Caroline Brettell and James Frank Hollifield, *Migration Theory: Talking across Disciplines*, 3rd ed. (New York: Routledge, 2014).

For the first peopling of America, be careful of competing arguments about exactly who the first Americans were, particularly about earlier or separate migration steams, whether Kennewick Man on the West Coast or cross-Atlantic movements seen in East Coast archeological sites—much less the periodic re-emergence of *Chariots of the Gods* explanations of human development in the Americas. For two mainstream and readable introductions, see J. M. Adovasio and D. R. Pedler's *Strangers in a New Land: What Archaeology Reveals about the First Americans* (Richmond Hill, ON: Firefly Books, 2016); and Brian M. Fagan's *The First North Americans: An Archeological Journey* (New York: Thames and Hudson, 2012). The *Smithsonian* magazine often has good, well-written discussions of archeological debates, but it, too, was sidetracked by the Kennewick Man controversy. For general global patterns in migration, a good standard source is Stephen Castles, Hein de Haas, and Mark J. Miller, *The Age of Migration: International Population Movements in the Modern World*, 5th ed. (New York and London: Guilford Press, 2013).

CHAPTER 1: A WORLD OF MIGRANTS, A NATION OF IMMIGRANTS

There are numerous books on the early migrations to North America, how they created the United States that we know today, and how the established Americans reacted to the new ones. For the early debates about immigration in the colonies and the United States, see especially Susan Forbes Martin, *A Nation of Immigrants* (Cambridge: Cambridge University Press, 2011); and Aristide R. Zolberg, *A Nation by Design: Immigration Policy in the Fashioning of America* (Cambridge, MA: Harvard University Press, 2006). For a solid guide to the documents associated with these policies, see Michael C. LeMay and Elliott Robert Barkan, *U.S. Immigration and Naturalization Laws and Issues: A Documentary History* (Westport, CT: Greenwood, 1999). For general histories of immigration, see especially Roger Daniels, *Coming to America: A History of Immigration and Ethnicity in American Life*, 2nd ed. (New York: Harper Perennial, 2002); and David M. Reimers, *Still the Golden Door: The Third World Comes to America*, 2nd ed. (New York: Columbia University Press, 1992). For more evocative discussions of immigration during the great surge before restriction, two especially good classic sources are Oscar Handlin's *The Uprooted: The Epic Story of the Great Migrations that Made the American People*, 2nd ed. (Boston: Little, Brown, 1973); and the work of Jacob Riis, documenting the complexity, diversity, concentration, and often squalor of immigrant New York at the end of the 1800s, including an extraordinary set of photographs. There are various editions of Riis's work—*How the Other Half Lives: Studies among the Tenements of New York* (Ann Arbor: University of Michigan Libraries, 2011), for example—but ones that include a broader range of his photographs are more useful. For a classic consideration of Polish migration at roughly the same time, see William Isaac Thomas and Florian Znaniecki, *The Polish Peasant in Europe and America: Monograph of an Immigrant Group* (various editions, originally Boston: Richard G. Badger, 1918).

Regarding the specific cases highlighted in this chapter, useful sources on the Irish and Germans at midcentury are Cecil Woodham-Smith, *The Great Hunger: Ireland, 1945–1849* (London: Penguin, 1991; originally London: Hamish Hamilton, 1962); Edward Laxton, *The Famine Ships: The Irish Exodus to America* (New York: Henry Holt, 1998); Kerby A. Miller, *Emigrants and Exiles: Ireland and the Irish Exodus to North America* (New York and Oxford: Oxford University Press, 1985); Mischa Honeck, *We Are the Revolutionists: German-Speaking Immigrants and American Abolitionists after 1848* (Athens: University of Georgia Press, 2011); and Don Heinrich Tolzmann, ed., *The German-American Forty-Eighters: 1848–1998* (Indianapolis: Max Kade German-American Center; Indiana University–Purdue University, 1998). The discussion of the last slave ship is from Sylviane A. Diouf, *Dreams of Africa in Alabama: The Slave Ship "Clotilda" and the Story of the Last Africans Brought to America* (Oxford: Oxford University Press, 2007). A very good source for the long and convoluted history of Asians in America, including the Chinese as discussed in the text, is Ronald T. Takaki, *Strangers from a Different Shore: A History of Asian Americans*, rev. ed. (Boston: Little, Brown, 1998).

CHAPTER 2: THE REOPENING OF THE UNITED STATES: REFUGEES AND IMMIGRANTS

In many ways, the opening of the immigration gates after the Second World War had its roots in the denial of refugees in the late 1930s. For a discussion of that refusal, see the work of David S. Wyman, especially his early book *Paper Walls: America and the Refugee Crisis, 1938–1941* (New York: Pantheon Books, 1985). For the issue of displaced persons after the war, see Mark Wyman, *DPs: Europe's Displaced Persons, 1945–1951* (Ithaca, NY: Cornell University Press, 1998). President Truman's concern with the issue can be seen in some of the online resources of the Harry S. Truman Presidential Library and Museum. The library sponsored a conference on Truman and the DPs, and the edited results appear in Roger Daniels, ed., *Immigration and the Legacy of Harry S. Truman* (Kirksville, MO: Truman State University Press, 2010). Three general sources on refugees in the United States that discuss these early arrivals along with later groups, especially Cubans and Vietnamese, are Gilbert D. Loescher and John A. Scanlan, *Calculated Kindness: Refugees and the Half-Open Door, 1945 to the Present* (London: Collier Macmillan, 1986); Norman L. Zucker and Naomi Flink Zucker, *The Guarded Gate: The Reality of American Refugee Policy* (San Diego: Harcourt Brace Jovanovich, 1987); and David W. Haines, *Safe Haven? A History of Refugees in America* (Sterling, VA: Kumarian Press, 2010).

For the rise of immigration, especially with the 1965 changes to immigration law, an excellent place to start is John F. Kennedy's *A Nation of Immigrants*, rev. ed. (New York: Harper Perennial, 2008). It invokes the great American immigration tradition and lays out the basis for the changes in immigration law that would only be passed after his assassination. For the period that has followed, there is now a very comprehensive literature on immigration, on immigrants, and on immigration policy. For general overviews of immigration, established historians like Leonard Dinnerstein, David Reimers, and Roger Daniels have made additional contributions beyond the books noted above. There are also many edited volumes that survey different immigrant (and refugee) groups. Although these tend to homogenize the experience of those from particular countries of origin, they can provide a very good sense of the diversity of migrant life. One volume that stresses the continuity of immigrant contributions to the United States is Diane Portnoy, Barry Portnoy, and Charlie Riggs, eds., *Immigrant Struggles, Immigrant Gifts* (Fairfax, VA: GMU Press, 2012). Another larger volume focused on post-1965 arrivals is Mary C. Waters and Reed Ueda, eds., *The New Americans: A Guide to Immigration since 1965* (Cambridge, MA: Harvard University Press, 2007). For similar profiles of refugee groups in more detail, see David W. Haines, ed., *Case Studies in Diversity: Refugees in America in the 1990s* (Westport, CT: Praeger, 1997). There are also useful overviews of migrants from specific countries, available online—particularly from the Migration Policy Institute (http://www.migrationpolicy.org).

CHAPTER 3: MIGRATION POLITICS AND POLICIES

Two earlier-noted books are especially helpful for tracing the continuities and changes in overall US immigration policy: Susan Forbes Martin, *A Nation of Immigrants* (Cambridge: Cambridge University Press, 2011); and Aristide R. Zolberg, *A Nation by Design: Immigration Policy in the Fashioning of America* (Cambridge, MA: Harvard University Press, 2006). Two other valuable sources from political science are Daniel J. Tichenor, *Dividing Lines: The Politics of Immigration Control in America* (Princeton, NJ: Princeton University Press, 2002); and Louis DeSipio and Rodolfo O. de la Garza, *US Immigration in the Twenty-First Century: Making Americans, Remaking America* (Boulder, CO: Westview Press, 2015). Since the debates on immigration policy are so vitriolic, it can be helpful to use sources that include both pro and con arguments on different aspects of immigration policy and public attitudes. One such effort is Judith Gans, Elaine M. Replogle, and Daniel J. Tichenor, eds., *Debates on U.S. Immigration* (Thousand Oaks, CA: SAGE Publications, 2012). That same pro-and-con approach can be developed by surveying the various advocacy and critique organizations that have strong online presences. Some are explicitly pro (for example, the American Immigration Council) and some explicitly con (for example, the Federation for American Immigration Reform [FAIR] and the Center for Immigration Studies). Others (for example, the Migration Policy Institute) aim for the middle ground, although remaining quite sympathetic to immigrants. The Pew Research Institute deserves note as an excellent research source for immigration, Hispanics, public policy and attitudes, and religion—which turns out to be very important for immigrants.

Underlying all the debates is a system of immigration policy that has results that sometimes make sense and sometime do not, that sometimes reflect rational goals and sometimes more hidden group interests. Chapter 2 of this book has suggested that one good way to look at immigration policy is to see who actually gets in. Probably the single-best source is the government's annual *Yearbook of Immigration Statistics* from the Department of Homeland Security; find the latest and earlier editions online at https://www.dhs.gov/immigration-statistics/yearbook. The USDHS website also offers a variety of research briefs that provide excellent overviews of who is arriving from where and what some of their general characteristics are. In addition, that site has very good and explicit discussions of exact US policies both on who gets in and who naturalizes. So if you have a question about actual policy, go to the government sources rather than to the organizations that provide commentaries on those policies.

CHAPTER 4: TO LIVE: MOVING FORWARD
BUT LOOKING BACK

The importance of simply surviving through the migration process is clearest for refugees. Two volumes that cover the ground well on refugee flight and resettlement are Mary Pipher, *The Middle of Everywhere: Helping Refugees Enter the American Community* (New York: Harcourt, 2003), and Caroline Moorehead, *Human Cargo: A Journey among Refugees* (New York: Picador, 2006). However, even the transition for nonrefugee immigrants can be complex and uncertain. The full spectrum of immigrant lives is perhaps best appreciated through literature. Classic examples of immigration literature that are used at different points in this text, and are worth a full reading, include Willa Cather's *My Ántonia* for its depiction of life on the plains (originally Boston: Houghton Mifflin, 1918), Drude Krog Janson's *A Saloonkeeper's Daughter* for the way life in the old and new countries was intertwined (original Norwegian publication in 1887; first English translation, trans. Gerald Thorson, Boston: Johns Hopkins University Press, 2002), Upton Sinclair's *The Jungle* for its portrayal of the range and hazards of immigrant jobs (originally New York: Doubleday, Jabber, and Company, 1906), Stephen Crane's *Maggie: A Girl of the Streets* for its sharp portrayal of social collapse in American cities (originally published by the author under a pseudonym, Johnston Smith, 1893), and Anzia Yezierska's *Bread Givers: A Novel* for its insight into the competing pressures of gender and generation within immigrant families (originally Garden City, NY: Doubleday, Page and Company, 1925). All are available in various formats, including online free availability for most. The exception is *A Saloonkeeper's Daughter*, which is based on a relatively recent translation. There is also more recent fiction that is directly relevant to the complexity of immigrant lives. Three titles that may work particularly well in classes are Cristina García's *Dreaming in Cuban: A Novel*, for the interplays of gender and generation, economics and politics (New York: Ballantine Books, 1992); Jhumpa Lahiri's *Interpreter of Maladies*, for the travails of even middle-class immigrants (Boston:

Houghton Mifflin, 1999); and Viet Thanh Nguyen's *The Sympathizer*, for the many contortions of personal and political commitments (New York: Grove Atlantic, 2015).

To explore further the specific case examples in this chapter (Soviet Jews, Cubans, Cambodians, and Salvadorans), see Steven J. Gold, *From the Workers' State to the Golden State: Jews from the Former Soviet Union in California* (Boston: Allyn and Bacon, 1996); Guillermo J. Grenier and Lisandro Pérez, *The Legacy of Exile: Cubans in the United States* (Boston: Allyn and Bacon, 2002); María Cristina García, *Havana USA: Cuban Exiles and Cuban Americans in South Florida, 1959–1994* (Berkeley: University of California Press, 1997); Sarah Streed, *Leaving the House of Ghosts: Cambodian Refugees in the American Midwest* (Jefferson, NC: McFarland, 2002); Sucheng Chan, *Survivors: Cambodian Refugees in the United States* (Urbana: University of Illinois Press, 2004); Cecilia Menjívar, *Fragmented Ties: Salvadoran Immigrant Networks in America* (Berkeley: University of California Press, 2000); and Susan Bibler Coutin, *Exiled Home: Salvadoran Transnational Youth in the Aftermath of Violence* (Durham, NC: Duke University Press, 2016). See also the general suggestions for chapter 2 about edited volumes on recent immigrants that provide shorter overviews of particular groups.

CHAPTER 5: TO WORK: GREAT OPPORTUNITIES BUT HEAVY COSTS

The literature on work spans a broad range of disciplines. For economist views on immigrant work and how it affects (or doesn't) the overall US economy, see George J. Borjas, *Immigration Economics* (Cambridge, MA: Harvard University Press, 2014) or *We Wanted Workers: Unraveling the Immigration Narrative* (New York: W. W. Norton, 2016), and see also Philip L. Martin, *Importing Poverty? Immigration and the Changing Face of Rural America* (New Haven, CT: Yale University Press, 2014). For more sociological consideration of immigrant employment, see Roger David Waldinger and Michael Ira Lichter, *How the Other Half Works: Immigration and the Social Organization of Labor* (Berkeley: University of California Press, 2003); and Alejandro Portes, ed., *The Economic Sociology of Immigration: Essays on Networks, Ethnicity, and Entrepreneurship* (New York: Russell Sage, 1998).

There is also much information, analysis, and dispute on immigrant work available online. Extensive data on immigrant labor patterns are available through the US Census's Current Population Survey (https://www.census.gov/programs-surveys/cps.html), the best source for tracking changes in overall employment among both the native- and foreign-born, and its American Community Survey (https://www.census.gov/programs-surveys/acs/), which provides broader social and economic information on both the native- and foreign-born. The websites are accessible and include tools for extracting detailed information on particular countries of origin, countries of ancestry, and ethnic/racial identification. (Note that "race" according to government definitions often includes issues that are technically more a matter of cultural attachment than biological origins.) One potential problem is that these data, unlike data on formal immigrant admissions, include unauthorized migrants. So data on "employment patterns of immigrants" from these sources tend to include the economic situation of both those legally admitted and those who are unauthorized.

To explore further the specific case examples in this chapter (Iranians, Indians, Ecuadorans, and Koreans), see Ron Kelley, Jonathan Friedlander, and Anita Y. Colby, *Irangeles: Iranians in Los Angeles* (Berkeley: University of California Press, 1993); Anny P. Bakalian and Medhi Bozorgmehr, *Backlash 9/11: Middle Eastern and Muslim Americans Respond* (Berkeley: University of California Press, 2009); Pawan Dhingra, *Life behind the Lobby: Indian American Motel Owners and the American Dream* (Stanford, CA: Stanford University Press, 2014); Vivek Bald, Miabi Chatterji, Sujani Reddy, and Manu Vimalassery, eds., *The Sun Never Sets: South Asian Migrants in an Age of U.S. Power* (New York: NYU Press, 2013); Ann Miles, *From Cuenca to Queens: An Anthropological Story of Transnational Migration* (Austin: University of Texas Press, 2004); Jason Pribilsky, *La Chulla Vida: Gender, Migration, and the Family in Andean Ecuador and New York City* (Syracuse, NY: Syracuse University Press, 2007); Kyeyoung Park, *The Korean American Dream: Immigrants and Small Business in New York City* (Ithaca, NY: Cornell University Press, 1997); and Pyong Gap Min and Samuel Noh, eds., *Second-Generation Korean Experiences in the United States and Canada* (Lanham, MD: Lexington Books, 2014).

CHAPTER 6: TO BELIEVE: HOPES, DREAMS, AND COMMITMENTS

Although this chapter takes the issue of beliefs in a somewhat eclectic direction, most of the relevant literature is based in a more conventional notion of religion and is often split between those who take religion as a core part of life and those who see it more as a refraction of social and cultural forces. Some useful sources are Gurinder Singh Mann, Paul David Numrich, and Raymond Brady Williams, *Buddhists, Hindus and Sikhs in America: A Short History* (Oxford: Oxford University Press, 2007); Richard Alba, Albert J. Raboteau, and Josh DeWind, eds., *Immigration and Religion in America: Comparative and Historical Perspectives* (New York: NYU Press, 2008); Peter Kivisto, *Religion and Immigration: Migrant Faiths in North America and Western Europe* (Cambridge: Polity, 2014); and Pierrette Hondagneu-Sotelo, ed., *Religion and Social Justice for Immigrants* (New Brunswick, NJ: Rutgers, 2006). To consider a wider range of commitments, compare Edwidge Danticat, *Create Dangerously: The Immigrant Artist at Work* (New York: Vintage Books, 2011); the classic but still-interesting autobiography by Michael Pupin, *From Immigrant to Inventor* (various editions, originally published New York and London: Scribner, 1923); and John Bul Dau, *God Grew Tired of Us*, with Michael S. Sweeney (Washington, DC: National Geographic, 2007). The invocations of meaning found respectively in art, in business, and in social commitment provide a beginning point for considering what it is that immigrants value and the degree of their commitment to it.

To explore further the specific case examples (Mexican and Vietnamese Catholics, Sudanese Christians, and Bosnian Muslims), see Alyshia Gálvez, *Guadalupe in New York: Devotion and the Struggle for Citizenship Rights among Mexican Immigrants* (New York: NYU Press, 2009); Leah M. Sarat, *Fire in the Canyon: Religion, Migration, and the Mexican Dream* (New York: NYU Press, 2013); Peter C. Phan, *Vietnamese-American Catholics* (New York: Paulist Press, 2005); Jon Holtzman, *Nuer Journeys, Nuer Lives: Sudanese Refugees in Minnesota* (London: Routledge, 2015); John Bul Dau and Martha Arual Akech, *Lost Boy, Lost Girl: Escaping Civil War in Sudan* (Washington, DC: National Geographic, 2010); Reed Coughlan and Judith Owens-Manley, *Bosnian Refugees in America: New Communities, New Cultures* (New York: Springer, 2006); and Fethi Keles, *Ways to Refuge: Bosnians in Central New York in Ethnographic Perspective* (PhD diss., Syracuse University, 2014), http://surface.syr.edu/cgi/viewcontent .cgi?article=1054&context=etd. For the specific details on how Bosnians and Sudanese identified themselves in government surveys, see chapter 4 in David W. Haines, *Safe Haven? A History of Refugees in America* (Sterling, VA: Kumarian Press, 2010).

CHAPTER 7: TO BELONG: ASSIMILATION, ADAPTATION, AND ACCOMMODATION

The issue of belonging is both one of immigrants' own sensibilities and of the receiving society's notions of proper immigrant behavior. It is also an issue that is both individual and group based, so an attention to different disciplinary perspectives can be especially helpful. A few places to start are Deborah Reed-Danahay and Caroline Brettell, eds., *Citizenship, Political Engagement, and Belonging: Immigrants in Europe and the United States* (New Brunswick, NJ: Rutgers University Press, 2008); Dolores Inés Casillas, *Sounds of Belonging: U.S. Spanish-Language Radio and Public Advocacy* (New York: NYU Press, 2014); Sujey Vega, *Latino Heartland: Of Borders and Belonging in the Midwest* (New York: NYU Press, 2016); Carola Suárez-Orozco, Marcelo M. Suárez-Orozco, and Irina Todorova, *Learning a New Land: Immigrant Students in American Society* (Cambridge, MA: Belknap Press, 2010); and Faith G. Nibbs and Caroline Brettell, eds., *Identity and the Second Generation: How Children of Immigrants Find Their Space* (Nashville, TN: Vanderbilt University Press, 2016). For an introduction to the sociological notions of assimilation, see the classic assessment by Milton Myron Gordon in his *Assimilation in American Life: The Role of Race, Religion, and National Origins* (New York: Oxford University Press, 1964) and the more recent analysis by Richard Alba and Victor Nee, *Remaking the American Mainstream: Assimilation and Contemporary Immigration* (Cambridge, MA: Harvard University Press, 2005). This is also a topic that is well addressed in literature and autobiography, so see again the further sources suggested for chapter 4.

To explore the case examples (Mexicans in Los Angeles, Cubans in Miami, Yucatecans in Dallas, and Koreans in Washington), see Alejandro Portes and Alex Stepick, *City on the Edge: The Transformation of Miami* (Berkeley: University of California Press, 1994); María Cristina García, *Havana USA: Cuban Exiles and Cuban Americans in South Florida, 1959–1994* (Berkeley: University of California Press, 1997); Manny Diaz, *Miami Transformed: Rebuilding America One Neighborhood, One City at a Time* (Philadelphia: University of Pennsylvania Press, 2012); Rafael Alarcón, Luis Escala, and Olga Odgers, *Making Los Angeles Home: The Integration of Mexican Immigrants in the United States* (Oakland: University of California Press, 2016); Roger Waldinger and Mehdi Bozorgmehr, eds., *Ethnic Los Angeles* (New York: Russell Sage Foundation, 1996); Enrique C. Ochoa and Gilda L. Ochoa, eds., *Latino Los Angeles: Transformations, Communities, and Activism* (Tucson: University of Arizona Press, 2012); Rachel H. Adler, *Yucatecans in Dallas, Texas: Breaching the Border, Bridging the Distance*, 2nd ed. (N.p.: Routledge, 2007); and Francine Curro Cary, ed., *Washington Odyssey: A Multicultural History of the Nation's Capital*, rev. ed. (Washington, DC: Smithsonian, 2003). For the discussions of Yucatecans and Koreans, I am completely in the debt to the aforementioned work by Rachel H. Adler—*Yucatecans in Dallas, Texas*—and that of Young A. Jung on Koreans in Washington, particularly the topic of Jung's 2014 dissertation at George Mason University, *Emplacing Parenting: Migration and Belonging among Korean Gireogi Families.*

Index

References to figures and tables are in italics. Unless specified otherwise, national labels (e.g., Irish, Indians, Germans) refer to people in the United States rather than in their country of origin.

About the Author

David W. Haines is professor emeritus at George Mason University and co-president of the Association for the Anthropology of Policy. He has twice been a Fulbright scholar (South Korea in 2004 and Western Europe—England, France, the Netherlands—in 1987 and 1988) and is past president of the Society for Urban, National, and Transnational/Global Anthropology (SUNTA) and founding member of George Mason's Diversity Research Group.

His publications include several edited volumes on refugees and immigrants, a historical monograph on Vietnamese kinship, and numerous articles in professional journals on migration, kinship, and governance. His most recent books are *An Introduction to Sociocultural Anthropology: Adaptations, Structures Meanings* (2nd ed., 2017); *Wind over Water: Migration in an East Asian Context* (coedited with Keiko Yamanaka and Shinji Yamashita, 2012); and *Safe Haven? A History of Refugees in America* (2010).

Professor Haines was a recipient of George Mason's Teaching Excellence Award in 2003 and has taught in the areas of general anthropology, refugees, migration, East Asia, and information technology.